BA

Stuart Valentine studied economics at the London School of Economics. He worked in the Economics Department of Midland Bank from 1964 to 1976, and is now Economic Adviser to the Stock Exchange. He has been Visiting Lecturer at the City of London Polytechnic, and writes regularly for banking publications.

Stan Mason has pursued a varied career, including posts with HM Customs and Excise Intelligence Branch, the Ford Motor Company and Midland Bank, where he has worked in branches, in the Marketing Department and for the Corporate Finance Division. He is currently Head of Research and Information in the Business Development Division.

TEACH YOURSELF BOOKS

BANKING

Stuart Valentine
BSc. (Econ), AIB

and

Stan Mason
FIB, ACIS, Dip.M, M.Inst.M,
M.Inst.AM, FBIM

TEACH YOURSELF BOOKS
Hodder and Stoughton

First published 1976 as
Basics of Banking
2nd edition 1981
3rd edition 1984

British Library Cataloguing in Publication Data

Valentine, S. P.
Banking.—3rd ed.—(Teach yourself books)
1. Banks and banking—Great Britain
I. Title II. Mason, S.
332.1'0941 HG2988

ISBN 0 340 35622 7

Printed and bound in Great Britain for
Hodder and Stoughton Educational,
a division of Hodder and Stoughton Ltd,
Mill Road, Dunton Green, Sevenoaks, Kent,
by Hazell, Watson & Viney Ltd, Aylesbury, Bucks.
Photoset by Rowland Phototypesetting Ltd
Bury St Edmunds, Suffolk

Contents

Preface

Banking is intended to be of assistance to those students who are taking *Elements of Banking* as part of a BTEC course in Business Studies, especially to those who are intending to make banking a career, and pursue further banking studies through the Institute of Bankers' examinations. In writing with the students' needs in mind, we have nevertheless tried to provide a readable account of the banking system which will be of use and interest to the non-specialist in helping him understand the workings of this increasingly complex subject.

If readers believe that banking is a staid unchanging subject, those working in banking can assure them that they themselves have difficulty in keeping up with developments, and numerous changes have had to be incorporated in the text during writing. No doubt further changes will occur before publication, but that is one of the perils to be faced by anyone brave enough to write a book of this sort. The reader is encouraged to keep abreast of recent developments by using sources of reference such as the financial press and up-to-date statistical publications, such as *Financial Statistics* and the excellent *Bank of England Quarterly Bulletin*.

Stuart Valentine
Stan Mason

Acknowledgments

In preparing this revised edition, we have been given help and cooperation by a number of people and organisations, particularly with the reproduction of statistical information.

In particular we should like to thank the following: The Bank of England for permission to reproduce the Weekly Return as Table 16.1, and for information derived from the *Bank of England Quarterly Bulletin* for Tables 14.2 to 14.4, 15.1 and 15.2; HMSO for permission to reproduce information derived from *Financial Statistics* in Tables 12.1 to 12.3; and finally Colin Jones, editor of *The Banker*, for permission to reproduce information from the November 1983 annual survey of overseas banks in London, as Table 13.1

Our thanks, too, to those who stimulated and encouraged us to carry out a full revision of the book, checked details and pointed out errors. Those which remain are, of course, entirely our responsibility. A last word of thanks to Ann Hanson for all the additional typing and photocopying which was necessary to put this new edition in a form fit to send to the publishers.

An Historical Introduction

What is a bank?

In writing an introductory book about any subject, a definition of the subject is a necessary starting point. In the case of banking, this task seems simple at first. The reader knows what a bank is; he probably uses one for many of his financial transactions, such as paying household bills, drawing cash and perhaps having his salary paid directly into his account. But in defining banking, this simplicity is indeed deceiving. The Bills of Exchange Act 1882, for example, which provides the basic legal framework governing cheques, and is thus an Act with which bankers are involved every day, defines a banker as someone who carries on the business of banking. To say the least, this is not altogether enlightening as a definition and until the passing of the Banking Act 1979, there was much dispute as to who could be called a banker and who could not. Nevertheless, it is well established that banking consists of three basic functions: the acceptance of deposits from customers, the transfer of these deposits from one account to another (or their withdrawal in the form of notes and coins) and the lending of money by way of loan or overdraft to customers (although the Banking Act does not regard the transfer function as an essential qualification). This will serve as our working definition. But before discussing the banking system as it now exists, let us look briefly at the historical development of banking in England.

Early history

Modern banking in this country, as in many European states, has its origins in the finance of foreign trade. In the great medieval trading states of Venice, Genoa and later Florence, a need arose to exchange one currency with another and the early money-changers also began the practice of accepting deposits of cash and valuables for safe-keeping. The merchants and money-changers of these cities also undertook the financing of commerce at the great medieval trade fairs, thus helping their fellow traders as well as themselves to sell their goods.

As these merchants prospered, they were also called upon to provide finance for the rulers of the states in which they were established, and often became closely involved in financing the running (and the wars) of their own and other countries. Because of the power these financiers could wield, and the pressure they no doubt frequently exerted as creditors, they were seldom popular. Readily identifiable groups, such as the Jews, were persecuted and sometimes expelled, and the laws against usury were strict. Such laws did not, however, prevent the practice of borrowing and lending money nor interest being demanded and paid, and an Act of 1545 eventually made the charging of interest on loans legal in England. A maximum rate of interest was then fixed at 10%, although this rate was changed from time to time by subsequent Acts of Parliament. Not until 1854 were the usury laws finally repealed and the maximum legal rate of interest abolished.

Since modern banking originated in the cities of northern Italy, it is not surprising that some of its basic vocabulary has Italian roots. The word 'bank' itself comes from the Italian word 'banco' meaning a bench. It was at benches that the early Italian bankers carried out their original function of money-changing. The word 'bankrupt' has the same origin, and refers to the practice of breaking the money-changer's bench to indicate that he was no longer able to honour his obligations and therefore unable to continue his business.

After the Jews were expelled from England by Edward I in 1290, money-lending activities were carried on by the Lombards, who were already established in England. The Lombards, so called because of their northern Italian origins, were principally merchants from the states of Genoa, Lucca, Florence and Venice and were important financiers in many European states. The name

'Lombard Street' in the heart of the City of London is a permanent reminder of the importance of these early Italian merchant/financiers.

The seventeenth century

The practice of banking in England as we know it today – the accepting of deposits, the making of loans and the transfer of funds – evolved during the seventeenth century with the growth of the goldsmith-bankers who had by that time taken over from the Lombards as major financiers in England. As the merchants of London prospered before the Civil War, so they required a place of safe-keeping for their money and valuables. Where could be better for this purpose than the Tower of London? The Royal Mint was at that time housed in the Tower, and surely no place in London was more secure than that ancient fortress. Safe it may have been from outside attack, but in 1640 King Charles I requisitioned £200 000 of coin and bullion which had been deposited there. Although Charles I later repaid the money, with conditions, the merchants were reluctant to trust the Mint with their cash again, and an alternative was sought.

The London goldsmiths provided the answer. Because of the nature of their trade, their premises had to be secure, and even before the 1640 seizure, there is evidence that they had accepted coin on deposit from their customers. The earliest known deposit receipt is dated 1633 and issued by Hoare's, a well-known name in the City even today. But after the incident of 1640, and then the uncertainties of the Civil War, the goldsmiths rapidly developed the business of receiving deposits from their customers and issuing receipts for them. At first these receipts were little more than warehouse receipts entitling the holder to the return of his actual deposit, but they later became 'promissory notes', giving the holder a promise that he would be able to withdraw, on demand, a sum equivalent to that deposited. Gradually these notes, instead of being redeemed for gold each time a debt had to be paid, themselves began to circulate among the merchants of London in settlement of their debts. Thus these receipts became the forerunners of the modern banknote.

Around 1670, the words 'or bearer' were added after the name of the original depositor and they became 'bearer instruments', thus making them easier to transfer and giving them a greater circulation. Although in practice they had become 'negotiable' instruments, transferable merely by delivery, it was not until 1704 that negotiability of these banknotes was recognised by law. Earlier, in 1670, the 'drawn note', or cheque, was introduced, enabling a depositor to transfer a part of his balance to a creditor and thus discharge his debts.

Before the end of the seventeenth century, the practice of placing money with a goldsmith with a given notice of required repayment had emerged, thereby originating what we today call 'deposit accounts'. The goldsmith also began to function as a lender of money, both to the Government and to private merchants to carry on and expand their trade, thus following the tradition of the Jews and the Lombards. Thus, before 1700, the essential foundations of today's banking system were in place: the receiving of surplus cash on deposit, redeemable either on demand or at a period of notice, the transfer of these balances between one account-holder and another, and the on-lending of cash in excess of that likely to be drawn at any one time to borrowers who used it in the development of their business. In addition, the private banknote was already in circulation. This aspect of private banking in London was to diminish substantially in the following century as England's first 'public bank', the Bank of England, gradually took over the function of exclusive note issuer.

The foundation of the Bank of England

In 1694, the Government of the day, in need of funds to pursue the war against France, wished to raise finance from the wealthy merchants of London. Partly because of the seizure of funds from the Mint in 1640 and a 'stop' on payments by the Exchequer imposed by Charles II in 1672, Government credit was not very high and a number of schemes were proposed to enable the necessary funds to be raised. The one adopted was put forward by William Paterson: in return for a loan of £1 200 000, bearing interest at 8%, the subscribers, who were limited to a maximum subscription of £20 000 each, were allowed to form themselves into a joint-stock company under the title of 'The Governor and Company of the

Bank of England'. In return for the loan, the Bank of England was granted a number of privileges including the right to issue notes payable on demand up to the maximum amount of the Bank's capital.

From its inception, the Bank of England held a privileged position in English banking. It was the only joint-stock bank in existence, the private banks all being no more than partnerships, and it was also closely involved with the financing of the Government.

The foundation of the Bank is noted here in its historic context. Today, it performs functions which are very different from those of an ordinary commercial bank. The present structure of the Bank of England and the essential functions it now performs are discussed in Chapter 16.

The eighteenth and nineteenth centuries

As early as 1697, only three years after the establishment of the Bank of England, an attempt was made by a further Act of Parliament to confer a monopoly on the Bank, and this monopoly was strengthened in the early years of the eighteenth century. Under these enactments, no other joint-stock bank could be established so long as the Bank of England remained in existence, and the monopoly of joint-stock banking thus granted to the Bank of England was to last for well over a hundred years. Private banks were allowed to continue their business and to issue their own banknotes, but they had to be partnerships, and were limited to not more than six partners. Such legislation ensured that these private bankers remained small and hence were no threat to the power and influence of the Bank of England. In addition to the powers already possessed, the Bank's position *vis-à-vis* the Government was further strengthened in 1715 when it acquired the power to manage the National Debt, a power it still continues to exercise.

As a result of the power and influence conferred on the Bank of England, its notes had a wide currency in London, and soon superseded the issues of the private bankers. During the next few years the note issue of the private bankers declined, but the banking partnerships continued to accept deposits from their customers, paying gold or notes on demand, and providing transfer facilities.

The introduction of the 'drawn note' or cheque in the seventeenth century has already been mentioned, and the cheque system developed rapidly in the eighteenth century. In order to facilitate the exchange of cheques drawn on each other, the London private bankers established a Clearing House in 1773. This increased the ease of transfer and allowed the individual banks to keep a smaller total of cash in their tills with which to meet withdrawals and transfers.

Operating outside the London area was an ever-increasing group of bankers, called the country bankers, who occupy an important place in the history of banking in this country. The development of industry in the North and Midlands needed to be financed and the early providers of such finance were wealthy local merchants who had added a rudimentary banking service as an adjunct to their main business before the end of the seventeenth century. Thus the early country banking activities were financed by mercers, grocers, tax-collectors and lawyers, among many others. The increase in the numbers of these country bankers was rapid, particularly after 1750. At that time, probably less than twenty banking firms were in existence outside London, but it is estimated that by 1820 there were nearly 600 such firms in operation.

Most of the country bankers used a London agent, either a bill-broker or a London private banker, of which there were about sixty in 1820. The role of these agents was to provide the country bankers with the means of cheque-clearing and also to act as a channel of funds between them. Country bankers in the predominantly agricultural areas usually had surplus funds to invest, whereas the more industrialised areas were usually in need of funds to expand investment. The London agents, by acting as intermediaries between these two groups, ensured that the surplus cash of one was channelled to the other for investing in the growth of industry.

Like other banking firms, the country bankers were limited to a maximum of six partners, but entry into banking was as easy as entry into any other trade. Banking partnerships were allowed to issue their own notes, provided they had a licence to do so. The system was, therefore, small scale and fragmentary and, not surprisingly, relatively unstable. Between 1809 and 1830, commissions of bankruptcy were issued against over 300 country banks including eighty in the years 1825 and 1826 alone.

In response to this instability, the principle of joint-stock banking, which applied only to the Bank of England under the jealously guarded monopoly, was extended by an Act of 1826 which allowed the establishment of note-issuing joint-stock banks, situated outside a radius of sixty-five miles of London. The principle was further extended in 1833, when joint-stock banks were allowed to be established within a sixty-five mile radius, providing they did not issue their own banknotes. At the same time, Bank of England notes were made legal tender for the first time. Although the Bank of England thus lost its position as the only joint-stock banking organisation, the privilege of note issue was strengthened.

The rapidly fluctuating economic conditions of the 1820s were attributed by many people to the relatively unrestricted right to issue banknotes and the problems caused by over-issue. During the 1830s, concern continued to surround the amount of the note issue, and in what is probably the best-known piece of banking legislation, the Bank Charter Act 1844, provisions to control the note issue more closely were laid down. These eventually led to the Bank of England acquiring a monopoly of the note issue in England and Wales. The Bank of England was divided for accounting purposes into two Departments, the Issue Department and the Banking Department. A weekly return had to be issued (and still is) showing the position of the two. The Bank was allowed to issue banknotes only to the value of its gold holdings, except for a small amount of £14m which could be backed by Government securities instead of gold. This extra amount – based on trust, rather than on gold – was called the fiduciary issue. Those private or joint-stock banks of issue which were already in existence, of which there were about seventy, were not permitted to increase their note issue above the level at the time. Any banks established subsequently were not allowed the right of note issue, and on amalgamation, or opening of an office within sixty-five miles of London, a bank lost its right of issue. Because of the rapid amalgamation of both joint-stock and private banks in the later nineteenth and early twentieth centuries, the number of note-issuing banks rapidly declined, and eventually, when Fox, Fowler was absorbed by Lloyds Bank in 1921, the last private banknote issue in England ceased.

The Acts of 1826 and 1833 had allowed the establishment of joint-stock banks, but the owners of the capital of these organisations remained liable to the full extent of their personal wealth in the event of the bank's failure. Although the principle of limited liability had been given to the Bank of England at its establishment, not until 1858 was it extended to other joint-stock banks, which eventually took full advantage of the privilege.

In the mid-nineteenth century, the structure of banking was still based on unit banks, that is, a structure in which a large number of individual banks operated with relatively few branches. In 1880, approximately 160 banks were operating in England and Wales, but thereafter the situation began to change rapidly. The transformation of British banking by way of amalgamation reached its height from the 1880s onwards, and was virtually completed in the early years of the twentieth century.

The twentieth century

Such was the pace of amalgamation that by 1918 the number of banks had been reduced to around forty, and the system was dominated by the 'Big Five' – Barclays, Lloyds, Midland, National Provincial and Westminster. At that point, a Treasury Committee, the Colwyn Committee, recommended that no further amalgamations should take place among these major banks. A number of mergers subsequently did take place between the major banks and some of the smaller ones, so that the total number of clearing banks was reduced to eleven, but the situation remained virtually unaltered until the 1960s.

When a smaller bank was absorbed, it usually kept its own identity within the larger group. The banks also sought amalgamations and affiliations with the banks in Scotland and Northern Ireland: thus the Clydesdale Bank and the North of Scotland Bank were absorbed into the Midland, and British Linen Bank by Barclays. In the reverse direction, Royal Bank of Scotland took over the small English banks Glyn, Mills and Williams Deacon's thus giving the Scottish bank membership of the Bankers' Clearing House in London. The Scottish and Irish commercial banks have a somewhat different history from that of the English banks, and among the differences now apparent is that they are still permitted, within limits, to issue their own banknotes. Although the Scottish and Irish banks have become linked with the English banking groups, they still retain their own identities.

The Bank of England was nationalised in 1946, but this development made little difference to the banking system, as the development of the Bank as the country's central bank had occurred gradually over the preceding century, as is discussed more fully in Chapter 16, and the Bank of England Act 1946 did little more than confirm the existing situation.

The basic commercial banking structure remained unaltered, however, until 1967. In that year, a report on bank charges was published by the National Board for Prices and Incomes. The Board ranged much more widely than the restrictive title of its report, and discussed competition between the banks in critical detail. One statement made in paragraph 154 of the report was to have far-reaching effects; it stated: 'The Bank of England and the Treasury have made it plain to us that they would not obstruct some further amalgamations if the banks were willing to contemplate such a development.'

Within a few months, the National Provincial Bank and Westminster Bank announced plans for a merger. The Government, with the power to refer the proposed merger to the Monopolies Commission for investigation, chose not to do so. But almost immediately, Barclays Bank and Lloyds Bank, which had both been interested in acquiring Martins Bank, one of the smaller of the clearing banks, announced a proposed merger of all three organisations. The Government promptly referred the proposal to merge Barclays, Lloyds and Martins banks into one group to the Monopolies Commission which, by a majority, recommended that the proposal to merge Barclays and Lloyds should not be allowed, but that a merger of Martins with one of the two should be permitted. The Government followed the Commission's findings, and Barclays, in the event, took over Martins and absorbed its branches into the main Barclays network. National Provincial and Westminster, now merged into National Westminster Bank, also carried out a full-scale re-organisation, merging their branch networks under the common name, and including in the re-organisation the branches of the District Bank, which, although acquired by the National Provincial Bank in 1962, had hitherto kept its own identity. Some further re-organisation took place among some of the other banks. Williams Deacon's, Glyn Mills and the National Bank, all owned by the National and Commercial Banking Group, merged to become

Williams and Glyn's Bank. In Scotland, the Bank of Scotland and British Linen Bank merged in 1971, and in Northern Ireland, Northern Bank and Belfast Banking Company merged under the title Northern Bank in 1970.

In addition, there are several other groups of banks which play a part in the UK banking structure, including the merchant banks and overseas banks. These are described in Chapter 13. However, the British retail banking system now consists of the so-called 'Big Four', Barclays, Lloyds, Midland and National Westminster, together with Williams and Glyn's and Coutts, which, although a member of the National Westminster group still retains its separate identity. The Co-operative Bank, Trustee Savings Banks and National Girobank are also now members of the Bankers' Clearing House, and other smaller commercial banks may join in due course. The major banks are now engaged in a wide variety of different financial activities both at home and overseas. They operate over 12 000 branches and employ over 250 000 people in the UK, a far cry indeed from the goldsmiths' shops, woollen mills and mercers' premises where it all began.

Questions

1 Explain the role of the goldsmiths in the history of banking in Britain.
2 Trace the steps by which goldsmiths' receipts developed into modern banknotes.
3 How did the country bankers of the eighteenth and nineteenth centuries employ surplus deposits? What role was played by London 'bill-brokers' in this process?
4 Describe the development of English banking, referring to any legislation which assisted it.
5 What changes took place in the structure of English banking in the nineteenth century which made it a more stable system?
6 Describe the process by which the Bank of England gradually acquired a monopoly of the note issue.

1

The Qualities and Functions of Money

Money is defined as anything which passes freely from hand to hand and is generally acceptable in the settlement of a debt. In many countries, the monetary system has been built on a base of precious metals such as gold or silver, but cowrie shells, salt and many other things can be, and have been, used as money. Although a primitive trading economy can be carried on without the use of money, historically at an early stage of a civilisation's development, something – and it does not really matter what that 'something' is – will begin to perform the various functions of money. Indeed, it is true to say that an economy cannot progress beyond an elementary stage unless such a development occurs.

Consider the situation which preceded the introduction of money. The situation is usually known as a system of barter. Under this system, trade is difficult but not impossible. The first problem is one we refer to as the 'double co-incidence of wants', which means that not only must one man have goods which a second man requires, but also that the second man must have goods which the first is willing to take in exchange. Let us take a simple example. A farmer growing wheat might wish to introduce some variety into his diet and so decides that he would like some fish. He therefore looks for a fisherman and if he is lucky, he will find a fisherman who not only has some fish he is willing to sell, but also requires some wheat. In this event, exchange can take place with little trouble. But supposing the fisherman has surplus fish but he wishes to buy wool, rather than wheat. In that case the farmer will have to find a third person who has wool to sell and wishes to take wheat in exchange.

Thus he would have to exchange his wheat for wool before he could obtain the fish which he really requires.

A further complication occurs with a barter system of exchange. That is the question of price. Assuming that a barter deal can be arranged between two parties, an exchange rate or price has then to be agreed. How much wheat is to be given for a given quantity of fish? Neither wheat nor fish will be of a standard or unchanging quality, so that the two participants in the deal will spend much time haggling over a price, taking into account the quality of their respective wares.

In the above example, both fish and wheat can be fairly easily sub-divided into relatively small units, but in many instances this might not be possible. Take, for example, the case of a man who wishes to buy fish in exchange for a cow. He will have to accept a vast quantity of fish in exchange for his cow, because clearly the cow cannot be 'sub-divided' into small units without losing its 'utility'.

The point need not be laboured further. Barter is a possible means of trade, but is slow, cumbersome and inefficient. People living in a pre-monetary barter society usually have to be part-farmer, part-fisherman, part-hunter, part-builder and so on.

This illustrates one of the further drawbacks to a barter system, and a more fundamental one. Because a man has to divide his time between many different tasks, he cannot concentrate on that activity which he performs best, leaving others to specialise in the tasks in which they are most skilled. Thus specialisation of labour cannot take place to any great extent under a barter system. Adam Smith in his classic book *The Wealth of Nations*, published in 1776, described, in a frequently quoted passage, how the output of pins produced by a given number of people could be substantially increased if the job were split into several distinct stages and an individual concentrated on performing just one of the stages before passing the partly finished pin to someone else who dealt with the next stage of its manufacture.

That is one example of the division of labour. Another is for one person to concentrate on being, let us say, a farmer, another a builder, a third a doctor, and so on. It is quite clear that the problems of barter, difficult enough even in the example of the farmer and the fisherman, become impossible when one thinks of a doctor trying to provide his services on a barter basis. Similar difficulties would confront teachers, dentists (and even authors). In order that an economy may progress from the simple provision of basic needs, something has to replace barter, to act as an intermediary separating the buying and the selling transactions. Such an intermediary – which we call 'money' – enables a man to receive payment for the goods or services he has provided, and to purchase, at a time he chooses and from whom he chooses, the goods or services he requires for his own use. Otherwise the society will remain small, fragmentary and inefficient in its use of resources.

The qualities of money

Whatever comes into use as money must possess certain qualities. The most important of these qualities is that of *acceptability*: anything which is acceptable as money *is* money, and thereby fulfils the definition of money used at the beginning of this chapter. Anything which is *not* acceptable as money is *not* money and cannot be used as such. Thus, acceptability is the key.

Several other qualities are aids to acceptability. These are given below.

Scarcity

For any substance to be acceptable as money it should be relatively scarce. It should not be *too* scarce, because if it were, the substance itself is likely to be hoarded and therefore not pass freely from hand to hand. It addition, it would tend to be extremely valuable and could not easily be sub-divided into smaller amounts for everyday transactions. Diamonds, or any precious stones, for example, would fall into this category. On the other hand, a commodity should not be too freely available. If a commodity used as money could be obtained in substantial and inexhaustible quantities by everybody, the goods which could be bought with that money would rise, and go on rising, in price. As prices increased, the value of each individual unit of money would fall and eventually those who had goods to sell would be unwilling to take that particular form of money in exchange for them. The commodity would, therefore, have become unacceptable as money and thus it would have ceased to be money, as it would no longer be taken in payment for goods and services.

Divisibility

The second subsidiary quality which anything used as money should possess is that of divisibility. We saw earlier how a cow cannot be sub-divided without at the same time losing all of its value. Any commodity to be used as money must be capable of being divided into a convenient number of smaller units so that transactions of smaller value can be carried out. Thus, in the UK, the major unit of money is the pound sterling. Since decimalisation of the currency in 1971, the pound can be sub-divided into 100 pence, or 200 half-pence. Each penny is worth one-hundredth of a pound, and a total of 100 pence will be just as valuable and will purchase exactly the same amount of goods as will a £1 note. Thus our present currency achieves the quality of divisibility without any loss of value.

Durability

A futher quality which money should possess is that of durability. The commodity used as money should not wear out quickly, nor should it deteriorate in quality as it becomes older. The quality of durability can easily be seen if we compare a coin to a piece of fish. The former is hard-wearing and can last for a hundred years, perhaps more, but a piece of fish is useless as a means of exchange after a few days.

Portability

To be used as money, a commodity should be easy and convenient to carry about. Money is required for many everyday transactions, and it would clearly be inconvenient to use as money any object which was heavy and bulky to carry. Thus, as an aid to being acceptable as money, the object should possess the quality of easy portability.

Homogeneity

Put into more simple terms, this means that each unit should be exactly the same as every other unit. Again taking an example from our own money, a one-shilling piece, minted in 1925, will be accepted for the same value as a one-shilling piece dated 1966 or indeed an equivalent decimal 5p coin dated 1974. Thus any unit of money, whenever it was made, should be equivalent to every other unit of the same face value.

Intrinsic value

In the early days of a monetary economy, it is usual to find that the commodity which is used as money has some value in itself, apart from its use as money. Precious metals, such as gold and silver, have therefore often become the basis of a country's monetary system. The use of anything with such intrinsic value is an aid to acceptability. People accept the metal because they know that it is of some value – as jewellery for example – even if it were to cease to be used as money. As a monetary society develops, intrinsic value no longer becomes so important as a quality of money, and the widespread use of pieces of paper (banknotes) and book-keeping entries (bank deposits) as money in modern times illustrates the point. Nevertheless, the importance of intrinsic value in the early development of money should not be forgotten. A commodity having these qualities and circulating in exchange for goods can thus be called money. Other commodities might possess some of the qualities of money; for instance, as we have already seen, diamonds possess intrinsic value, but are not available in sufficient quantities to enable them to circulate freely. Pebbles would have the qualities of durability and, to some extent, portability, but anyone could pick up pebbles in almost unlimited quantities, and they would therefore soon become unacceptable as money.

The functions of money

Anything possessing all these qualities can be used as money, but we have so far only touched briefly on why we need money. We must now examine the functions that this commodity which we call 'money' performs. These functions are usually summarised as follows:

1 A medium of exchange;
2 A unit of account;
3 A store of value;
4 A standard of deferred payment.

1 Money as a medium of exchange

We have seen above the sort of problems which confront anyone wishing to trade in a system of barter. To progress beyond this elementary stage of development, man needs to develop a 'vehicle' to make the business of trade easier, and it is probably to perform the function of a medium of exchange that money first came into being. To go back to our earlier example, the wheat farmer in a monetary economy will sell his wheat for money, and he will keep that money until he wishes to purchase a quantity of another commodity. This 'waiting period' may be a few minutes or it could be several months. Note that what the farmer uses as money is not wanted for its own sake; he accepts the commodity only because he knows that someone else will take it from him in exchange for goods which he does require, such as fish, at the time he requires them. Again referring back to our earlier example, the farmer, unable to effect a direct exchange of wheat for fish, had first to exchange some of his wheat for wool before being able to purchase the fish he wanted. In a rudimentary way, the wool in this example was being used as money, because it was purchased, not for its own sake, but because the farmer knew that on that particular occasion, the wool would be acceptable in exchange for the fish he required. So the first function of money is that of a medium of exchange.

2 Money as a unit of account

Closely linked to its function as a medium of exchange, money also acts as a unit of account, enabling a pricing system to come into being. Under a barter system, every single commodity has to have a price in terms of every other commodity. Thus a given quantity of wheat would have a separate exchange rate in terms of fish, wool, meat, weapons and everything else. Furthermore, because many commodities deteriorate rapidly, the quality of wheat, fish, meat, etc. would have to be taken into account in every individual transaction. In other words, each unit of a commodity is not homogeneous, not identical to other units of that commodity in all respects.

By introducing a monetary unit, all prices can be expressed in terms of that 'common denominator', each good has its price, and different qualities of the product can be accurately reflected by being given a higher or lower price. In addition, the unit of account function enables accurate accounts to be kept. More fundamentally, future projects can be assessed in terms of a common denominator, which enables a choice to be made between one and another. Without a common denominator, it would be impossible to compare the returns on, say, building a power station and building several schools. Even money acting as a unit of account may not be perfect in doing this, but it is much better than any alternative.

It is usual, although not essential, that whatever acts as a medium of exchange should also act as a unit of account. So in this country we use pounds and pence to carry out our transactions, and our book-keeping records, too, are kept in terms of pounds and pence. Until the decimalisation of the pound in 1971, we had one small example in which the unit of account and the medium of exchange were not the same. That example was the guinea. Prices, especially those charged by professional advisers, were often denominated in guineas, as, for some curious reason, were women's clothes, but not for many, many years had the guinea existed as a medium of exchange. It is also possible that at a time when the value of the medium of exchange is falling rapidly in value – a condition we refer to as hyper-inflation – contracts are priced in terms of something which is more stable in value. At the time of the hyper-inflation in Germany in the early 1920s, contracts were often drawn up in terms of US dollars, so that a different and more stable base was used as a unit of account than the medium of exchange.

3 Money as a store of value

The third function of money is that it should enable people to set a given amount aside for future use without, in the meantime, having lost any value; to act, in other words, as a store of value. We mentioned earlier that for a commodity to act as money it should be durable, and we contrasted it with fresh fish, which rapidly deteriorates in quality and therefore decreases in value as a medium of exchange the older it becomes. But although money is durable in the physical sense, it is not durable in another sense. To understand this we must realise that money is only a claim to goods and services; money is valuable only in terms of the amount of goods and services it will buy. Its value lies in the purchasing power which it gives an individual – the command it gives him over real goods and services within an economy. If there are no goods or services available to purchase, then money is useless and valueless.

So if the prices of goods and services are rising in terms of money, then each individual unit of money will buy less than before and is therefore depreciating in value. We call this situation *price inflation*, a gradual and steady erosion of the value of money as a result of a continuing increase in the average level of prices in an economy. If money is falling in value, it is clear that a given amount will not purchase as much in five or ten years' time as it does now. In this sense money can be said not to be durable, and certainly acts less efficiently as a store of value.

Thus we may say that although the store of value function is attributed to money, it will perform this function only at a time of stable prices. To use money as a store of value in times of a steady rise in prices, or indeed of a steady fall in prices, is rather like trying to measure the length of a table with an elastic tape measure. Anyone doubting this should consider the difference if he were told today that a man was earning £1000 a year after tax and if he had been given that same information in 1914. Goods, which in that year cost £100, would today cost well over £1000. How much more purchasing power did £1000 give in 1914 than it does today!

4 Money as a standard of deferred payment

Lending and borrowing agreements are drawn up in terms of money, and when money is used in this way it is said to be acting as a standard of deferred payment. In a hire-purchase agreement, for example, the amount borrowed, plus interest, is repaid by a given number of payments of fixed amounts, denominated in terms of money. In some ways, the standard of deferred payment function is almost a sub-division of the unit of account function but is usually given separate treatment.

These, then, are the functions which money performs in a modern economy, although as we have seen it carries out some of them less efficiently than others. To summarise, by performing the functions described, money overcomes the various disadvantages of barter. It generalises purchasing power, enabling decisions to be made on the basis of a common denominator. By separating the buying of goods from the selling of goods, it enables specialisation of labour to take place, whereby a man can concentrate on doing what he is best at, in exchange for money, and allows a much wider range of goods and services to be made available than would ever be possible under barter. Finally, by enabling accumulation of savings money provides the means whereby investment in an economy can take place, so increasing the amount of goods available in the future.

Present-day forms of money

So far, we have discussed money in general and largely theoretical terms. Let us now look at money today. The examples we shall use will be drawn primarily from the experience of the UK, but the broad outline of the forms of money which we now use is of general application.

Money consists of coins, banknotes and, most important of all, bank deposits. Today, bank deposits account for over 80% of the money supply, but this was not always so. In fact, coin, which is now of relatively small importance in the economy, was until quite recently the main form of money in use in this country. The history of coins in use as money in Britain goes back many centuries. Coins were certainly used in Roman times and probably even earlier. During the Roman occupation and afterwards, coins were usually made of silver, but gold coins were known in this country by the thirteenth century. Nevertheless, it is unlikely that a large number of the population used them very much. Under the feudal system, payment was usually made 'in kind' to workers on the lords' lands, and it was probably only the lord himself, selling surplus crops for money, who dealt in silver and gold coin. The eventual breakdown of the feudal system and the development of a money economy were closely interlinked; the one could not have come about without the other.

Until the fourteenth century, gold was not used in England as an everyday medium of exchange, because its intrinsic value was too high to enable small transactions to take place in exchange for it. When gold later became used as coinage, both silver and gold circulated side by side for a considerable period of time; and it was not until the nineteenth century that gold became the primary metal, while silver continued to be used in our coinage until the mid-twentieth century. Today, however, neither of these metals is used in coins, which are made of base metals with little intrinsic value. Coins today are thus mere tokens.

Until the beginning of the seventeenth century, coins were the only form of money in circulation in England. Then the banknote was introduced, referred to already in the history of the London banks in the Introduction. At first, banknotes were simply receipts and circulated because they were more convenient than using coin and thus were not considered as money but simply a claim to money itself, which was in the form of gold and silver coin. Notes were at all times convertible back into coins, and indeed woe betide the banker who was unable to honour his obligation to redeem his notes for gold and silver when called upon to do so. So long as banknotes were simply a claim on gold and not circulating very widely, they presented no threat to the growth of the supply of money, which remained under the direct control of the Government, through the Mint, with severe penalties for forgery. When banknotes began to be more freely acceptable as a means of settlement, and there was less demand to redeem them for gold, the Government sought to control their issue more closely. In order to control the supply of notes, the Bank of England was given increasing powers which enabled it to become, eventually, the sole issuer of banknotes in England and Wales.

Until 1914, except for brief periods of national crisis, the Bank of England's notes, like those of the goldsmith-bankers, were fully redeemable for gold on demand. At the outbreak of the First World War, the Bank of England again suspended the convertibility of notes into gold. This was meant to be a temporary suspension which would be lifted again as soon as the war was over, but in fact it has never since been possible to walk into the Bank of England and exchange a £5 note for the equivalent of gold. For a brief period from 1925 to 1931 it was possible to purchase gold from the Bank in 400-ounce bars, but since 1931 the Bank of England notes have been completely inconvertible. They have become not claims to money in the form of gold and silver, but money in themselves.

The notes which we now carry are no better than the paper they are printed on. The legend on the £1 note, 'I promise to pay the bearer on demand the sum of £1', means nothing except that the Bank of England will give you another £1 note in exchange for a surrendered one. The quality of acceptability can be clearly seen in the case of the inconvertible banknote. It circulates in payment for goods and services, not because it has any intrinsic value, nor because it can be exchanged for something of intrinsic value such as gold. Although notes are legal tender up to any amount, even having the benefit of legal tender is not conclusive. Bank of England notes circulate in settlement of debts merely because those taking them in payment know that they will be able to use them to purchase goods and services which they require in due course. They circulate as money because they are acceptable as such, and for no other reason.

As late as 1914, despite the fact that banknotes had been in existence for about 300 years, coins still predominated as a source of money. At the outbreak of war, coins in circulation totalled over £160m but notes accounted for only £40m. Only with the withdrawal of gold coin from circulation during the war did this situation change.

But in fact both these forms of money had already been overtaken in importance by the third element of money supply, namely bank deposits. In 1914, bank deposits already totalled £1000m and had already become the principal form of money. This remains so today, and indeed the importance of bank deposits has increased even further. Today, total sterling bank deposits with the clearing banks amount to around £60 000m, whereas notes in circulation total only about £11 000m, and coin a mere £500m. These figures do, however, only give an approximation of the size of each element in relation to one another. They are always changing, particularly during a period of high inflation.

'Near-' or 'Quasi-money'

The forms of money described above are those which in a developed economy perform all the functions of money. Some other forms of asset perform some of the functions of money but not all of them, and these assets are known as 'near-money' or 'quasi-money'.

We saw above that bank deposits, transferable by cheque or other instrument of transfer, are generally acceptable as a means of payment. In this context, however, some doubt exists about whether money kept on deposit account or in other forms of 'time-deposit' is money in the full sense or not. The argument in favour of deposit account balances being included as money is that they are so easy to transfer to a current account that in practice they are freely available for almost immediate transfer. On the other hand, it is argued that deposit account balances cannot be called money because they cannot be transferred directly by cheque – banks will not issue cheque books against deposit accounts – and the deposit account balance has to be converted into a current account balance before it can be truly used as money. There is no hard-and-fast answer to this problem, but certainly the UK in its narrow definition of money supply, called M_1, includes in the total only notes and coin held by the public and sterling 'sight' deposits of the private sector (i.e. deposits repayable on demand and not subject to a period of notice).

Other types of deposit are almost as liquid as current account bank deposits, but, like deposit account balances, lack the quality of direct transferability in settlement of a debt. Included in this category are deposits with savings banks, building societies and instalment credit finance companies. Building society deposits, for example, are effectively withdrawable on demand; although a period of notice is officially required, for small sums this is rarely imposed and immediate cash withdrawals are permitted. It is also possible for a depositor to ask the building society to draw a cheque in favour of a named payee, but the cheque is drawn not on the building society itself, but on the building society's own current account with a clearing bank. In both these instances, the building society deposit has had to be converted into a full form of money – either cash or a current account deposit – before it can be used to settle a debt. Thus, although a building society deposit performs the store of value function quite as efficiently as a bank deposit, it lacks the essential transferability quality and is therefore an example of near-money.

Other assets count as near-money, because although acceptable in settlement of debts, they are not immediately available. Included in this category would be bills of exchange, which become payable not at sight but at a date in the future. Thus they are not acceptable in the immediate settlement of a debt and hence are another form of near-money.

Questions

1 What functions does money perform?
2 What qualities are necessary if an object is to be used as money?
3 What forms of money exist in Britain today?
4 What is meant by 'convertibility' of banknotes? Are Britain's notes 'convertible' now?
5 What is meant by the 'intrinsic value' of money? To what extent, if any, does Britain's money possess intrinsic value?
6 Explain, with examples, what is meant by 'near-' or 'quasi-money'.

2

Bank Accounts

Types of accounts

The principal types of accounts available to customers of the banks are:

1 Current accounts;
2 Deposit accounts;
3 Savings accounts;
4 Student accounts;
5 Loan accounts;
6 Personal loan accounts;
7 Revolving credit schemes;
8 Budget accounts.

Current accounts

The main features of a current account are:

(*a*) The balance standing to a customer's credit on current account is repayable on demand, and there is a right to draw cheques.

(*b*) A customer may be granted an overdraft. This means that cheques may be drawn up to an agreed limit beyond the amount standing to the credit of the current account. Normally, banks do not pay interest on sums standing to the customer's credit.

(*c*) The relation between banker and customer, although legally expressed to be that of debtor and creditor, is in practice a close, personal one – and as confidential as that between doctor and patient, or solicitor and client.

A new customer will be given a paying-in book and will be shown how to fill up the credit forms (known as Bank Giro Credits), so that cash is distinguished from cheques. The counterfoils, which are receipted by the bank cashier, provide a record of amounts deposited. Cash and cheques can be paid in at any branch of the bank or, if there is no branch at the particular place where the customer happens to be, then at a branch of another bank. In either case, the amount will appear on the credit side of the account within a few days. In the case of overdrafts, the bank charges interest on a day-to-day basis but, if a customer overdraws the current account without the bank's prior agreement, an offence is in fact committed, and could lead to proceedings under the terms of the Theft Act 1968.

Deposit accounts

The main features of a deposit account are:

(*a*) The balance standing to a customer's credit on deposit account is repayable upon personal application after a stated period of notice – usually seven days.
(*b*) The customer has no right to draw cheques.
(*c*) The bank allows interest on sums standing to the customer's credit at a rate which varies from time to time.
(*d*) The bank does not usually charge commission on a deposit account. If services, such as collection of dividends or the payment of standing orders, are undertaken, the customer will normally have a current account as well as a deposit account, and commission may be charged as a result of the current account's additional use.

A deposit account gives safety of capital, but not capital appreciation, combined with virtual repayment on demand. It is particularly suited to customers who wish to earn some interest but who may need to draw out cash fairly quickly. In the past, deposit account customers were issued with passbooks, giving details of money lodged and withdrawn. Most depositors nowadays receive statements produced by computer, similar to those issued for current accounts. Cheques, postal orders and other types of credit instrument may be paid in for collection and credit to a deposit account. As with current accounts, the customer can pay in his cash or other items at any branch of the bank for the credit of his account at the particular branch where the deposit account is kept. Alternatively, deposits may be made at a branch of another bank, which will see that the money reaches the customer's account – provided that the deposit credit slip is filled in correctly with all details.

Savings accounts
These accounts are a special type of deposit account which are intended primarily for small savers. The rate of interest on savings accounts is usually a little lower than that on deposit accounts. Some banks allow the full deposit rate of interest on savings account balances in excess of a certain amount.

Student accounts
Many years ago student accounts began to interest the banks as it became recognised that students were:

(*a*) A comparatively untapped source for obtaining new bank accounts;
(*b*) A method of obtaining accounts of potential industrialists and businessmen who would become, eventually, a good source of contact for banking services within their companies or firms;
(*c*) A group which the banks actually desired to assist.

Most banks define students as men and women engaged in courses of full-time study at universities or other recognised institutes of further education. As most students receive a grant by cheque it is necessary for them to use a bank account to utilise it. No commission is charged on student accounts provided they are not overdrawn. In addition, there are arrangements for loans to be made to certain types of student where interest is charged at very low rates during the period of study and repayments are deferred until the course of study has ended.

Accounts do not necessarily have to be kept at a bank or branch near the university, college or polytechnic, and the banks are willing to make any reasonable arrangements throughout their branch networks for students.

There is generally a great deal of competition between banks during the summer and early autumn for student accounts. As inducements, two leading banks have offered book vouchers;

another offered quality ball-pens and clip-boards; and all the main banks advertise widely to attract students to bank with them.

Loan accounts

The overdraft is the most usual method of lending money to a customer on current account, but sometimes it is desirable to advance a fixed sum by way of loan account, the proceeds being credited to the customer's current account. Interest is calculated on the amount of a loan outstanding on a daily basis and, usually, repayment of the loan is made by periodic transfers of fixed amounts from the current account to loan account.

Personal loan accounts

The special features of personal loan accounts are that no security is required, and arrangements are made for repayment of the loan together with interest by equal monthly instalments over a pre-arranged period of time. In this way, the total amount to be paid by way of charges is known at the outset. As a general rule, the loans range from a minimum of £50 increasing to a maximum of about £1000. As the name implies, this service is intended primarily for financing items of domestic expenditure – for example, buying of furniture, personal goods or a motor car.

Revolving credit schemes

Some banks offer revolving credit schemes. These normally involve loans repayable by regular monthly instalments, but they differ from other loans repayable by instalments in two respects. First, the borrower need not take up the full amount of the loan at the outset. Second, as repayments reduce the indebtedness, the loan can be 'topped-up' by borrowing more, provided that the total debt outstanding does not exceed the agreed credit limit.

Budget accounts

In 1967, some banks introduced a new form of account for personal customers, called a 'budget account', to pay personal and household expenditure, such as electricity and gas bills, rates, season tickets, car insurance, school fees, etc. The total amount of these items is estimated for the year, and the customer makes payments out of this account as and when they fall due. Each month, the customer transfers one-twelfth of the estimated total for the year from his current account so that, after 12 months has passed by, the whole amount is repaid.

Opening an account

When a private individual wishes to open a current account there are four major matters regarding the new customer which the bank must consider:

1 Is the prospective account holder a bona fide customer? There have been many cases where a dishonest person has succeeded in opening an account under an assumed name, solely for the purpose of obtaining money to which he, or she, is not entitled.
2 Is the prospective customer a proper person to conduct a bank account? The referee or person introducing the new customer should be in a position to say whether he is a fit and proper person to have a bank account.
3 Does the person opening the account have the authorisation to do so? Normally, a prospective customer calls at the bank to open an account personally. Occasionally however, some third party states that he is authorised to open an account for a person. Requests of this nature should always be treated with extreme caution.
4 Is the prospective customer employed by someone else? The new customer should be asked whether he is employed and, if so, the nature of the employment and the name of the employer.

References

Before opening an account for a private person the banker has to obtain, and take up, a reference or an introduction from an established customer of either his or another bank. The reference should be checked in the case of an introduction by a stranger.

There are many dangers in opening an account for a stranger without first obtaining references or an introduction. For example, the person may be an undischarged bankrupt and there are several risks, especially for a banker, in having business relations with such people. The person may be an infant, in law, in which case any overdraft will not be enforceable against him. If the banker has any doubts about a person's age, further enquiries must be made. A secondary purpose of obtaining a satisfactory reference is to try to ensure that the new customer is a suitable person to be trusted with a chequebook. A specimen must be taken of each customer's signature. Some banks have all signatures in a signature book but the more usual and convenient method is to take all signatures on individual cards which also incorporate details of each customer's full name, address and occupation.

Statements and balances

Computerisation has transformed the banks' book-keeping systems, the issue of statements and the handling of cheques. It involves one or more centralised posting centres where computers are housed, each serving many hundreds of branches and dealing with many thousands of customers' accounts. Most banks already have a number of computer centres operating in key centres, with other complexes handling specialised accounting operations such as those connected with international operations. A customer may ask for his statement of account at any time, but the frequency with which the statement is sent regularly depends on the number of transactions, and varies according to circumstances and the customer's own wishes. In all cases, however, it is preferable and usual for statements to be sent out at regular intervals, so that they can be agreed by the customer. In the customer's own interests, and to preserve the confidential relationship and proper secrecy about personal affairs, very precise written instructions are required by the bank before any other person is allowed access to the statement. Banks are often placed in a difficult position by a customer ringing up to ask for the balance of the account. It is not always possible to identify a voice over the telephone, and if the bank seems unduly cautious by insisting on proper identification it is not because of any lack of desire to help, but for the customer's benefit alone.

Closing an account

The severance of relations between the banker and his customer by drawing out the full amount standing to the credit of a customer's account, either by the customer's own act, or at the request of the banker, closes the account. When, as sometimes happens, a banker wishes to close an unsatisfactory account, he usually sends written advice to the customer that he will not receive any further credits on the customer's behalf, and requesting the customer to withdraw the balance; or, alternatively, stating that he will honour only those cheques up to the limit of the credit balance. It is not desirable, and in fact would be unwise in such circumstances for the banker to send the customer a cheque for the balance. A banker is not entitled to close an account without giving such reasonable notice as will obviate any damage to the customer's credit. But a customer may close an account merely by presenting a cheque made out for the balance on the account, usually informing the bank of this intention and returning unused cheques. A banker cannot prevent a customer from withdrawing his balance and closing his account even when, for example, there are bills running under discount for the customer and on which, therefore, he is contingently liable.

A banker is bound to 'stop' an account continuing in the event of notice of the death, mental incapacity or bankruptcy of a customer or, in the case of a limited company, notice of voluntary liquidation or the making of a winding-up order; the service of an order of the court; and notice of an assignment to a third party of the balance standing in the customer's favour. Secured accounts will nearly always be stopped when some event happens which decreases the value, or affects the availability of, the security. For example, a current account secured by a mortgage would be stopped as soon as the banker received notice of a second charge upon the security. Where an account is covered by a guarantee or other security given by a third party, the account would be stopped on receipt of notice of the death, mental incapacity or bankruptcy of the guarantor or the person who deposited the security.

Questions

1 What are the main features of a current account?
2 How does a 'revolving credit' scheme operate?
3 What does a banker have to consider when opening an account?
4 Is it possible for a banker to close the account of a customer with or without notice?
5 For what reasons is a banker bound to 'stop' an account?

3

Cheques and Bank Cards

A cheque is defined as an 'unconditional order in writing addressed by one person to another, signed by the person giving it, requiring the banker to pay on demand a sum certain in money to or to the order of a specified person or to bearer'.

The person who draws a cheque is known as the drawer and the person to whom the cheque is made payable is known as the payee. The banker on whom the cheque is drawn is called the drawee bank.

A person may draw a cheque payable to himself, in which event the drawer and the payee are the same person.

Within the terms of the relationship that exists between a banker and a customer, there is a duty by the banker to honour cheques drawn upon him by the customer, according to the credit money available in the customer's account, or within any agreed overdraft limit.

As has been mentioned already, millions of cheques are passed through the clearing system each day, the majority of which are paid and debited against the credit balances held on customers' accounts. Unpaid cheques are returned with a reply indicating the reason for return. There are many impediments which may cause a cheque to fail to be paid. Generally, these are as follows:

1 The legal definitions which relate to cheques according to the Bills of Exchange Act 1882 and the Cheques Act 1957;
2 Certain situations which may arise, such as the death, mental incapacity or bankruptcy of the customer, entailing immediate action to be taken by the banker.

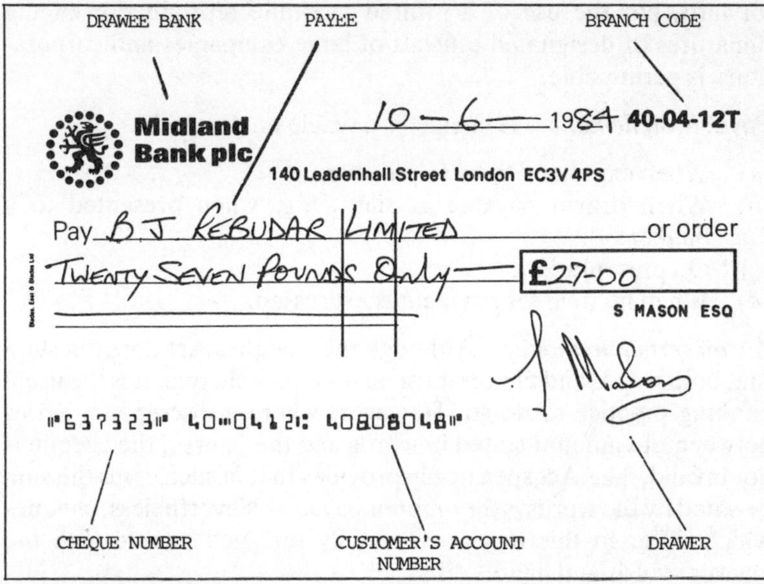

Conditions of use

To be legally acceptable, all cheques must be:

Unconditional If the banker is ordered to pay conditionally, on the payee performing an act or deed, the instrument is not a cheque because it is not unconditional.

In writing A cheque should be drawn in ink, although it is permissible to use a typewriter to enter all the details. If it is written in lead pencil, however, a banker will normally return the cheque.

By one person to another An instrument drawn by a banker upon himself is not a cheque because it is addressed to himself. However, an individual may draw money on a cheque signed by himself as it becomes a valid order for the payment of money under the provisions of the Cheques Act 1957. Banker's drafts drawn by one branch on the head office or on another branch are not cheques, because the head office and all the branches are considered to be one institution, whereas the drawer and the drawee must be distinct parties.

Signed by the person giving it This would appear to be straightforward, but the use of a printed facsimile reproduction of the signatures of designated officials of large companies and corporations is permissible.

Payable on demand A cheque is payable on demand:

(*a*) When expressed to be so payable;
(*b*) When drawn payable at sight, e.g. when presented to a banker;
(*c*) On presentation;
(*d*) When no time for payment is expressed.

A sum certain in money Although the Cheques Act does not state that both words and figures must be used on a cheque, it is the usual banking practice to do so. However, where a discrepancy arises between the amount stated in words and the figures, the cheque is not invalid. The Act specifically provides that in such cases the sum denoted by the words is the amount payable. Nevertheless, cheques which differ in this way are normally returned unpaid with the answer 'words and figures differ'.

Payable to a specified person or bearer Some people fill in cheques 'to cash or order', but where a cheque is not made 'payable to bearer', the payee must be named or otherwise indicated therein with reasonable certainty.

Note: There is no legal requirement to date a cheque and the Bills of Exchange Act 1882 provides that it is not invalid merely because the date is missing. In practice, however, the cheque may be returned by the drawee banker with the answer 'date required'.

A cheque is issued when the drawer parts with it to another person, with the intention that the proceeds of the cheque shall be paid to the person, or to his order, or to bearer. The drawer is not liable upon a cheque until it has been issued, or is precluded from denying its issue. A cheque is duly issued even though the drawer was induced by fraud to issue it.

Crossed cheques

The drawer of a cheque should take all possible precautions to ensure that persons who are not entitled to it cannot obtain value for it. By crossing a cheque, the drawer will make it more difficult for a fraudulent person to obtain value for it. A thief, for example, would be unable to obtain payment for it by presenting it at the counter of the drawee banker. Instead he would either have to clear the cheque through a banking account in his own name or an assumed name, in which case he may be subsequently traced and prosecuted. Alternatively, he may compound the felony by forging the payee's endorsement on the cheque and obtain value by handing it to a third party.

The Bills of Exchange Act 1882 identifies the law relating to crossed cheques, as follows:

(*a*) If a cheque is crossed generally, it should be presented by, and paid only to, a banker.
(*b*) If a cheque is crossed specially, it should be presented by, and paid only to, the banker named in the crossing, or to his agent for collection, being a banker.
(*c*) A cheque which is crossed specially to more than one banker, except when crossed to an agent for collection, being a banker, must not be paid.

A banker disregarding any of these rules will be liable to the true owner of the cheque for any loss which may be sustained.

Crossings can be either general or special. A general crossing consists of two parallel lines across the face of the cheque with or without the words '& Co.' and 'Not Negotiable'. The effect is that the cheque may not be cashed over the counter of a bank but must be paid into a banking account for collection. A special crossing consists of the name of a particular bank written across the face of the cheque, with or without the parallel lines, and the words '& Co.' and 'Not Negotiable'. Its effect is that the cheque can only be paid into an account at that bank.

The words '& Co.', which are optional and have no legal significance, are a relic of earlier days when most bankers were private firms and the drawer of the cheque, not knowing his payee's bankers, would put in '& Co.', leaving a space before it for the addition by the payee of his banker's name.

The words 'Not Negotiable' added to the crossings are the best possible safeguard when a cheque is sent through the post. Not only must a cheque so crossed be paid into a banking account, but also no one can obtain a better title to it in law than that possessed by previous persons. Anyone who receives it subsequent to its theft,

Examples of cheque crossings

General crossings

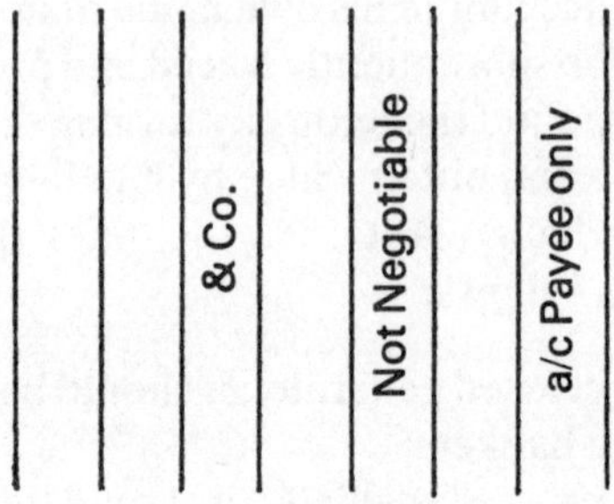

Special crossings

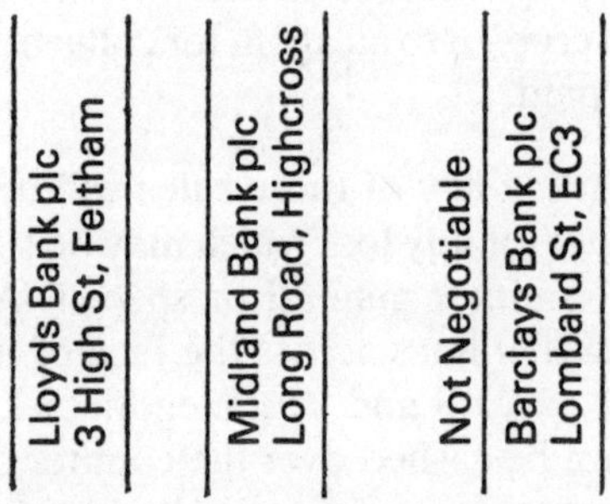

has no better title than had the thief, who, of course, had none at all. Even if the cheque is paid before the loss is discovered, the true owner can recover the amount from the person to whose account it has been credited. However, the words 'Not Negotiable' have no significance apart from the recognised crossings, and if the words appear on the cheque without the parallel transverse lines, or without the name of the banker written across the cheque, the words 'Not Negotiable' alone do not make the document a crossed cheque. The addition to either a general or special crossing of the words 'A/c. Payee Only' ensures that the collecting bank will credit the cheques to the account of the payee and no one else. Failure to do so is negligence, rendering the bank liable for conversion.

Authorisation to cross cheques is defined as follows:

1 A cheque may be crossed generally or specially by the drawer.
2 Where a cheque is uncrossed, the holder may cross it generally or specially.
3 Where a cheque is crossed, the holder may cross it specially.
4 Where a cheque is crossed generally or specially, the holder may add the words 'Not Negotiable'.
5 Where a cheque is crossed specially, the banker to whom it is crossed may again cross it specially to another banker for collection.
6 Where an uncrossed cheque, or a cheque generally, is sent to a banker for collection, he may cross it specially to himself.

Negotiability

The characteristics of negotiable instruments, including cheques, are as follows:

1 A negotiable instrument, like the money which it represents, may pass from hand to hand by delivery, or by delivery with endorsement.
2 The holder may sue without notice to the person liable to pay.
3 The transferee of a negotiable instrument is presumed to have given consideration, i.e. money or value.
4 A holder in due course, which is identified below.

A holder in due course is 'a person who has taken a bill complete and regular on the face of it, providing that he took it (a) before it was overdue, and without notice that it had been dishonoured, if such be the case; and (b) that he took it in good faith, and for value, e.g. money, goods or a service, without notice of any defect in the title of the person negotiating it'. Hence, a negotiable instrument is one that can be transferred to convey a perfect title to the holder.

Endorsement

An endorsement may be defined as the signature of a cheque (usually on the back) by the holder, or his duly authorised agent, followed by delivery of the instrument whereby the holder of a cheque payable to his order negotiates it to another person, who takes it as a new holder.

Before 1957, every cheque had to be endorsed before being paid into an account. The Cheques Act 1957 held that where a banker in good faith and in the ordinary course of business pays a cheque drawn on him which is not endorsed or is irregularly endorsed, he does not, in doing so, incur any liability by reason of the absence of, or irregularity in, endorsement.

An endorsement may be blank or special: A *blank* endorsement specifies no endorsee and its effect is to make the instrument payable to bearer. It may be converted into a special endorsement by the holder writing above the endorser's signature a direction to pay the cheque to, or to the order of, himself or some other person. A *special* endorsement specifies the person to whom, or to whose order, the instrument is to be payable. For example, with a cheque endorsed 'Pay to Jones' or 'Pay to the order of Jones', the endorsee may further negotiate it by endorsement and delivery.

There may be certain difficulties regarding endorsement according to the titles of individuals, or companies, and some of these are listed below:

Cheques payable to	*Endorsement should be*
Tom Jones	Tom Jones or T. Jones
Tom Jones, Esq.	Tom Jones or T. Jones
Mr T. Jones	Tom Jones or T. Jones
Dr T. Jones	Tom Jones, T. Jones or T. Jones, MD
Capt. T. Jones	Tom Jones, T. Jones or T. Jones, Capt.
Mrs Rebecca Jones	Rebecca Jones
Mrs Jones	R. Jones
Mrs Tom Jones	R. Jones, wife (or widow) of Tom Jones
Miss Rebecca Harris (since married)	Rebecca Jones, née Harris
T. Jones & Co.	T. Jones & Co. or T. Jones & Co.–H. Farmer, Proprietor
T. Jones & Co. Limited	For and on behalf of: T. Jones & Co. Limited H. Farmer, Secretary

Banker's authority to pay

Revocation

The banker is under obligation to his customer to honour his cheques provided that (a) the balance of the account is sufficient to meet the cheque, or that the customer has authority to overdraw, and (b) the cheques are correct in form.

However, a banker's authority to pay a customer's cheque is revoked:

1 By countermand of payment, that is, where the customer orders the bank not to pay a cheque which he has already issued;
2 By notice of the customer's death;
3 In addition, each cheque has to be examined for the following details by which the banker would be affected legally:
   (*a*) The date: the cheque must not be paid if it is 'post-dated' or 'out of date';
   (*b*) The name of the payee must be entered;
   (*c*) The words and figures, which must be the same;
   (*d*) The signature of the drawer, which must be the same as the customer's specimen signature held by the bank and not be forged;
   (*e*) Any alterations made by the drawer of the cheque must be initialled;
   (*f*) The absence of mutilation;
   (*g*) The endorsement, if any, which should appear correctly;
   (*h*) That the customer has sufficient credit to meet the amount of the cheque;
   (*i*) That there are no restrictions with regard to the payee or in the crossing;
   (*j*) That there is no other reason why the banker should not pay.

In each of these cases, failure by the banker to act appropriately may cause loss to the bank, either by having to repay the value of the cheque to the customer or from litigation by the customer. At the same time, it is not sufficient for a customer to write out cheques without care for the details, as negligence may cause the cheque to be returned or allow another person to alter it fraudulently. In the last case, for example, it is extremely likely that the writer of the cheque will be liable for the loss. Therefore, both the customer and the banker have a responsibility in relation to the issue and payment of cheques, and both must take care.

The following circumstances also compel the banker to refuse payment of his customer's cheques:

(*a*) Notice of a customer's mental incapacity;
(*b*) Notice of any order of the Court, such as 'garnishee order' which restrains the customer from drawing on his account;
(*c*) Notice of bankruptcy;
(*d*) Notice of the winding-up of a company under the Companies Act;
(*e*) Knowledge of any defect in the title of the presenter of the cheque.

The drawer is the only person who can instruct a banker not to pay. The customer's right to countermand payments exists up to the time of payment. This is so even if the banker has told the holder that the cheques will be paid on presentation.

Forgery

If the signature of the drawer is forged, and the banker pays out the customer's money on the authority of the forged signature, the banker cannot usually debit his customer with the money paid out. The mandate on which the banker has acted is not his customer's mandate. Nevertheless, there may be exceptional circumstances which will enable the banker to debit his customer with a cheque bearing a forged signature:

1 The customer by his conduct may have misled the banker, causing him to pay the cheque when otherwise it might have been refused. For example, if he does not repudiate the signature as soon as the forgery came to his notice, and the banker pays it when otherwise he would have returned it.
2 If the banker is thereby prejudiced in any action he may take against the forger.
3 If by some act, or by his conduct, the customer has induced the banker to believe that the signature was a genuine one. For example, a cheque may have been forged by the wife of the customer, for the sake of expediency.

All practicable steps should be taken to prevent blank cheques getting into the wrong hands:

(*a*) Chequebooks should not be handed out to new customers until satisfactory references have been obtained.

(*b*) Chequebooks should be issued to the customer personally, or to a known representative, against a properly signed order.
(*c*) Customers are warned not to give blank cheques to strangers.

A careful record is made of cheques which are reported lost or stolen. Special care is given to cheques which were obviously not issued to the customer himself, e.g. those which he has apparently borrowed from a customer or another branch, the name of that branch having been altered. Cheques for substantial amounts, or with unusual payees, are closely examined on presentation.

Fraudulent alteration

The fraudulent increase of the amount of a cheque is a material alteration, and the banker cannot normally debit the customer's account.

It has been established that:

1 The customer owes a duty to the banker to use reasonable care in drawing cheques so as not to facilitate addition or alteration.
2 The banker is justified in declining to pay a cheque if there are reasonable grounds for suspecting that it has been tampered with, or if it is couched in an unusual or irregular form, but his answer on the cheque should not be detrimental to the customer's credit-standing.

The *bank* will stand the loss if the alteration is apparent, *or* if the alteration is non-apparent, and the drawer used due care. The *drawer* will stand the loss on failure to exercise care and if the alteration is non-apparent.

All material alterations on a cheque must be made with the drawer's assent, confirmed by a signature or initials alongside each alteration. Any material alterations made without this assent render the cheque void. If there are two or more signatories on the cheque all must join in the confirmation. Alterations on cheques on behalf of limited companies and other corporate bodies must also be confirmed by all signatories to the cheque.

Mutilation

If a drawer tears a cheque in such a way that its condition is clear evidence that he intended to cancel it, the banker must suffer any loss that may be incurred by his paying it to a person who has put the pieces together and presented the cheque. If the payee accidentally tears it in two before presentation, he must get the drawer's confirmation, or the collecting banker's guarantee, before the drawee banker will pay it. Generally, the cheque is returned by the banker on whom it is drawn, marked 'mutilated cheque'. A cheque torn, but not quite in two, would usually be paid, although the banker would actually be quite justified in returning it, marked as above; in all cases of doubt this is the safest course to follow.

Lost or stolen cheques

If a customer loses either his chequebook or any individual cheque, or has them stolen, it is important to countermand payment immediately by giving the bank written instructions to that effect. Speed is vital on these occasions and, on receiving a message, the bank will postpone payment pending confirmation in writing. The cheque number must be quoted and, in the case of a cheque already issued, the date, the amount and the name of the payee must be given. Where a cheque has been lost before it is overdue, the person who was the holder of it has the right to apply to the drawer for another cheque for the same amount. Normally he must give an undertaking to the drawer to indemnify him against all persons, in case the cheque alleged to have been lost should be found again. If, on request, the drawer refuses to give a duplicate cheque, he may be compelled to do so. A holder, however, has no right to apply to an endorser to make a fresh endorsement on the duplicate cheque.

Post-dated cheques

Cheques on which the date is made out for some future time are called post-dated cheques; for example, when a cheque written on the first of the month bears a date later in the month. The effect of this is that the cheque cannot be paid until the date arrives. Although cheques are not invalid because they are post-dated, they may involve the paying banker in substantial loss if payment is made before the due date because:

(*a*) The customer may countermand payment at any time before that date;

(*b*) The customer may die, or become bankrupt;

(*c*) If a post-dated cheque is paid and the banker subsequently dishonours other cheques which could have been paid, he will be liable to the customer for damage to the customer's credit.

Post-dated cheques are sometimes issued by creditworthy customers for quite genuine reasons, e.g. to give them time to ensure that goods supplied are satisfactory. In many cases, however, such cheques are issued by customers, with the object of obtaining additional time to provide funds to meet them.

Stale cheques

A cheque is overdue, or 'stale', when it appears on the face of it to have been in circulation for an unreasonable length of time. 'An unreasonable time' has never been legally defined but the question is an important one, for if a stale cheque is negotiated it can only be negotiated subject to any defect of title affecting it when it was due. By custom, most bankers return cheques presented six or more months after date, marked 'out of date', and require either the drawer's confirmation before payment or that the drawer alters the date and initials the alteration.

Issuing cheques

Each day, large numbers of cheques have to be returned because of carelessness or thoughtlessness on the part of the drawer. Properly, the banks return them marked 'post-dated', 'words and figures differ', 'signature differs', and so on. The correct date, the correct amount in both words and figures, the customer's signature in accordance with the specimen held by the bank, the correct name of the payee to prevent irregular endorsement and the avoidance of a blank space after the name to preclude unauthorised additions will all save trouble and loss of time if completed properly.

Some customers make a practice of drawing cash from their bankers by filling up an ordinary cheque form so that it reads 'Pay cash or order' or 'Pay wages or order'. Customers occasionally also use the words 'Pay cash or order' when they wish to make payments to third parties, especially when they do not want to reveal the names of the payees.

Technically, cheques made out in this way do not comply with the definition of a cheque because a correctly drawn cheque requires the banker to pay to, or to the order of, a specified person or to bearer. 'Cash' cannot be described as a 'specified person'. Instruments payable to 'Cash or order' or 'Wages or order' may be crossed generally, or specially, or 'Not Negotiable'.

Payment of salaries and wages

The Bank Giro system (see page 52) is used by large numbers of companies and other organisations for crediting employees' salaries direct to their banking accounts. This system benefits not only the companies which, otherwise, would have to make out cheques or pay over cash, but also the employees who can draw their cash requirements from the bank, pay their bills by cheque, and be assured that the balance of the money is safe from loss or theft.

Cheque cards

British banks started to issue cheque cards in 1965 and all the main commercial banks in Britain, with the exception of Barclays Bank which uses the Barclaycard credit card as a cheque card as well, agreed to issue a standardised form of cheque card.

A cheque card is a document made of plastic material issued by a bank, which enables the holder to cash cheques up to a stated maximum (£50 at present) at any branch of the issuing bank or of certain other banks with whom reciprocal arrangements have been made. In addition, the card is valuable when making payments to third parties, because it contains an undertaking to the payee of a cheque that the bank will pay any cheque not exceeding the stated maximum. The main regulations are as follows:

1 The cheque must be signed in the presence of the payee.
2 The signature on the cheque must correspond with the specimen signature on the card.
3 The cheque must be drawn on a bank cheque form bearing the code number shown on the card.
4 The cheque must be drawn before the expiry date of the card.
5 The card number must be written on the reverse of the cheque.

The great benefit of the cheque card is that many shops, restaurants and hotels which previously had refused, or had been unwilling, to accept cheques from strangers, can now do so, secure in the knowledge that no cheques offered by a customer holding a cheque card will be returned unpaid, unless the instructions have not been carried out.

Issue of cheque cards is by no means confined to the British banks. Banks on the Continent were quick to recognise that this idea also offered benefits to them and to their customers. The result was a profusion of cheque cards issued by different banks to their own customers, but, due to Exchange Control regulations, each card was usable only in the country of origin. As these regulations were eased, it became feasible to consider the introduction of a system whereby banks in several countries could cash cheques for holders of cheque cards from other participating countries. Out of this was born a scheme which allows a customer, who has a cheque card issued by a British bank, to cash cheques at any bank in Europe which displays a Eurocheque sticker in its window.

Credit cards

The Diners' Club Inc. was probably the first company to issue an all-purpose card, in 1950. This was followed by the Franklin National Bank of New York which adopted a credit card plan. About seven years later the American Express Company, the Bank of America and the Chase Manhattan Bank entered the credit field. In 1966, Barclays Bank became the first British Bank to introduce a credit card known as 'Barclaycard'. It should be pointed out, however, that Diners' Club and American Express cards are specifically travel and entertainment cards (T and E cards), and do not set out to offer any form of deferred or revolving credit as do credit cards.

In October 1972, the Access card was introduced by Lloyds, Midland, National Westminster and Williams and Glyn's Banks, together with the Clydesdale Bank, the Royal Bank of Scotland and the Northern Bank. Each of these banks is responsible for the issue of cards to its customers, and for fixing the credit limit for each customer.

Credit cards are designed to obviate the use of either cash or cheques and also, in some cases, to give some measure of credit to the cardholder. They are available for use only at those places (shops, hotels, restaurants, etc.) which have agreed to accept them, and where the credit cards may be accepted in place of cash for payment for goods or services. Credit cards operate quite differently from cheque cards. A cheque card guarantees payment of a cheque, whereas a credit card guarantees payment against a sales voucher signed by the cardholder. Each credit card bears a specimen signature of its holder and is 'embossed' by the issuing bank with the holder's name and number. When goods or services are supplied, the holder hands the card to a retailer who has agreed to join the scheme. The retailer places the card in a special imprinter machine, which records the holder's name and number on a sales voucher to which is added, by hand, the particulars of the transaction. The holder then signs the voucher, and the retailer compares the signature with that on the card. The special forms signed by the customer are then sent to the particular credit card centre. At the end of each month the customer receives a statement of expenditure, together with the relevant signed forms as confirmation of the purchase. The customer then pays by cheque direct to the credit card centre either the whole of the outstanding balance or a certain proportion which is indicated on the statement.

The main advantages of the credit card for the cardholder are that he can:

(*a*) Purchase goods or services at a large number of outlets without using cash or cheques;
(*b*) Obtain cash from a bank through the credit card;
(*c*) Make payments on the credit card account to provide more credit, up to the agreed limit;
(*d*) Settle the account of many purchases throughout the month with only one cheque;
(*e*) Obtain a period of free credit between the period of purchase and the time of payment.

The main advantages of the credit card to the retailer are that:

(*a*) Credit can be granted without the risk of bad debt.
(*b*) There is less risk than in handling cash.
(*c*) People tend to spend more generously when paying by credit card.
(*d*) He is likely to increase sales, as against competitors who do not accept credit cards.

Travellers cheques

Travellers' cheques are issued mainly for the convenience of individuals travelling abroad, and they are the usual method by which travellers take money abroad to provide for their expenses. Travellers' cheques issued in the UK are usually expressed in sterling amounts and are issued in fixed denominations such as £5, £10, £20 and £50. However, they are also available in other currencies, such as US or Canadian dollars, lire, pesetas, etc. Whatever the currency, each denomination has a distinctive colour, selected by the issuing bank, and the purchaser signs each cheque on issue as drawer in the presence of the issuing bank.

Travellers' cheques are normally exchanged for local currency at the cashing banker's rate of exchange for sight drafts in London. Normally, no commission is charged and the cashing banker makes his profit on the transaction in the rate of exchange. In most cases the holder cannot insist that a foreign bank cashes his cheques unless that bank is a correspondent authorised by the issuing bank for the purpose. It is a rare event for a bank or a third party to refuse to cash, or to accept in payment, travellers' cheques. At most a passport or some evidence of identity is required as a condition of cashing. The holder has to sign the cheque in the presence of the person cashing or accepting it and this signature must, of course, agree with the one already on the cheque. Travellers' cheques which have been issued, but not used, can be either paid into the holder's bank account or cashed by the issuing bank. If travellers' cheques are lost, any loss falls, in principle, upon the traveller; in practice most banks replace them free of charge. The chief advantages of travellers' cheques are simplicity, general acceptability, cheapness, and comparative safety. They are very convenient for a traveller who is moving about, whether at home or abroad. Hotels and shops are accustomed to accepting the cheques in payment, and they can be used in place of cash when the banks are closed.

Eurocheque cards

In 1983, Midland Bank devised a payment system for customers travelling on holiday or on business. The Eurocheque card offered the freedom to use cheques in many countries in the same way as ordinary cheques are used in the UK.

The benefits are as follows:

1 Eurocheques can be used in nearly forty European and Mediterranean countries.
2 Cash can be obtained from more than 185 000 bank branches.
3 Eurocheques are accepted by over 4½ million shops, hotels, garages, etc.
4 Currency cheques are guaranteed up to an amount agreed by participating banks – approximately £75.
5 In the UK, individual cheques are guaranteed up to £75.
6 There is no limit on the number of cheques that may be issued.
7 Cheques can be written in most European currencies.
8 Eurocheques are drawn on the current account, without the need to make advance payments.
9 Exchange rates are those prevailing upon presentation of cheques in the UK – avoiding having to accept rates of exchange offered by hotels, *bureaux de change*, etc.

The customer pays no charges in most countries. When cheques are received in the UK, a nominal charge is made for clearance plus a fee of 1¼% of the value of the cheque which is payable to the foreign bank for the work undertaken. A modest annual card fee is charged by Midland Bank to join the scheme.

Questions

1 What is the legal definition of a cheque?
2 What is the difference between a drawer and a payee?
3 Explain how a general crossing differs from a special crossing.
4 What effect do the words 'Not Negotiable' have on a cheque?
5 Explain the purpose of endorsing a cheque.
6 For what valid reason may a banker refuse to pay a customer's cheque?
7 Who stands the loss when a cheque is fraudulently altered?
8 How can post-dated cheques involve a banker in substantial loss if payment is made before the due date?
9 Explain the difference between a cheque card and a credit card.

4

The Clearing System

Clearing is a term used to describe the system of collecting payment for cheques paid into banks, and a cheque is cleared when it has been paid by the branch of the bank on which it is drawn. Clearing also takes place in respect of credit items.

The Bankers' Clearing House

The system known as the Bankers' Clearing House is believed to have begun as early as 1773. It originated when clerks from the various banks were required to take bundles of cheques for payment to the other bank offices. The clerks used to meet at a coffee house, and soon realised that, by an exchange of cheques among themselves, and the receipt or payment in cash of the difference due to or from each of the other representatives, there was really no need for them to call at each other's offices. The idea worked so well that it was shortly adopted officially by the London bankers. Soon after that, premises were bought and the Bankers' Clearing House was established. Despite the massive volume of paper and the huge sums involved, the bankers' clearing system works very smoothly. The Clearing House has an account at the Bank of England, as has also each of the clearing banks. The Bankers' Clearing House is now a limited company established in London, and its members are the clearing banks.

Millions of cheques are drawn by bank customers on their accounts each day and they are subsequently paid back into the banks. A cheque is drawn on a particular branch of a bank and it can be paid only at that branch. Therefore, either the cheque, if it is not 'crossed', must be taken to that branch for payment, or it may be paid into a bank account and the banker must present it for payment.

At one time, there were three clearings: town, metropolitan and country, roughly corresponding to branches in the City of London, the outer City and West End, and the remainder of the country respectively. There were, in addition a number of provincial clearing houses in large cities which dealt exclusively with cheques drawn on branches within each area and paid into other banks in the same area. The present system involves the Bankers' Clearing House dealing with cheques passing through:

(*a*) Town clearing;
(*b*) General clearing;
(*c*) Credit clearing;
(*d*) Bankers' Automated Clearing Services (BACS).

Town clearing

The Town clearing has always handled cheques drawn on branches within the City of London, but now it is restricted to cheques drawn on offices and branches in the City within easy walking distance of the Clearing House. Only cheques of £10 000 and over are eligible for the Town clearing, and they must be drawn on, and must have been paid into, one of these Town branches. All other cheques are cleared through the general clearing, or through Bankers' Automated Clearing Services. The Town clearing covers the financial operations of the City of London, including all the banks, the Stock Exchange, the insurance companies, shipping companies and other large financial institutions.

The Town branches sort out the cheques drawn on each of the other member banks, and make a list of the items together with a total amount. These are taken to the Clearing House where each bank has an established 'position'. The cheques are taken to the branches on which they are drawn to be examined before payment. It may not be possible to pay all the cheques, for one reason or another, and some will be returned unpaid. Any unpaid cheques, on which must be clearly marked the reason for non-payment, must be returned at the Clearing House, as quickly as possible on the same day, to the banks that presented them.

General clearing

The remainder of the cheques handled by the Bankers Clearing House are passed through the general clearing, which deals with a much greater volume of work than the Town clearing. Because of the large number of cheques passing through the general clearing, the banks deliver by van the cheques in plastic containers to the Exchange Centre at the Clearing House.

All general clearing cheques paid into a branch are sorted into bank order and sent, together with a machined-listing of individual cheque amounts and a grand total, to that bank's clearing department in London. This practice is followed by all branches throughout the country, and the clearing department of each of the banks amalgamates the bundles of cheques for each of the other banks, together with the listings received from the branches. A summary is made of the totals of those listings. Then, together with the cheques, they are taken to the clearing house for exchange. After the exchange, the listings, and any cheques received, go back to the clearing departments of the banks on which the cheques are drawn, where the total is agreed with the listings handed to them by the presenting banks. The cheques are sorted into branch order and the same day, by post, bundles of cheques are dispatched to the branches on which they are drawn.

The banks have special arrangements with the Post Office and, although there are occasionally unexpected delays, it usually takes a minimum of three complete days to clear cheques through the general clearing. On the day after receipt, cheques are delivered by the head office of the branch bank at which they were paid into the head office of the drawee branch. On the second day, they are received by the branch on which they are drawn. If a cheque cannot be paid, it is returned direct to the collecting branch, where it arrives on the third day. Thus a cheque paid in for the credit of an account on Monday will, if returned unpaid by the drawee branch, be received back by the presenting branch on the following Thursday. The intervention of Saturdays, Sundays and public holidays will lengthen this three-day period. If, after allowing for these and other possible delays, the cheque is not received back, it can be assumed to have been cleared.

Should a customer wish to know quickly whether or not a cheque is cleared, the branch can usually arrange for a 'special presentation', when the cheque will be sent direct to the drawee branch, thus bypassing the general clearing system.

Credit clearing

A most convenient method of transferring money from one bank to another is by means of credit slips. This occurs when a customer pays in money for his account at a branch other than his own, or when a bank makes a payment on behalf of its customer under a standing order arrangement.

In 1960, the credit transfer system was introduced, and this facility for transferring money was encouraged by the banks. It was made available to non-customers as well as to customers. The system enabled payments to be made direct to customers' accounts at any bank, making it unnecessary to purchase money orders, postal orders or to draw cheques to send money through the post. Coinciding with the introduction of the credit transfer system, a new clearing – for the exchange and settlement of credit vouchers – was added to the functions of the Bankers' Clearing House. This was called 'credit clearing' and is now part of the Bank Giro system. All branches remit to their clearing departments in the City bundles of credit transfers with detailed listings for each of the other banks. The clearing departments then amalgamate these bundles for delivery to the other banks at the Clearing House.

Bankers' Automated Clearing Services Limited (BACS)

The function of BACS, which forms part of the banks' money transfer services, has been defined by the Bankers' Clearing House as to 'process on behalf of the clearing banks, Bank of England, Scottish banks and their customers, magnetic tapes containing details of bankers' orders, Bank Giro Credits and direct debits'.

The introduction of magnetic ink characters at the bottom of cheques has helped to speed up the handling of the clearing. It has become possible, therefore, to improve the methods by which paper entries can be handled without the need for a separate piece of paper for each entry. For example, if a company wishes to make a payment to a person who has a banking account, this can be done by preparing a credit transfer; that is a paper voucher, which is cleared through the credit clearing and the funds placed to the account of the beneficiary. If the company has a computer, or buys 'time' on another company's computer, there is no longer any need for a paper voucher to be prepared. All the payments to be made by the company can be recorded on a reel of magnetic tape, or punched on paper tape, and passed to a special section in the Clearing House. The information received from the tapes each day is sorted by a computer into the various destination banks and branches. These entries are transferred to other magnetic tapes for each bank. Any customer may give instructions for payments to be made on a regular basis, direct to the bank account of another customer.

As well as customers, the banks themselves make use of BACS to reduce the volume of clerical work performed manually.

By the use of a system of tape exchange, whereby credit transfer slip entries are recorded on reels of magnetic tape and passed through the BACS, and by a process known as direct debiting, it is also possible for local authorities, insurance companies and similar organisations to collect payments due to them.

Daily settlement

At the end of each day, each bank will be due to receive, or to pay, money in respect of that day's Town clearing and of the previous day's general and credit clearings and computer bureau clearing.

Each bank compiles a daily settlement sheet which shows on one side the balances due to be received from other banks. These balances will be in payment for cheques delivered to other banks through the Town and general clearings, on Town clearing cheques returned unpaid, and for credit vouchers received from the other banks in the credit clearing. A similar settlement sheet is prepared by BACS showing its entries. On the other side, entries are made for the balances due to be paid to the other banks. The two sides are then totalled and a balance worked out which is, in fact, the net balance due to be received or paid by the bank in respect of all its transactions for the day.

Each clearing bank keeps an account at the Bank of England and the balance of the day's clearing operations is transferred to or from that account. It must follow, then, that the total balances paid by some banks must equal the total balances received by the other banks.

Bank Giro system

The term 'Bank Giro' was adopted by the clearing banks and Scottish banks in 1967 to describe the established credit transfer system and the newly introduced direct debiting system.

Credit transfer

Bank Giro Credits provide a simple, efficient method of transferring funds to the banking account of a customer of any bank in the UK as an alternative to paying by cheque.

Although the cheque has proved to be a convenient instrument for making payments, it has certain disadvantages, namely, signing, sending through the post, handling and risk. For example:

1 Each cheque has to be signed by or on behalf of the drawer.
2 Most cheques are sent by post to the payees; this is costly in terms of stationery and postage.
3 A cheque often passes through several hands, including the staff of the remitter and the staff of the recipient.
4 There is always a risk that a cheque may be stolen and misappropriated.

The credit transfer system avoids those disadvantages and provides a simpler, cheaper and safer method of transferring funds from one person to another. It may not, however, always be as convenient.

Credit transfers are initiated by the payer. Instead of drawing a separate cheque for each payment, a person having to make payments fills in a credit slip for each payment showing the name of the recipient, the amount to be paid, the name and address of the

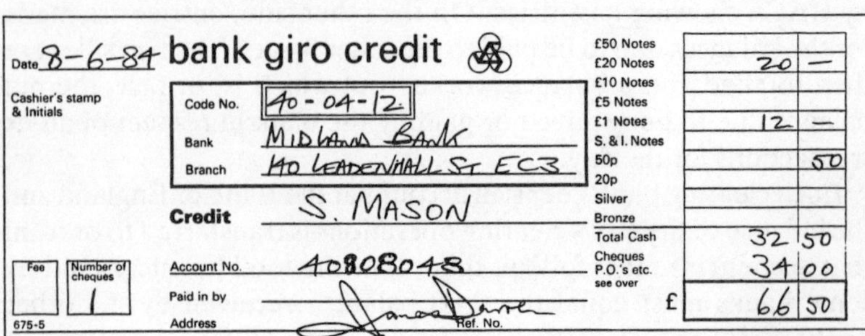

Date 8-6-84 bank giro credit

Cashier's stamp & Initials

Code No. 40-04-12
Bank MIDLAND BANK
Branch 140 LEADENHALL ST EC3

Credit S. MASON

Account No. 40808048
Paid in by
Address
Ref. No.

Fee | Number of cheques 1

675-5

	£	p
£50 Notes		
£20 Notes	20	—
£10 Notes		
£5 Notes		
£1 Notes	12	—
S. & I. Notes		
50p		50
20p		
Silver		
Bronze		
Total Cash	32	50
Cheques P.O.'s etc. see over	34	00
£	66	50

recipient's bank and the remitter's name. The credit slips are then sent to the payer's bank with one cheque to cover the total amount.

For the businessman, or the private individual who may have a number of payments to make, the Bank Giro system enables the customer to send one cheque to his bank for the total amount involved. Large numbers of payments tend to fall due at the beginning or the end of each month, and customers are encouraged to prepare the forms for the bank some days before payment is due. In the absence of postal delays or other exceptional problems, credits should reach their destination on the second business day after receipt by the bank.

Standing orders

Payment of fixed amounts on regularly recurring dates can be made by standing order. A standing order, or 'banker's order' as it is sometimes called, is a written instruction given by a customer to the bank to make a series of payments on his behalf when they fall due. The value of this service is considerable since it relieves the customer of the need to remember to make each payment. It also saves correspondence, the writing of cheques and the cost of stamps. Finally, it prevents the irritation or embarrassment of further demands, avoids any loss that might be caused by failure to make payment, and offers the customer maximum freedom from the responsibility of sending the payments.

Direct debiting

In 1967, the clearing banks and the Scottish banks introduced a new service known as 'direct debiting'. By this system, the person to whom the payment is to be made initiates the payment.

The creditor initiates a debit slip for an amount which is owed to him, and sends this debit slip to his debtor's bank through his own bank. Clearly, this system cannot be used without a potential debtor's prior authorisation but, if such an authorisation can be obtained, it is a useful system for business, such as insurance companies, who can then initiate debits for payments of premiums.

A particular advantage that direct debiting has over standing orders is that while the latter can be used only for fixed amounts at fixed intervals, the former can be used, additionally, for varying amounts at varying intervals.

The bank customer who initiates the debits is required to execute an indemnity addressed to all the clearing banks and the Scottish banks. By the terms of this indemnity the creditor agrees to keep each bank indemnified against all actions, claims, damages, costs and expenses arising directly or indirectly from such debiting. The creditor, in his turn, authorises each bank to admit, compromise or reject any claims without reference to the creditor.

Having executed this indemnity, the creditor obtains the agreement of the persons or companies whose accounts are to be debited. They sign a special form of standing order addressed to their own bank, authorising their accounts to be debited.

At specified times, the creditor lists the direct debit forms, which are encoded in magnetic ink characters, and delivers them to his own bank. His account will be credited with the total amount, and the debits distributed to the banks to whom they are addressed. If a debit cannot be paid because of lack of funds, it is returned unpaid.

There are certain advantages enjoyed by the creditor in this method:

1 It ensures that sums owed to him are paid promptly.
2 Unpaid debts are returned quickly.
3 The administration required for checking payments is minimal compared with that required for the standing order system.

Questions

1 Define the four main types of clearing system
2 How is it possible for a cheque to bypass the clearing system?
3 What is the purpose of a credit transfer?
4 Explain what happens in the clearing if a cheque is not paid, and the timing involved.
5 For what purpose are standing orders used in banking?
6 Can you describe the functions of BACS?
7 How does a direct debit differ from a standing order?

5

Bills of Exchange and Other Documents

Bills of exchange were in use long before cheques, and they were first mentioned in history in connection with the merchants from Lombardy. In those early days, the bill of exchange was not a negotiable instrument and, if stolen, could not be recovered by the true owner from the person who had taken it in payment of debt. During the thirteenth and fourteenth centuries they were not even legally transferable, but the custom of merchants in treating them as credit instruments, and in transferring them from one person to another in payment of debts, caused the Law Courts to regard them with more favour.

Eventually, in 1663, endorsement was permitted and an inland bill of exchange made payable to bearer received legal recognition, not as a negotiable instrument, but merely as a document on which actions could be brought to the courts.

It was 1758 before banknotes were given the status of negotiable instruments. This was followed in 1764 by bills of exchange and promissory notes, when the law finally recognised the value of these widely used commercial documents. In general terms, bills of exchange are used mainly to finance international trade. The main functions of a bill of exchange are:

(*a*) To enable exporters of goods to obtain cash as soon as possible after they have exported their goods;
(*b*) To enable importers to defer payment at least until they receive the goods;
(*c*) To defer payment until they have sold the goods and obtained

the proceeds. This object is attained by 'discounting' or 'negotiating' bills.

The bills of exchange illustrated below indicate that there are the same parties to a bill as there are to a cheque, but a cheque is always drawn upon a banker. The person who draws a bill is known as the drawer; the person on whom it is drawn is called the drawee and the person to whom it is drawn payable is known as the payee.

Example 1

> Sugar Street, Tysdale
> 6 June 19--
>
> £300
> On demand pay to James Bliss or order the sum of three hundred pounds.
> For and on behalf of John Fisher Plc,
> John Fisher
> Director
>
> To Alexanders Plc,
> Monument Street, London

In the second example the bill has been accepted by the drawee. When the drawee accepts a bill, he is known as the acceptor.

Some differences which exist between cheques and bills are as follows:

1 A bill may be drawn upon any person, whereas a cheque must be drawn upon a banker.
2 A bill may be payable on demand or at a fixed or determinable future time, whereas a cheque must be payable on demand.
3 If a bill is not payable on demand, it is usually accepted, whereupon the acceptor is the party primarily liable to the holder. A cheque is not usually accepted, and the drawer is the party primarily liable.
4 A bill must be presented for payment when due, or the drawer will be discharged from liability to pay. Under the Limitation Act, the drawer of a cheque is not discharged for six years.
5 There is no provision which enables bills to be crossed, whereas cheques may be crossed.

Example 2

Accepted payable at XYZ Bank
Sugar Street, Tysdale. For and on
behalf of Alexanders Plc.

Signed: A. Alexander, Director.

Sugar Street, Tysdale
6 June 19--

£300
Two months after date to James Bliss or order the sum of three hundred pounds.
For and on behalf of John Fisher Plc,
John Fisher
Director

To Alexanders Plc
Monument Street, London

6 There is no statutory protection for a bank which pays bills domiciled with it (a domiciled bill is one payable elsewhere than at the business or private address of the drawee), but banks are protected, subject to certain conditions, when paying cheques drawn upon them.
7 The provisions of the Cheques Act 1957, relating to the abolition of endorsements, apply to cheques but not to bills.

Acceptance of a bill

The requisites of a valid acceptance are:

(*a*) It must be written on the bill and be signed by the drawee. The mere signature of the drawee is sufficient.
(*b*) It must not express that the drawee will perform his promise by any other means than the payment of money.
(*c*) The acceptance must be completed by delivery of the bill or notification that it has been accepted.

An acceptance of a bill of exchange is either general or qualified. A general acceptance assents, without qualification, to the order of the drawer. A qualified acceptance, in express terms, varies the effect of the bill as drawn.

There are five sorts of qualified acceptances:

1 *Conditional acceptance* is one which makes payment dependent on the fulfilment of a condition, e.g. 'Accepted payable on delivery of 200 tons of jute'.
2 *Partial acceptance* is an acceptance to pay part only of the amount for which the bill is drawn, e.g. a bill drawn for £200, but accepted for £100 only.
3 *Local acceptance* is an acceptance to pay only at a particular specified place, but unless the words 'and not elsewhere' or 'and there only' or their equivalent be inserted, the acceptance is a general one.
4 *Acceptance qualified as to time* is an acceptance to pay at a longer or shorter time than that specified in the bill, e.g. a bill drawn payable six months after date, but accepted payable nine months after date.
5 *Acceptance qualified as to parties* is illustrated by a bill drawn on X, Y and Z, on the acceptance of X only. However, if X had authority to accept on behalf of all the drawees, and he did this, the acceptance would not be qualified.

Presentment for acceptance is legally necessary:

(*a*) Where a bill is payable after sight; presentment for acceptance is necessary in order to fix the maturity of the instrument;
(*b*) Where a bill expressly stipulates that it must be presented for acceptance;
(*c*) Where a bill is drawn payable elsewhere than at the residence or place of business of the drawee.

Except in these three cases, it is not obligatory to present a bill for acceptance. The holder may await the maturity of the bill and then present it for payment. As a rule, however, it is presented for acceptance to secure the liability of the drawee. Alternatively, if the drawee refuses to accept the bill, the holder then has an immediate right of recourse against the drawer and endorsers if the appropriate steps are taken.

Discharge of a bill

Discharging a bill is the performance, setting free or payment of a bill, after which all rights are 'extinguished'.

A bill may be discharged:

1 By payment of the bill in due course to the proper person;
2 By the acceptor becoming the holder of the bill in his own right at or after maturity;
3 By waiver;
4 By cancellation;
5 By material alteration.

1 Payment by, or on behalf of, the acceptor at or after maturity to the holder in good faith, and without notice of any defect in his title, always operates as a discharge.
2 If the bill is negotiated back to the acceptor, or before maturity, he may (if the form of the bill permits) re-issue and further negotiate it, but he is not entitled to enforce payment against any intervening party to whom he was previously liable.
3 To waive means to relinquish, to give up claim to. Thus, a bill is discharged by the holder, at or after maturity, giving up the bill to the acceptor or to the party to be discharged, or else absolutely renouncing his rights against the acceptor. The renunciation must be in writing.
4 Cancellation of the bill by the holder is a discharge of the bill, and if a person's name is cancelled, that person is discharged and so is any endorser who would have a right of recourse against him, unless the cancellation was unintentional, made by mistake or made without the holder's consent.
5 A material alteration is one which in any way alters the operation of the bill and the liabilities of the parties, whether the change is prejudicial or beneficial. Material alteration of the bill without the assent of all parties liable voids the bill, except as against the parties who made or assisted to the alteration and subsequent endorsers.

The following alterations are material:

(*a*) Any alteration of the date;
(*b*) The addition of a place of payment where the bill was accepted generally;
(*c*) A particular consideration substituted for the words 'value received';
(*d*) Conversion of 'three months after date' into 'three months after sight';
(*e*) Alteration of the crossing of a cheque;

(*f*) Alteration of a specified rate of interest or rate of exchange;
(g) Joint promissory note converted into a joint and several promissory note, or a new maker added;
(*h*) Alteration of the number on a Bank of England note;
(*i*) Place of payment added without the assent of the acceptor to a bill which has been accepted generally.

Endorsement of bills

There are five kinds of endorsement of bills:

1 Conditional;
2 In blank;
3 Special;
4 Restrictive;
5 Partial.

1 A conditional endorsement is one which makes the transfer of the property in a bill dependent on the fulfilment of a stated condition.
2 An endorsement in blank specifies no endorsee, and a bill so endorsed becomes payable to bearer.
3 A special endorsement specifies the person to whom, or to whose order, the bill is to be payable. When a bill has been endorsed in blank, any holder may convert the blank endorsement into special endorsement by writing above the endorser's signature a direction to pay the bill to, or to the order of himself, or some other person.
4 An endorsement is restrictive which prohibits the further negotiation of the bill or which expresses that it is a mere authority to deal with the bill, as thereby directed, and not a transfer of the ownership.
5 A partial endorsement purports to transfer:
(*a*) to the endorsee a part of the amount payable;
(*b*) to two or more endorsees separately.

Conditional orders

A conditional order is a document ordering payment which is subject to the fulfilment of a condition. A cheque itself may be a conditional order, for example, where it states on it that payment is not to be made unless an attached receipt form is signed.

A conditional order may be crossed like a cheque, for the Cheques Act extended the provisions of the Bills of Exchange Act to protect bankers. However, conditional forms of cheques are objectionable for many reasons and bankers usually require an indemnity in connection with these documents.

Dishonour of a bill

Most bills are accepted when presented for acceptance, and duly paid when presented for payment. Occasionally, however, acceptance or payment is refused, and the bill is then said to be dishonoured by non-acceptance or by non-payment, as the case may be. As a general rule, the person who presented the bill must give notice of dishonour to prior parties and take the appropriate steps to have the bill 'noted' or 'protested'. (Noting is a minute made by a notary public on a dishonoured bill. This is sometimes followed by a formal document called a 'protest', bearing the seal of the notary and attesting that the bill has been dishonoured.) Failure to take the proper steps promptly may have serious consequences. An immediate right of recourse against the drawer and endorser accrues to the holder if the bill is dishonoured.

Bankers' drafts

There are certain types of transaction for which payment by cheque is not usually acceptable. For example, on purchase of a house, a solicitor acting for a seller will not normally hand the title deeds to the purchaser's solicitor in exchange for a cheque, for he has no guarantee that it will be paid on presentation. To save the inconvenience of having to draw out a large sum of money, a bankers' draft is obtained. In exchange for a cheque in its favour, the bank supplies its customer with a draft drawn on itself made payable to the person who is to receive the money. As this draft is signed on behalf of the bank, it is treated as being equivalent to cash.

These are two types of bankers' drafts. First, there is the type of draft drawn by one bank upon another. Second, there is the type of draft where the same bank is both drawer and drawee. Usually, such drafts are drawn by a branch of a bank upon its head office (or vice versa), or upon another branch.

If a demand draft drawn on a bank by one of its own branches has a forged endorsement, the person in possession of the draft cannot compel the banker to pay it. However, a bank should not stop payment of a draft drawn by a branch on the head office, or on another branch, other than in exceptional circumstances, e.g. where there is definite evidence that the endorsement is forged.

The duties of the paying banker in relation to bankers' drafts are similar to those which govern the payment of cheques. The banker on whom a draft is drawn must be satisfied that it is drawn by duly authorised officials and the particulars of the draft must correspond with those given in the advice which he will have received by post.

Bankers' drafts should always be crossed: as a general rule the safest crossing is 'Not Negotiable. Account Payee Only'.

Dividend warrants

A dividend warrant is the payment by a company of the dividend due to a shareholder. Dividends are paid to shareholders after income tax at the full standard rate has been deducted.

Sometimes, there are words on a dividend warrant which indicate that it will not be honoured after a certain period, usually three months, from the date of issue, unless it is returned to the company for confirmation.

A dividend or interest mandate is a written authority addressed by the person who is entitled to receive dividend or interest payments, to the company or authority making such payments, requesting and authorising that company or authority to make the payments to the bankers of the person entitled to receive them. The system is advantageous to the shareholder or stockholder because:

1 There is less risk of loss.
2 The customer does not have to take, or send, the warrants to the bank personally.

The system is advantageous to the company or authority concerned, because they merely issue one cheque in favour of their own bank in respect of all dividends mandated to the accounts of shareholders and stockholders. The relevant vouchers are then passed through the credit clearing.

Postal and money orders

Postal and money orders are purchased at post offices for remittance of small sums of money. Postal orders of various denominations up to £10 are available: the sender of a postal order should enter the payee's name on the order in ink and is recommended to fill in the name of the post office of payment, if this is known. Money orders can be obtained for any sum which does not exceed £50. On the purchase of a money order, the order itself is handed to the purchaser to be sent to the payee, and at the same time an advice note is sent by the issuing post office to the paying post office.

Postal orders and money orders may be crossed, and although this means that such orders must be paid through a bank, they are not covered by the crossed-cheque sections of the Bills of Exchange Act 1882. Furthermore, they are not cheques or bills of exchange, since they are drawn by one post office on another, and are not within the Cheques Act 1957.

Bankers accepting postal orders (but not money orders) for customers are protected against the true owner by the Post Office Act 1953. The banker is protected whether or not he has been negligent or has acted in the ordinary course of business, and whether or not the postal order is crossed. But as bankers usually do not merely collect such instruments for their customers, but credit them as cash, they lose the protection of this section and, should the order prove to be stolen, the banker would be liable in an action for conversion. If his right of recourse against his customer should prove worthless, the money would be lost. When a postal order is presented for payment by a banker, the payee of the order need not have filled in his name in the stipulated place or have signed the receipt at the foot of the order, provided that the name of the presenting bank is stamped on the face of the order.

Both postal orders and money orders are marked 'Not Negotiable' and they must be presented for payment within six months of the date of issue.

Coupons

Coupons are detachable certificates for the payment of interest on bonds, debentures, etc. They are issued in sheets, each separate coupon being numbered with the same number as the relative bond or certificate, and also with a number indicating the order in which it is to be detached for payment, for example 'Debenture No. 156. Interest Coupon No. 4.' The place of payment is also indicated on the coupon. Each coupon entitles the holder to interest for a certain period, usually six months, and when due it is cut off and presented for payment. The dates of payment are generally stated on the coupons, but where no date is given it is announced in the press.

Customers should not be credited with the value of coupons on foreign bonds presented for payment until the banker has received advices of the net amounts realised. These cannot be readily calculated beforehand owing to differences in income tax deductions and, in some cases, to fluctuations of the rate of exchange. Difficulties arise when bonds are sold while the current coupon is in the banker's hands for the purpose of collection. This is due to the fact that the price of the bonds on the Stock Exchange includes the current coupon, the value of which is not deducted until the due date of payment. If the holder sells the bond without the current coupon, the full amount of the interest the coupon represented has to be paid over to the buyer and, as the holder will receive only the proceeds of the coupon less income tax, he has to adjust matters in his annual income tax return.

Questions

1 What is a bill of exchange?
2 Describe how a bill can be materially altered.
3 What term is used when acceptance or payment of a bill is refused, and what steps must be taken?
4 What are the requirements for a valid acceptance of a bill?
5 When is presentment for acceptance legally necessary?
6 How can a bill be discharged?
7 Can you name the five kinds of endorsement of a bill?
8 Explain the use of bankers' drafts.

6

Bank Advances

Apart from the clearing banks' distinctive money transmission role, their other main function and commercial object is to lend. It has long been accepted that they provide the cheapest, most convenient and efficient source of short-term credit for all sectors of the economy. More specifically, they are the main external source of working capital for industry and trade. The clearing banks are responsible lenders in that they endeavour to give full weight to official policy objectives, to social considerations and to the interests of the borrowers themselves.

The terms on which banks accept money from customers determine the terms under which they can lend. If the banks 'borrow' on a short-term basis, i.e. on current account, they cannot, generally, lend on a long-term basis, since they must be able to meet demands for immediate repayment of money lodged.

Principles of bank lending

In weighing up an application from a customer for a loan, the bank manager has to consider the basic principles of bank lending. There are no rigid rules, and no proposal is likely to fulfil every canon of good lending. Each case is judged on its merits. In the practical competitive field, advances have sometimes to be made and risks accepted, but normally the prudent banker expects a proposal to comply with the following basic principles.

Safety

As the banker is lending his customers' deposits, which are largely repayable upon demand, the requirement of safety is obvious. The advance has to be granted to a sensible borrower upon whom the banker can rely to repay the debt, from a reasonably certain source, within a relatively short time. As an insurance against any unexpected development, approved security of adequate value is usually requested to ensure the complete safety of the debt. There are many points for enquiry and negotiation under this simple heading before the banker can be satisfied that the advance will be safe.

Desirability

Banks are expected to restrict advances to those needs which are considered desirable to the nation's economy. Detailed policy in this respect varies according to monetary conditions existing at the time of the advance, but clearly it is essential to know the purpose of the advance. Apart from any question of government controls and directions, it is not the normal function of a banker to finance speculative enterprises or gambling.

Profitability

There would be little point in making a loan unless it yielded profit to the bank. This requirement is self-explanatory and dependent upon the customer and the negotiations. Therefore the principles to be followed will cover the following points:

(*a*) The customer must be trustworthy, of good character, integrity and business ability.
(*b*) The customer must be able, as well as willing, to pay.
(*c*) Collateral security, if any, must be acceptable banking security, with an adequate margin of value as cover for the advance taken.
(*d*) Lending should be as widespread as possible.
(*e*) Unless special arrangements are to be made, advances should be of short-term nature.
(*f*) Advances should, where possible, be of a self-liquidating character, or the source of repayment reasonably sure.
(*g*) The total of advances granted must not affect the ratios adversely.

The customer's requirements

When an approach is made by a customer for a loan, the banker seeks to obtain, at the initial interview, all the information required to enable him to decide whether or not the proposal merits support, and to assess the risk factor. Where the lending is to be wholly or partly without security, particular care is necessary in assessing the proposal, because there is little or nothing to fall back upon if the borrower fails to repay. The relationship between banker and customer is essentially a personal one based on mutual confidence, and a frank and detailed discussion of the borrower's requirements and prospects is essential at the outset. The customer who is open and wholly honest about his finances will always be treated with greater understanding – and, perhaps, sympathy – than will the customer who deliberately withholds relevant facts.

The customer's trustworthiness

The banker should have complete confidence in the integrity and ability of the customer to use the money to advantage and to repay it within a reasonable period. In the absence of such confidence it is preferable to decline to lend, no matter how much security may be available.

A good banker will know his customer and be able to judge his integrity and ability from past dealings, and from information already available, supported by the new facts brought out in the interview.

Ability of customer to repay

Having enquired about the customer's personal details, the manager will assess the customer's ability to repay. He will need to know:

(*a*) Is the customer's financial position satisfactory, as shown by his statements of account?
(*b*) Is repayment possible from present income?
(*c*) Is the customer taking into account certain intangibles, e.g. overtime, commission, etc., which could be stopped suddenly?
(*d*) Does the customer have secure, full-time employment?

Sanctioning advances

The ultimate responsibility for all the bank's business rests with the directors. They formulate and declare its policy, which is put into practice by the general managers through the administrative machinery. While the directors must keep in close touch with the day-to-day problems affecting banks and banking they generally delegate most of the responsibility for the granting of advances to the management.

Working immediately under the general management and their assistants, who may be based in the head office or in local or regional head offices, are officials designated 'advance controllers', or, 'branch superintendents'. They, and their staff in turn, deal with all the problems of smaller lending in the branches under their direct supervision.

Most banks carry the delegation of sanctioning power still further by giving their branch managers certain discretionary 'limits', fixed individually, according to the experience of, and confidence in, each manager. These limits are usually divided into 'secured limits' and 'unsecured limits'; a higher figure being allowed where the advance is backed by adequate security.

The branch manager, in granting an advance under his discretionary powers, must act within the framework of policy directives passed on to him through his general managers. He must also, of course, observe the general principles of sound lending.

The form of bank advances

Bank advances to customers may be made in the following ways:

1 Overdraft;
2 Various forms of loan;
3 Discounting bills;
4 Various other services, e.g. factoring can provide for a customer to receive 80% in advance on invoices; and hire purchase, or instalment finance, is technically a loan.

Overdrafts are the most common means of borrowing from a bank. They have the appearance of utter simplicity to the customer, who is permitted to overdraw a current account into debit up to an agreed sum. As interest is charged on the daily 'cleared' balance, the customer has the advantage of paying interest only on the actual amounts borrowed from day to day and not on the arranged advance for the whole period. This system is particularly suitable for the trader, whose borrowing for working capital will normally fluctuate daily within the arranged limit. Thus, where the normal turnover of a business is on a monthly basis, there is likely to be a certain time in the month when the borrowing is at its peak. Payment is then received for goods delivered or services rendered, and part or all of the borrowing is repaid. Conversely, as wages are paid, and materials purchased, week by week, so the overdraft may well increase until the next month's accounts are collected and the account is again in credit.

With other businesses, or trades, this turnover, or 'time-cycle', may be much longer – say every three, six, nine, or even twelve months. With others it may be even shorter. Some wholesale merchants may turn their stock over every week. The arable farmer, on the other hand, may have an overdraft that increases month by month in the early part of the year as he pays for seeds, fertilisers and wages. Repayment is made when his crops have been harvested and sold.

Whatever the time-cycle, a healthy business should reflect this swing in the account. In-and-out borrowing from the bank, within an arranged maximum figure, has the advantages of flexibility and comparative low cost. Borrowing by means of an overdraft from a bank is, generally, the cheapest form of borrowing, since the rate of interest is usually lower than can be obtained elsewhere and the customer pays interest only on the money actually used in the business, as distinct from loans obtained from some other sources, where interest has to be paid on the full amount from the moment the loan is granted.

A healthy swing of the balance may show that money is going out and returning with profit. On the other hand, an overdraft which steadily rises and sticks at the 'limit' may be a danger signal.

From the bank's point of view, one major disadvantage of an overdraft advance can be the comparative difficulty in obtaining periodic and permanent reductions in the borrowing. On some occasions this can be done only by reducing the 'limit' and insisting on its strict observance even, maybe, to the point of refusing to meet cheques, payment of which would cause it to be exceeded. A minor point which aggravates this difficulty is that interest and commission debits automatically increase the debt.

Interest rates
It is not possible to give hard-and-fast rules about interest rates, as these vary considerably. The rate charged for a particular lending proposition will depend upon many factors. The most important are the period of time for which the advance is required, the purpose for which the money is required; the reputation and standing of the customer, the competitive situation; and the general level of interest rates in the country and each bank's own base rate, to which all its interest rates for lending are related.

For example, a 'blue-chip' company, well-established on the Stock Exchange, may be granted a loan at, say, 1% over 'base rate', whereas a sole trader who has a day-to-day business, such as window-cleaning, may have to pay 4% or 5% over base rate. Bank advances to first-class discount houses, finance houses, insurance companies and the like are at very 'fine' rates indeed.

Loans
The personal loan, revolving credit and budget account schemes are based upon the personal integrity of customers and not on the material security which they can provide. The personal loan service was introduced to help with such lump-sum payments as those for home repairs and decorations, the purchase of cars, furniture or household appliances, and professional equipment. The amount of the loan has to bear a reasonable relation both to the purpose for which it is required and to the customer's means. The rate of interest is fixed for the whole period of the loan, unlike normal bank advances (where the rate is linked to base rate) and is added at the outset. Repayment is usually made by monthly instalments under a standing order. The loan is automatically discharged if the borrower dies, and thus no liability will fall on the estate.

Revolving credit schemes have been introduced both by clearing banks and by a number of instalment finance companies.

Customers using this service pay an agreed amount each month (usually varying from £10 to £30) by standing order, transferring the monthly payment from current account to a special type of loan account. The bank then agrees a borrowing limit on the loan account, which is often equal to 30 times the agreed monthly payment. So, a customer paying £15 a month immediately obtains access to credit up to £450. Most schemes have a maximum limit of £1000. Depending on the actual system adopted, the customer obtains use of the loan either by a transfer to current account, where an ordinary chequebook can be used, or by using a special chequebook issued for use only on the revolving credit account.

Advantages for the customer using this type of account are:

1 The drawing facility is continuing, readily available and can be used for any purpose.
2 There is no need to renegotiate a new loan for each present or future need.
3 There is a fixed monthly payment which covers repayment of both principal and interest, so that customers know the precise amount of their commitment each month.
4 The cost of borrowing, varying from 1¼% to 1½% a month, is less than most forms of instalment finance.
5 In some cases, when the borrowing facility is not required, the monthly transfers create an interest-bearing savings account.

Discounting

This is a special form of advance with peculiar characteristics, which may not even be recognised at first sight as borrowing. Nevertheless, it is, in essence, a form of borrowing and one which combines most of the desirable features of a bank advance.

Briefly, an advance is made on the face value of the bill against the security of the liability of the parties to the bill, or promissory note, being discounted. The banker must be careful to retain the customer's liability by insisting on the endorsement of the instrument by him. The amount charged as 'discount' may be regarded as interest charged on the amount advanced until the maturity of the bill or note. The merits for the bank of this form of lending are:

1 The advance is, generally, short term, provided it is a 'trade bill' representing a trading operation and part of working capital.
2 The advance is self-liquidating, in the sense that payment of the bill to the banker on its due date repays the debt.
3 The banker can arrange his total portfolio of bills so that some are maturing almost every day, and thus provide the desirable feature of a continuous turnover of funds.

4 Interest is a simple calculation on the amount of the bill and the time it has to run from the moment the money is lent.
5 Security cover is obtained through the liability of all the parties to the instrument, i.e. those who have signed as acceptor, as drawer or as endorser. The names of the acceptors and the drawer are collateral security to that of the borrowing customer, who should sign as endorser.

Application for a loan

Each branch manager will have his own style of conducting an interview. No hard and fast rules can be laid down, for each customer must be treated in an individual manner according to his temperament and needs. One manager's method may be to concentrate on putting the customer at his ease and then get him to talk easily and naturally, putting his proposal in his own words. Such a manager will skilfully guide the proposer by a brief question or two until he has a complete picture of the proposition. Another manager may have to identify the salient points from a flood of unconnected facts quoted by a garrulous customer. Yet another might have to prise the information from a shy or reticent applicant. Whatever the case, it is easy to miss the important facts in the course of a long and, perhaps, partly irrelevant conversation.

When written down, relevant information about the advance can be expected to identify the following facts:

1 Name;
2 Address;
3 Amount required;
4 Purpose;
5 Duration;
6 Scheme of repayment;
7 Source of repayment;
8 Security offered;
9 Present loan or overdraft, discount or credit – if any;
10 Rate of interest;
11 Amount of income;
12 Source of income;
13 Any other resources.

By this time, the manager should be in a position to judge whether the proposition is one that the bank can consider and, assuming that he is satisfied, and that the amount lies within his discretionary powers, the customer will be given a decision straightaway. Where the application must be submitted to a local or regional head office, the final decision must not be pre-judged. However, if the manager is not completely satisfied, he will examine the branch records for further information, as follows:

Credit items

(*a*) Income from salary, pension, commissions, dividends or properties;
(*b*) Repeated credits from sale of stocks or shares might mean living on capital;
(*c*) The weekly takings of a business;
(*d*) Unusual and non-recurring credits may show the sale of assets, such as property or a motor car.

Debit items

(*a*) Cheques payable to bookmakers indicate gambling on a regular basis (small payments to football pools will not be regarded too seriously!);
(*b*) Rent cheques or mortgage repayments give a clue to household costs;
(*c*) Cheques for 'expense account' activities may indicate a mode of living;
(*d*) Insurance premium payments may put the manager on the track of additional security;
(*e*) In a shopkeeper's account, payees' names on cheques will indicate his suppliers, while the amounts may provide clues about stocking levels;
(*f*) Property deals may be indicated.

Balances

(*a*) A steadily declining balance could be the result of living beyond income;
(*b*) A dormant balance tells nothing, but raises a host of queries;
(*c*) Salary all spent earlier and earlier each month is a danger sign;
(*d*) Trends in the swing of a business account balance may give a clue as to the health of the business.

Other information

(*a*) The absence of normal items running through an account, or ceasing to appear there, such as:
   (i) Income from salary, pension or other previously regular credits;
   (ii) Repayments to hire purchase or loan companies;
   (iii) Normal periodic payments not made, e.g. rent, insurance premiums;

(*b*) Evidence from other sources of reference:
   (i) Items in the bank's safe custody registers;
   (ii) Records of bankruptcy or County Court judgements, published in Stubbs' Gazette;
   (iii) Records of guarantees given;

(*c*) Information from professional credit agencies;

(*d*) Information available in public registers, such as the Companies Register;

(*e*) Reports in trade journals or in newspapers;

(*f*) Trading figures and balance sheets;

(*g*) Evidence of bank accounts elsewhere.

Some customers omit the formality of asking the branch manager for a loan and overdraw their accounts without permission from, or even warning to, their banks. Where customers do this they run the risk of having their cheque returned unpaid and marked 'Refer to drawer'.

The best advice for any customer in need of temporary assistance, or in any way worried about his financial position, is to have a chat with his bank manager and explain the position. Whether borrowing from the bank is on loan account or by overdraft on current account, the interest is generally debited half-yearly, towards the end of June and December, except on personal loans.

Credit scoring

A credit scoring system is a statistically based management tool for forecasting the outcome of extending credit to individuals. It begins with the applicant being asked to fill in a questionnaire, and scores are given for answers to each question. The scores for each of the answers are then added to give a total credit-risk score, which is designed to measure the chance of default if credit is granted.

The following example shows the characteristics which a typical credit scoring scheme is likely to take into account.

Applicant's characteristics

1 Geographical location;
2 House ownership/tenancy;
3 Has a bank account and will pay by credit transfer;
4 Business capacity;
5 Time in present employment;
6 Amount of loan required;
7 Present age.

Each category will attract a credit-risk score from which analysis can be made.

There are several stages in developing and checking a credit scoring scheme:

1 Information about past good and bad borrowers must be collected for analysis.
2 Questions on the application form which are good predictors of creditworthiness must be identified.
(Scores are then developed for these discriminating characteristics.)
3 As an initial check, the scores are applied to other good and bad accounts in the records.
4 The next step is the selection of a cut-off score, i.e. a score at which applicants are considered too risky to be accepted.
5 As a final check, the scoring scheme can be introduced alongside normal lending techniques to ensure that the decisions implied by the scores are acceptable to the management of the loan scheme.

Credit scoring is generally considered in relation to the decision to accept or reject a potential borrower. Other values of the scheme are as follows:

(*a*) Selective reduction of bad debts during times of credit restriction;
(*b*) Improved profit forecasting and hence control;
(*c*) Detection of changes in creditworthiness of applicants;

(*d*) Control of individual credit officers (if necessary);
(*e*) More economic use of additional credit enquiries;
(*f*) Charging interest rates on the loan to reflect the credit risk of the borrower;
(*g*) Determining optimum credit limits for borrowers;
(*h*) Measuring the effect of promotional and advertising schemes;
(*i*) Providing a management information service to senior executives.

Bridge-over loans

There are many occasions when temporary finance is required, perhaps urgently. A temporary advance of this nature is termed a 'bridge-over'. For example, a bank may be asked to provide, as an interim measure, finance to build a factory or install machinery, or for some other capital purpose, where an assurance is given that fresh share capital is to be introduced shortly, or that a long-term mortgage or debenture loan is being arranged to provide permanent finance. For personal customers, a bridge-over loan may take other forms as, for instance, when an advance is made pending realisation of investments, receipt of proceeds of property sales, of maturing life policies, or for the purchase of one house before another has been sold, and so on.

Many private house buyers find it difficult to arrange for the purchase of their new property to coincide exactly with the sale of their existing property, and it is essential that they should have finance to 'bridge' this time gap. Before this, they will probably have to put down a deposit (usually 10% of the purchase price) when the contract to buy is signed. This, also, will require ready cash, and the bank will generally help as well as with 'bridging finance', although a condition will usually be that the contract for the sale of the customer's existing house has already been signed.

'Banks rely on solicitors to a great extent in 'bridge-over' advances for property, and if a particular firm is not known to the bank already, a status enquiry should be made early in the negotiations as to their professional standing.

The deposit money will be advanced only when the branch manager is satisfied on the following three points:

1 Soundness of the proposition, including availability of any new mortgage;
2 Receipt of a solicitor's undertaking to account for the net proceeds of sale, based on an exchange of sale contracts;
3 Reliability of the solicitor.

Additionally, the bank must obtain control over the deeds which will be conveyed into the customer's name upon purchase. It should:

1 Obtain its customer's instructions to his solicitor to hold the deeds to the order of the bank upon purchase;
2 Obtain the solicitor's undertaking to comply;
3 Ensure that the property is insured for full market value against fire at contract stage.

The purchase money can then be paid by the bank (with its customer's authority) direct to the solicitor against his undertaking. 'Bridge-over' advances are by nature short-lived. Deposit advances last for no more than about a few months; completion moneys will often be lent for only a few days. Nevertheless, considerable work may have been involved which may not be remunerative if interest alone is charged. A suitable arrangement fee is often negotiated, therefore, at the outset to ensure that the bank obtains a fair return and the customer knows his total financial commitment.

Long-term lending

For many years, the object of the banker was to 'borrow long and lend short' and this axiom prevented borrowing becoming hard-core. The reason for this ideal situation was to lessen risk by lending for a short period, retrieving the money, relending it, and so on. In our advanced society, there have been greater demands for lending to industry and the banks have had to reconsider their attitude. In the 1970s, medium-term lending was adopted which added a new dimension to the existing arrangements of overdrafts and loans and this has gained a firm foothold during the decade. However, even the term of borrowing from two to ten years was sometimes insufficient for the needs of certain companies which encouraged the banks to extend the scope more widely to encompass long-term lending.

The essential purpose of entry into this market related to the provision of finance for those businesses which, due to limitation of size, had no direct access to the capital markets. It was directed principally, but not exclusively, at small/medium-sized businesses, including private companies, partnerships and sole traders aiming on a selective and secured basis, to make loans available for periods of 10 to 20 years in support of new capital expenditure projects. A scheme of this nature evidenced the recognition of the banks with regard to the needs of the smaller business sector wherein borrowers preferred to spread repayments over a longer period than had been possible under traditional banking criteria. It also reflected the desire of the clearing bank to obtain increased market shares in a very competitive atmosphere.

Most banks actively apply their medium-term loan schemes to all borrowers, with a view to meeting the needs of those customers whose cash flows permit repayment within a period of 10 years or, where the period of the loan is indicated, as in the case of plant and machinery, by the useful working life of the asset being purchased. The long-term loan scheme was designed to offer assistance for the purchase of property, or from the ownership of existing property, with the respective deeds being legally charged to banks in support of the borrowing.

Long-term lending, by its nature, involves higher interest rates and fees, and the bases on which these charges are structured vary from time to time with market conditions. Nevertheless, in some cases an important and competitive innovation includes a willingness to offer the borrower the choice of a conventional floating rate (linked to base rate) or, for those borrowers who wish to establish their costs with certainty at the outset, a fixed interest rate for the duration of the loan. Repayments are made usually on an annually reducing basis, although in some instances an initial 'rest' period of up to two years is allowed to match the customer's cash-flow pattern until the new project begins to generate profitably.

Banks and house mortgages

Primarily the province of the building societies, the house mortgage market was penetrated by the banks in 1979. There was no intention of competing directly with the building societies, and efforts were made to fill the gap in the £20 000 and over mortgage market where credit restrictions and policies made it difficult for mortgage loans to be obtained.

The American banks were the first to arrive on the scene, and Lloyds Bank was the first British bank to enter the market in force in January 1979. They offered to lend sums of £25 000 and over, setting £20m aside for the scheme. After only four months, however, they injected a further £20m and lowered the minimum threshold to £20 000. Conditions are very similar to those imposed by the building societies, based on 2½ times the borrower's annual income, up to about 80% of the purchase price, and repayable over twenty years. The banks waive time requirement of a previous saving record provided that the borrower is an acceptable customer, although even non-customers may be successful.

Williams & Glyn's and Midland Bank were the next to announce schemes. The former allocated £10m to mortgages ranging from £20 000 to £150 000, at an interest rate of 3% above base rate. The latter introduced a scheme which offered two extra attractions: a repayment period of twenty-five years as opposed to twenty years and an interest rate of only 2½% above base rate. Then Barclays launched the strongest attack on the home loan market, offering mortgages from £10 000 to £100 000 on terms which effectively matched those offered by the building societies.

The Trustee Savings Bank set aside 3% of its deposit base for mortgage lending in November 1979. It limited mortgage advances to a maximum of £30 000 but the sum available then, at £166m, was more than double the amount ear-marked for this purpose by all other UK banks put together.

The building societies did not decry the banks' intrusion into their territory at a time when funds were short and mortgage queues lengthened. The general contention was that the banks might force house prices to spiral, or that competition from the banks could lead to a reduction in the present figure of more than 300 building societies, as the smaller societies failed to maintain business at economic levels. On the other hand, the banks still face a number of disadvantages. The interest rates charged by some banks are higher than those charged by building societies, who benefit also from the composite tax rate (the tax the society pays on behalf of its investors).

Supervision

It might be assumed that once a lending proposition has been agreed it is only necessary to review the facility annually. Unfortunately, a variety of unexpected events can combine to modify the trend of borrowing and it may be necessary for a branch manager to have frequent discussions with customers when overdraft limits have been exceeded, when trading conditions have changed or because of failure to comply with an arrangement to produce certain trading figures at regular intervals.

Each bank has its own standard procedures for doing this, and each branch manager will develop his own methods of maintaining surveillance.

Records

Among the records which a bank branch will normally keep about advances are the following.

Full security records. This will include all the supplementary records and diary notes necessary to keep control of the value of the cover.

Particulars of sanctions. It is usual to keep this information on cards sorted in alphabetical order for ease of reference. On the cards will be recorded the dates of the sanctions, the amounts, time-span, security and rates of interest.

Diary cards. These will take care of renewal and expiry dates and also times of promised reductions. The manager will retain his own record of interviews and telephone conversations. Some banks also keep an information sheet for each borrowing customer on which all details relating to the loan, its inception and subsequent history are recorded in an abridged form, so that the whole history of the advance can be seen at a glance.

Daily surveillance and control

This is primarily the responsibility of the branch manager who will carefully collect and file any facts and information he may glean about his customers, and particularly his borrowers. He can, of course, receive valuable help from his staff; indeed, he is expected to delegate much of the detailed work and maintenance of records.

The accountant, who will deputise during the manager's temporary absence from the branch, must have a knowledge of all the facts relevant to branch advances. Access must be available to all the manager's notes and reports of interviews.

The securities clerk is responsible, generally, to deal with security deposited. A good securities clerk can relieve his manager of anxiety with the completion of the bank's charge over security and of the maintenance of adequate cover. The system of record should be such that, for example, any insurance premium not paid on its due date is immediately noticed and the necessary action taken. Also, an eye must be kept on any deterioration of security values, which should be reported to the manager when the margins of cover required appears to be in danger. There should also be a periodic and regular valuation of property in the security register, undertaken either by the manager or by the manager of the branch nearest the property.

Cashiers. The intelligent and alert cashier can be the eyes and ears of the manager in daily dealings with customers. Knowing the borrowing accounts, a report will be made of any unusual features of payments in, or withdrawals. In order to avoid undesirable overpayments, all cashiers should be in possession of a list of these customers who are nearing their 'limits' and who should not exceed them. Such names would be in addition to the usual short list of doubtful customers whose accounts are marked 'Not to overdraw' which, to be of maximum assistance, must be kept up to date and under constant review.

An important part of the work of bank inspectors during their periodic, but irregular and unannounced visits to branches is to make a detailed examination of borrowings and all records connected with them, as well as the security held for each account.

Bank inspectors may work under the control of an inspection department, centralised at the head office, or under a chief inspector responsible directly to the general managers, or they may work directly under the control of a superintendent of branches or controller of branches.

For advances sanctioned by head office, an inspector's main concern is to see that the security is present, in order, and as described in the information given to the control department. He will also review the pattern of the borrowings themselves and all the relevant facts about them, judging whether the branch manager's expressed opinion and recommendations are justified. Minor points about the security are dealt with directly at the branch, but any serious omissions or differences of opinion with the manager's judgement will be commented on by the inspector in his report at the completion of his visit.

Questions

1. What points must be considered when an application has been made for a loan?
2. Can you illustrate the merits of discounting?
3. What is the use of credit scoring in banking?
4. What is the purpose of a bridge-over loan?

7

Borrowers

Types of borrowers

This chapter deals, briefly, with the following types of borrowers:

1 Personal;
2 Limited companies;
3 Partnerships;
4 Joint accounts;
5 Trustees;
6 Executors;
7 Liquidators and receivers;
8 Unincorporated societies or clubs;
9 Local authorities;
10 Building societies;
11 Solicitors;
12 Minors.

Personal borrowers

Very few people realise how much credit they rely on throughout a period of even one month. Many people deny that they are involved at all yet, on a short-term basis, they accept credit for gas, electricity, rent, telephone, hotel bills and even milk, because they use the services first and settle the bills at a later date.

Everyone is a consumer buying goods and services – the difference depends on the extent of the credit and, perhaps, on whether the goods and services are essential or merely luxuries.

The main forms of personal credit are as follows:

(*a*) Overdrafts;
(*b*) Personal loans;
(*c*) Revolving credit accounts;
(*d*) Budget accounts;
(*e*) Hire purchase;
(*f*) Credit sales;
(*g*) Credit cards;
(*h*) Monthly accounts;
(*i*) Finance house loans;
(*j*) Money lenders;
(*k*) Pawnbrokers;
(*l*) Trading checks;
(*m*) Hiring;
(*n*) Home shopping and mail order.

The growth in consumer lending by the banks became substantial on the introduction of Competition and Credit Control in 1971. This period of growth was accompanied by considerable development in the techniques of lending available at the banks, and in the marketing of the services they provide.

As a result of developments all the big banks became equipped, in one way or another, with a comprehensive range of consumer finance techniques. The range of lending services available from the banks is still based on the overdraft system which remains competitive with most alternative sources of personal finance. For most consumer finance purchases, however, the banks are more inclined to promote the alternative lending packages, even though they are rather more costly to the borrower.

The prime example is, perhaps, provided by the personal loan technique, which has advantages with its fixed advance commitment and regular payments for financing large purchases such as cars. Though more expensive than the overdraft, the bank personal loan is often significantly cheaper than alternatives, such as instalment credit provided through the retailer.

The credit card, in contrast, provides a convenient method for a number of small purchases, settling them all with one monthly cheque, effectively giving up to six weeks' free credit. Beyond that, it offers the opportunity to expand the credit with considerable flexibility in the use of the finance.

In addition to this technique, a number of banks and many large finance houses also offer a revolving credit facility where a credit limit is provided up to a given multiple of an agreed monthly repayment figure, giving a flexible method of financing the purchase of consumer durable goods.

In the matter of taking security for the personal customer, banks prefer to take security for substantial loans, wherever it is available. However, much depends on the creditworthiness of the customer. If it is considered that the customer will not be able to meet the required payments, even though he has more than sufficient security to cover the advance, the banker should have no qualms about refusing the loan. He will be doing the customer no favour by acceding to the loan request which, subsequently, would lead to hardship and misery in getting repayment.

Limited companies

The first questions which are likely to be asked by the branch manager when presented with a borrowing proposition from a limited company are:

(*a*) Has it power to borrow?
(*b*) Is there any limitation to the amount it can borrow?
(*c*) Any limitation as to security?
(*d*) Is the purpose of the borrowing within its power?

The answers should be found in the Memorandum and Articles of Association of the Company which must be carefully examined.

The files at Companies House will reveal:

(*a*) Its capital structure;
(*b*) The names of the directors and their shareholding;
(*c*) The names of other shareholders and their holdings;
(*d*) Special resolutions passed altering the constitution of the company;
(*e*) Total mortgages;
(*f*) The latest balance sheet;
(*g*) A copy of the Memorandum and Articles of Association.

To facilitate the extraction of information during this search, most banks issue a printed form for use for this purpose. The branch bank adopts the following procedure when granting a loan:

(*a*) The Memorandum and Articles of Association are obtained.
(*b*) A copy of the last balance sheet, duly certified by the auditors, and a copy of the trading and profit and loss accounts for the period are requested.
(*c*) A certified copy of the resolution of the board authorising the borrowing must be forwarded.
(*d*) If there is a limit on the borrowing powers of the company or the directors, the company secretary must send a certificate stating that the proposed advance is within the powers.
(*e*) The branch must check that the security offered, if any, is in order, and prepare any necessary charge forms.
(*f*) The branch must make a search, before accepting security, to see whether any prior charge exists.
(*g*) The charge form must be executed properly. If under seal, that the seal is properly affixed according to the relevant Article of Association; or where under hand, that it is signed by the duly authorised official, or officials. A certified copy of the resolution giving this authority should be obtained.
(*h*) The charge must be registered within 21 days of its creation. This may be done by the bank or by the company's solicitor, but in either case a certificate of registration should be obtained and retained with the charge form.

Partnerships

It is usual to obtain an undertaking when a partnership account is opened, signed by all partners agreeing to be jointly and severally liable for any debt on the partnership account. The partners may then be sued either jointly or severally, and the banker will have the right to set-off any credit balances on the partners' separate accounts against a debt on the firm's account. Even so, all general partners should sign a specific form of charge pledging the firm's property, even when a mandate is held which only gives one partner authority to bind the firm. Any change in the partnership brought about by death, bankruptcy or retirement of a partner dissolves the old firm and the account must be broken, particularly if it is desired to preserve the liability of an outgoing partner. A distinction should be made between security which is part of the partnership assets and security which is the property of one of the partners, for there will be a difference in proof in the event of bankruptcy proceedings.

Joint accounts

On a joint account, joint and several liability should be established in any borrowing, and this is usually provided for by the mandate obtained when opening the account. This preserves not only the bank's right against each holder's estate in the event of his death or bankruptcy, but will also give the right to as many rights of action as there are parties to the account. Also, in certain circumstances, it will give the bank a right of set-off in respect of any credit balances or any private account of the parties against a debt on the joint account.

If security is taken, the form of charge also establishes joint and several liability.

Trustees

All borrowing by trustees will be governed by statute or by the trust instrument if there is one. This should be examined to ascertain whether it gives power to borrow and to charge security, and in most cases the trust instrument should be submitted to the branch solicitors for their report on the powers written into it. All trustees must sign a form of charge over security deposited. Trustees are generally jointly liable only, unless the bank's mandate form, or the form of charge, establishes several liability.

Executors

The title and powers of executors date from the date of death, while that of administrators only from the granting of the letters of administration. Nevertheless, it is not the practice to allow borrowing by executors before they can show that probate has been obtained, except for the payment of capital transfer tax and expenses. If either executors or administrators wish to borrow for this purpose, their personal undertaking is obtained to repay out of the estate of the deceased and out of the first money coming to hand. It is, thus, a purely temporary borrowing, primarily on the personal responsibility of those who sign the undertaking. Since it must be for the specific purpose mentioned, the banker will want some evidence of the net value of the estate, so that the tax chargeable can be estimated. After grant of probate or letters of administration, the executors or administrators have power to borrow for the purpose of performing the duties of administration, but not for the purpose of carrying on the deceased's business as a going concern. Moreover, even where they are authorised by the will to carry on the deceased's business, they may not employ the private assets of the testator unless the will specifically gives them power to do so.

Liquidators and receivers

Liquidators are appointed to sell the undertaking and all the property of a company being wound up for cash, which is then distributed to creditors and members. In a compulsory winding-up, he has to borrow and pledge the assets of the company for purposes of winding-up the company without sanction of the court. A liquidator in a voluntary winding-up of either type – members' (where a declaration of solvency is made) or creditors' (where that declaration cannot be made) – may borrow; but the consent of the court may be required in the case of a creditors' voluntary winding-up, or of the committee of inspection, if appointed. In a members' voluntary winding-up the direction of the company in general meeting may be necessary.

As a rule, receivers have the power to borrow, but the appointing authority, whether a court or debenture holders, should consent. A receiver of the property is personally liable on any borrowing with a bank unless an agreement otherwise provides, the receiver having the right to be indemnified out of the assets administered by him.

Unincorporated societies or clubs

(such as amateur dramatic societies, football clubs, etc.)

An association of this kind cannot be sued for a debt, nor can any member of the committee, unless he assumes personal liability. In general, therefore, unsecured borrowing is not allowed. If an interested party is willing to give a guarantee or deposit specific security to cover the debt, it is as well also to obtain a certified copy of the committee's resolution authorising the borrowing.

Local authorities

In general, local authorities have powers to borrow conferred on them by various Acts of Parliament. Borrowing must be taken from the Public Works Loan Board unless the Treasury makes an exemption order. The exemption order enables a local authority to borrow from a bank, while various sections of the Government Acts allow temporary borrowing to be made from banks in certain circumstances.

Borrowing by local authorities may conveniently be considered under the following headings.

Long-term borrowing An exemption order, as mentioned above, sets out the manner, purpose and sources of the borrowing.

Temporary borrowing Temporary borrowing from a bank by way of a loan or overdraft is permitted, as mentioned above, without the consent of the sanctioning authority for the following purposes:

(*a*) For defraying expenses (including the payment of sums due by the council to meet expenses of other authorities) pending the receipt of revenues which are receivable by it in respect of the period of account in which those expenses are chargeable, and were taken into account in the estimates made by it for that period;

(*b*) Pending the raising of a loan which the council has been authorised to raise, for the purpose of defraying expenses intended to be defrayed by means of the loan.

Building societies

These may be incorporated or unincorporated. If the former, they may be permanent or terminating. A permanent society may borrow, in total, by way of deposits or loans, up to two-thirds of the amount secured to the society by mortgages from its members (less those more than 12 months in arrears, or in respect of which the society has been in possession for 12 months or longer). A terminating society, alternatively, may borrow up to a sum not exceeding 12 months' subscriptions on the shares for the time being in force, and its rules will show which alternative has been adopted. In each case the rules may vary or further restrict borrowing. Unincorporated societies also are governed by their own individual rules, which must be strictly observed.

Solicitors

A solicitor may not overdraw an account held specifically for a client. If any borrowing is taken it should be on his general account, and not taken on a client's account for a debt due on a general account. Where a separate trust account is open, however, where the solicitor is the trustee, borrowing may be allowed on this account, subject to the same considerations as any other trust account.

Minors (under 18)
Borrowing should not be allowed on an account maintained by a minor, except possibly against a guarantee or third party security, but the surety or third party should be made aware that he is liable as a principal and that he has no rights against the minor.

Secrecy

A banker's duty of secrecy to his customer is a legal duty implied in the contractual relationship between banker and customer. Breach of this duty gives a claim for nominal damages or, if the customer's reputation has suffered, for substantial damages. It is most important that this duty should be observed, for although the financial loss involved in nominal damages may be small, the damage to the banker's reputation could not be measured in monetary terms. Disclosure is justified:

1 Under compulsion by law;
2 Under a public duty;
3 Where the interests of the bank require disclosure;
4 Where made by the express or implied consent of the customer.

In addition, secrecy must be maintained, not only as to the actual state of the customer's account, but also with regard to any information derived from the account.

Credit and privacy

Following the growth of consumer credit in the UK, the expansion of personal credit produced some interesting implications especially in the area of individual privacy.

A credit-based consumer society must inevitably bring demand for information about an individual's financial standing. A free flow of information has existed between various business sectors for some time and, in the case of the banks, the advent of extensive computerisation may accelerate the trend.

The banks are an obvious source of information to those seeking to extract knowledge of the creditworthiness of an individual or commercial enterprise (see p. 98), but outside views on privacy can come sharply into conflict with the function of the organisations which operate as credit rating agencies.

The general policy line adopted by the clearing banks is that there is a legal obligation not to disclose customers' affairs without authority. In the case of the credit agencies there is no personal relationship, legal or commercial, of this kind.

Where the clearing banks may come under fire, though, is the practice of providing other banks with confidential information in response to enquiries from third parties. Thus, if an individual wishes to enquire into the credit status of another he can seemingly do so by investigations through his bank.

These inter-bank opinions are kept at a general level and expressed in conventional terms, and are given only to a controlled list of organisations.

The banks' point is that the practice of passing information is a well-established service. The Younger Committee on privacy, however, was concerned that the banks' standards of confidence should fall to a level lower than the acceptable. Moreover, the Younger Committee felt it right that any customer should have knowledge of disclosed information. Its recommendation was that 'the banks should make clear to all customers, existing or prospective, the existence and manner of operation of their reference system, and give customers the opportunity either to grant a standing authority for the provision of references or to require the bank to seek their consent on every occasion'.

Far and away the biggest threat to credit privacy comes from the credit-rating agencies.

Originally credit-rating agencies collected information and drew up registers recording facts about customer creditworthiness, but many companies have now branched out into debt collection. Subscribers, usually retailers, provide the agencies with their own credit experience and in return are entitled to facts on the financial standing of any potential customers.

Questions

1 When a limited company makes an application for a loan, what main questions must be asked by a banker?
2 Describe the operation of a 'partnership' account.
3 Can local authorities borrow from a bank? If so, what types of borrowing may be considered?
4 When must a banker disclose information concerning a customer?

8

Banking Services

The major banks provide a wealth of services, many of which are outlined in the various chapters in this book. However, there are some services which are ancillary services, which have not yet been specified, while others are worthy of mentioning in greater detail. This chapter deals with the following services:

1 Executor and trustee services;
2 Share registration and new issues;
3 Credit open arrangements;
4 Status enquiries;
5 Safe custody;
6 Hire purchase;
7 Block discounting;
8 Leasing;
9 Factoring
10 Insurance;
11 Cash distribution;
12 Customers' investments;
13 Financial Counselling;

Executor and trustee services

Most banks include an executor and trustee service as part of the normal facilities available to customers. The advantages to the customer appointing a bank as executor or trustee is that it provides:

(*a*) *Security*. It is an absolute safeguard against both negligence and fraud.

(*b*) *Continuity of Management*. It ensures continuity and avoids the possible anxiety and expense of choosing a new executor, or of appointing new trustees at a later stage.

(*c*) *Impartiality*. The bank ensures that instructions will be carried out with fairness and impartiality, combined with tact and sympathy.

(*d*) *Secrecy*. The staff of the bank is pledged to secrecy, and no information will be divulged except to those entitled to receive it.

(*e*) *Accessibility*. Delays due to illness or absence of individual trustees are avoided, and there are branches of the trustee department throughout the country.

(*f*) *Experience*. In addition to their own knowledge of trust law, accounting, taxation, exchange control, investment and property management, trust administrators in the bank are able to draw on the wide experience of their senior managers, and of experts in other specialised departments of the bank.

(*g*) *Administration*. This is in the hands of an individual administrator who, by becoming closely acquainted with the beneficiaries and their particular problems, can administer the estate with the same human understanding as a family trustee.

Executor and trustee services provided by the banks include the following.

Personal services

(*a*) Executor and trustee of wills;

(*b*) Administrator in cases where there is either no will, or no available executor;

(*c*) Attorney administrator;

(*d*) Trustee of:

- (i) Existing trusts;
- (ii) New settlements and trusts;
- (iii) Bequests to minors;
- (iv) Life assurance policies;
- (v) Special situations relating to the sale or development of land.

Management of investments

This is a service provided for the individual or for organisations.

Personal taxation

Adjustment and agreement with the Inland Revenue of income tax, capital gains tax, wealth tax and capital transfer tax.

Custodian trustee

(*a*) Under wills and settlements;
(*b*) Of assets belonging to societies, clubs, charities and other organisations.

Trustees for debenture holders

Wherever money is raised by the issue of debentures or the creation of loan stock, it is advantageous to secure the stock by a trust or covering deed, conveying property of the company to trustees in favour of the debenture holders, charging other property, and containing provisions regulating the respective rights of the company and the stockholders. This trust leads to the appointment of a trustee to act in protection of the interests of the lenders, and they are given extensive powers in order to fulfil a watchdog role on behalf of the subscribers.

Trustee for pension funds

Companies engaged in certain spheres of activity suffer severely because of the high rate of staff turnover. The setting up of a satisfactory pension scheme may be an incentive to employees to stay with the firm. If it is decided to set up a scheme which is wholly or partly on a self-invested basis then an expert view must be taken throughout its life on the suitability of the fixed interest stocks, equity shares and properties retained.

The introduction of government legislation from time to time may affect the basis of new schemes.

Trustees and share option schemes

Whereas a pension scheme usually extends to the majority of any group of a firm's employees, a 'share option scheme' can be limited to those employees who are considered by the board to be making a major contribution to the company's affairs. The shares of a scheme of this nature are vested in trustees who act in accordance with the terms of a trust deed, entered into with the company. This type of scheme may be affected by governmental legislation.

The private company

Varioux tax problems of considerable gravity and complexity can arise where there is, in a private company, a controlling interest or an interest amounting to control. Unskilled attempts to avoid the potential damage which may be caused by legislation may prove to be very costly in the end. Fundamentally, the solutions involve dispositions by the shareholder, but refinements include the creation of special trusts over appropriate blocks of the company's shares. These trusts are then administered for the benefit of families or employees, with the interests of the company remaining in mind. Legislation introduced as estate duty or capital transfer tax must be carefully interpreted.

Share registration and new issues

A specialised service offered by the banks is share registrations and the handling of new issues of shares. The banks act as registrar for customers, offering a complete company and local authority share/stock registration service which relieves company secretaries and treasurers of corporations of responsibility for all registration matters. In addition to the normal duties of maintaining registers of members, preparing dividend/interest payments, mailing notices and reports and attending at company meetings, the banks handle conversions of loan stocks, drawings of debentures, and carry out work on the registration of bonus, rights and other share/stock issues. In addition, they deal with local authority bond issues by the issue of certificates against payment, the subsequent payment of interest, and finally repayment of the bonds. New issues of capital by company customers are handled, involving invitations to the public to subscribe for the stock or shares, the application forms and prospectus details being obtainable from branches of the bank, in addition to being published in the financial and daily press. Through long experience of assisting companies which offer shares to the public, banks are able to handle not only the collection of applications, and issue of allotment letters, but also provide specimen documents for use by any of the companies' professional advisers. Introductions can be made to London brokers whenever necessary. Services are also available to assist a company engaged in a takeover, or making a rights or bonus issue to shareholders. The money subscribed on application and, later, on allotment, together with any further instalments, is sent on to the bank's new issue department, which sends out the allotment letters (or letters of regret) to applicants. Quite apart from the service of the particular bank's new issue department in preparing and dispatching allotment letters, a customer can always take an allotment letter to his own branch for guidance as to procedure, or for safe-keeping. On receiving written instructions from the customer, the branch will attend to the payment of any further instalments when they become due, debiting the amounts to the account. At the appropriate time, the document will be sent to the company to be exchanged for the new share certificate, which, if desired, can then be left with the bank. A service of value to customers living abroad is the registration of securities in the names of private nominee companies formed by the banks. By this means the collection of dividends and the purchase and sale of securities are simplified, and much time and correspondence saved as dividend warrants, dividend mandate forms and transfer forms do not have to be sent abroad.

Credit open arrangements

Banks will make credit open arrangements to allow customers to cash cheques up to an agreed weekly or monthly limit at a designated branch of the bank. This is a useful arrangement for customers who cannot visit their own branch and require a convenient cheque-cashing service on a temporary basis.

The procedure is quite simple. At his own branch the customer completes a form stating how much is required, for how long, where it will be wanted and giving a specimen signature. The form is sent to the branch named, where cash can be drawn up to the amount of credit.

Some large corporations and companies use the credit open system for paying salaries, wages and other regularly recurring payments. This involves the opening of a 'general credit' authorising the bank to pay, either at specified branches or at any branch, cheques up to a certain amount, provided that they are in order and signed by the requisite number of officials. Specimens of those signatures are provided. There may be a condition that only crossed cheques are to be paid, or different limits fixed according to whether they are open or crossed.

Large sums of money for wages and other disbursements are drawn every week by this means. For the customer going on holiday in the UK, there exists the convenience of being able to open a credit at any one of the thousands of branch offices of his own and other banks. This prevents the need for the customer to carry large amounts of money on a journey.

Status enquiries

Although a banker maintains strict secrecy about the affairs of his customers, an opinion on the financial standing of one of his customers can be provided, in confidence, in response to a request from another banker. The need for an opinion arises when a customer is contemplating entering into a business relationship with another person, firm or company with whom there have been no previous dealings, where knowledge of integrity and financial standing is required. The customer may be supplying goods or services on credit and will naturally wish to know whether it will be safe to do so. For example, if a person proposes to enter into an agreement such as a hire-purchase or tenancy agreement, the other party to the agreement may require a reference, preferably a banker, who would be prepared to give an opinion concerning the customer's financial standing. In such a case, the other party asks his own bankers to follow up this reference. They write to the bankers named, asking for an opinion in confidence as to the respectability and standing of the customer concerned, and further asking whether he may be considered trustworthy, in the way of business, to the extent of a certain sum of money. The reply or opinion will give a general indication of the creditworthiness of the customer, without, of course, giving any details of the account. A usual form of opinion is: 'Respectable, and considered good for your figures.'

There are a few well-known trade-protection societies which, being 'recognised' by the banks, can actually make their enquiries concerning customers direct to the banks; these enquiries are answered just as though they had been received from banks.

While bankers take every possible care to ensure that answers to status enquiries are given in such a way as to protect the interests both of their customers and those of the banks, claims are occasionally made by customers against the banks. Such claims are usually based on the allegation either that the banker made unauthorised disclosure of the customer's affairs, or the opinion given was unfavourable to the customer, that it was not justified, and that loss was suffered.

In the vast majority of cases, the practice of providing a status opinion about a customer, without that customer's express authority, does no harm at all. There are, indeed, many cases where a customer whose creditworthiness is the subject of enquiry does not even know that any enquiry is being made.

Safe custody

A useful service which a bank offers to customers is that of safe-keeping valuables of various kinds, such as jewellery, share certificates, life policies and title deeds. Generally, property left with a bank for safe custody is deposited in a locked box, the key of which is retained by the customer. Alternatively, items such as deeds, share certificates or life policies are often enclosed in an envelope which is sealed with sealing wax. In this case, the customer is usually asked to sign across the flap of the envelope. By taking charge of property in this way, the banker becomes a bailee, i.e. a person to whom goods are entrusted for a specific purpose. There are two kinds of bailee – gratuitous bailees and bailees for reward. Since the bank does not usually make a specific charge for taking care of its customer's property, it has been argued that the bank is a gratuitous bailee. Some authorities contend, however, that the practice of taking charge of their customers' valuables is so general that it is as a consideration for the customers' opening or continuing their accounts. Therefore, it is contended that the bank is a bailee for reward.

The difference has legal implications so far as certain claims relating to articles deposited are concerned. The banks are protected by law, however, if they take precautions by using the best methods available. The banks' vaults and safes are quite adequate for this purpose.

Customers who keep their valuables and important papers in

locked deed-boxes have access to them during normal banking hours. A customer who cannot visit his bank personally may give written authority for some other person to have access to the box on his behalf, but he would not be expected to send the key to the bank with instructions for removal of items, or even opening the box, by bank officials. The bank does not wish either to have knowledge of the contents or, in respect of articles lodged for safe custody, access to them.

In addition to articles of intrinsic value, bearer securities may be left with a banker for safe custody, and to enable the bank to detach coupons in respect of dividend or interest and to present them for payment. Payments of capital will also be sent direct to the bank when bonds are redeemed. By virtue of the Exchange Control Act 1947, most bearer securities had to be kept with 'authorised depositaries', and no payment of capital or interest could be made except to, or to the order of, the authorised depositary (generally a bank). But these measures ended in April 1980.

It is the usual practice when accepting safe custody articles from joint account customers, partnerships or limited companies, to obtain specific instructions concerning the persons to whom the articles may be returned.

A small number of bank branches provide safe deposit facilities. Here, in specially built strong-rooms, a depositor can rent, for a modest annual fee, a private safe containing a deed box. Each safe is under the sole control of the depositor concerned and can be visited at any time during banking hours. For those who desire complete privacy when dealing with the contents of their safes, individual rooms are available.

Hire purchase

Certain of the major banks have either taken an interest in a finance house, or have actually absorbed one within their organisations. The major service offered by finance houses is the provision of instalment finance credit, or 'hire purchase', as it is generally known.

Hire purchase is a form of credit where goods are supplied after payment of a deposit with an agreement to pay regular instalments over a period of time. The deposit paid helps to preserve, for the finance house, an interest in the goods throughout the period of hire, and the amount paid will depend on the nature of the equipment being purchased. At the end of the hiring period, legal title passes to the hirer on payment of a nominal sum. The length of hiring period, and the deposit required, depends to a large extent on the nature of the goods and, more particularly, on any government restrictions. If, during the period of hire, the hirer wishes to settle the agreement prematurely, a rebate of charges will normally be given by the finance house.

For companies, if ultimate ownership of equipment is an important factor, hire purchase (instalment finance) is one obvious choice of purchasing equipment, as the charges element of the agreement can be claimed against tax. After payment of an agreed deposit by the customer, the machine will be invoiced by the supplier to the finance house which then becomes the legal owner. Significant advance in hire purchase was made by the provisions of the Finance Act 1971, which enables a hirer to claim various tax benefits during the financial year when the contract is signed, irrespective of how many deposit or capital repayments have been made during that year. Prior to this enactment, when investment grants applied, the amount of these allowances which a hirer could claim for each financial year was directly in proportion to the capital repayments he had made. The revised situation allows hire purchase to rank level with any other form of borrowing.

Hire purchase has become an accepted feature of life today, even though the goods bought under such a contract remain the property of the seller until all the instalments have been paid. However, the last instalment includes a nominal sum which changes the contract from a hiring to an outright purchase.

The main items which comprise the basis for this type of credit are motor cars, furniture, television and other consumer durables for private individuals, and motor vehicles, plant equipment, office machinery and furniture for the business purchaser.

Block discounting

Many companies, especially in the retail trade, run their own credit facilities for their customers, providing, for example, television sets, washing machines and other household durable goods on hire purchase, credit sale or rental agreements. This can be expensive for the retailers, since cash has to be tied up in the goods, but specialist instalment credit companies can assist by providing block discounting facilities. Under such an arrangement, the instalment finance company will purchase approved 'blocks' of hire-purchase or rental agreements from the retailer, providing him with a substantial proportion of the purchase price in cash. The remainder of the agreed purchase price is paid in instalments to the retailer as he collects the accounts from his customers, which he continues to do as the agent of the finance company.

Leasing

The leasing of equipment is a relatively new service offered by banks in the UK, and is often provided through one of their associate or subsidiary companies. The major difference between leasing and various alternative methods of finance is that under a leasing agreement the ownership of the goods remains permanently with the lessor, while the lessee enjoys the use of them. The procedure is that the lessor buys the item of equipment required from suppliers of the lessee's choice and then leases it out to the lessee at an agreed rental. Almost any item may now be leased, from single items of equipment costing just a few hundred pounds, to machine tools, cranes and aeroplanes costing thousands or millions.

A lease usually runs for a period of three to five years, but this can be varied according to the expected life of the goods. Thereafter, the lessee can either return the goods to the lessor, or continue the rental at a nominal fee.

A leasing agreement has a number of advantages for the businessman. Because a lease is not a loan agreement, obtaining goods on lease does not count as part of a company's borrowing. By leasing goods rather than borrowing funds to buy them, the businessman has borrowing facilities available for other uses.

In addition, the tax position has to be taken into account. Investment allowances, designed to encourage businessmen to invest in capital equipment, are set against profits to reduce a company's liability to tax. The company owning the goods is able to claim the tax credit in the form of investment allowances, and under a leasing agreement this will be the leasing company. The tax credit element will be reflected in a lower rental payment. A businessman contemplating a leasing agreement will therefore have to balance the tax and investment allowance position before deciding whether to lease or to buy the equipment he requires.

Factoring

As in the cases of instalment finance and leasing, factoring is a further service available through the banks, but usually carried on by an associate or subsidiary company.

Under an ordinary factoring agreement, the customer 'sells' his trade debts to the factoring company (the factor). The latter takes over the customer's sales ledger, and becomes responsible for the collection of the debts; in the event of a buyer's default or insolvency, the factoring company will, in approved circumstances, guarantee payment of the buyer's debt to its customer. The advantages from the businessman's point of view are that he is relieved of the cost of administering his sales ledger, and is given a form of credit insurance by the factoring company.

This is not all. A further service available from a factoring company is that of pre-payment; this means that the factor will pay his customer a percentage of the total of his sales invoices, before payment has been received by the factor from the buyers. Naturally, the factor charges a rate of interest for the length of time he is advancing the money, but such an arrangement gives the customer a guaranteed cash flow at the time he needs it.

The usual factoring agreement described above involves the disclosure by a supplier to a buyer that a factoring company is being used. Some companies may not wish this to be known to their customers, and so a factoring company can also provide a confidential factoring service. The factor buys the book debt of the customer who continues, in this case, to run his own sales ledger, receiving payment in the usual way from his buyers. As the receipts from the sale of goods come in they are paid over to the factor by his customer to repay the funds advanced to him when the factor first bought the debts.

Factoring is not available to all companies. In order to enter into an agreement with a factoring company, a customer is usually expected to have an annual turnover of at least £100 000 or £250 000 when confidential factoring is required. He should also be supplying goods to a large number of buyers who, in turn, will be other companies, and not members of the public. Factoring is not, therefore, a service designed for a retailer.

Insurance

Although insurance for customers has been handled by bank managers for more than a century, the clearing banks declined to enter the insurance broking market in their own names until recently.

In the 1960s, Westminster Bank pioneered the change of policy by closing managers' insurance agencies and creating a centralised insurance department which continued after the merger with National Provincial. Barclays entered the field in 1970, setting up an insurance broking subsidiary with a network of field offices on a decentralised basis. Midland and Williams and Glyn's soon followed this pattern with some slight variations. Lloyds Bank introduced its insurance department through its trustee department.

The growing sophistication of insurance requirements is completely handled by large numbers of brokers, but individuals are often reluctant to refer to them. In the past, bank managers gave sound and constructive advice to their customers, but they were limited to placing business within the narrow confines of their own agencies. Understandably, their guidance was largely of a non-professional nature. However, with the formation of the insurance broking subsidiaries or departments, the customer can now expect to receive an insurance service that is professional, all-embracing and impartial.

The decentralised type of operation is based on offering service of two kinds: (a) from the central advisory point; (b) through regional or district representatives throughout the country. The insurance adviser in the field is at the disposal of the bank managers in his district. He is a man of wide insurance experience, well versed in all classes of the business, and with a background of insurance marketing. His main function is to provide a day-to-day service to his bank's managers, assist in the placing of business and, at a manager's request, advise and negotiate for customers direct.

The increasing complexity of fire and accident covers, packaged policies, legislation requiring the protection of special covers, and the wide variations in life assurance all demand considerable research and analysis. This is the area of responsibility for the central advisory team, where specialists maintain close liaison with the insurance market. While the field man can deal with the greater proportion of the type of business referred to him by the bank branches, the more complicated cases are referred to the head office organisation for processing.

In many cases, Quotel, a computerised service for life assurance quotations, is used, so that a list of leading insurance companies and their respective quotations can be produced within a few minutes of the enquiry.

Insurance is now marketed successfully through the massive spread of outlets of the clearing banks.

The simple forms of personal policies required for the protection of private dwellings and their contents, and travel, lend themselves easily to straightforward marketing. It is possible, also, to arrange agreed cover with leading insurance companies, either individually or through a consortium, using the bank as a 'brand' name.

The banks have a decided advantage because of the relationships they have built up with their customers over the years, but the field of the insurance is, to a clearing bank, an augmentation of the whole of its range of financial services. Where customers already receive service from competent professional advisers the bank manager will seldom make any attempt to upset this relationship.

Cash distribution

The banks provide a nationwide cash distribution service which is, perhaps, taken for granted to a greater degree even than the clearing system, and it enables cash to be made available through bank branches to every community of any size, to meet the needs of all types of customer. The provision of this service entails an extensive number of branches mainly for the convenience of the public, and although every opportunity is taken to rationalise the system and to minimise costs, it is expensive in terms of manpower, premises and security.

The clearing banks extend their money transmission service to foreign payments and receipts on a scale which is unmatched by other organisations. An efficient external payments system is indispensable to the conduct and development of the nation's foreign trade and investment overseas, and the banks operate such a system with the minimum of formality.

Many benefits are conferred on the trading community through the speedy provision, by the banks, of their cash requirements. Although there is a considerable saving in cash transactions by the crediting of salaries direct to banking accounts, very large sums of money are paid out every week over bank counters to meet wages. Customers requiring large sums usually send notification in advance so that branch banks get to know the cash requirements and so have no difficulty in supplying their customers' needs.

Some branches finish up each week with a surplus of cash; others pay out more than they receive. In some areas there is a big demand for one type of coin; in others for quite different ones.

The banks ensure that sufficient money of the right kind is always where it is wanted.

Apart from the reserves maintained at the head offices and at cash centres throughout the country, there is a continual movement of cash from some branches to head office, from head office to other branches; between branch and branch; and between bank and bank. The sheer weight of money alone, quite apart from its value, so transferred every week of the year is staggering, and represents a remarkable feat based upon years of experience.

Customers' investments

An important service which banks offer is assistance in the investment of money. A bank will handle, through stockbrokers, any new investment required by a customer, or will attend to the sale of securities or the reinvestment of the proceeds in other securities. These transactions, if carried out by the bank, may not cost the customer any more than if a direct approach had been made to a broker. However, it has long been an established principle of British banking that it is no part of a banker's duty or function to give advice on investments. The normal procedure is for the branch manager to obtain opinions from one of the bank's brokers as to certain lines of securities that would meet the customer's needs.

The banker, as his customer's agent, must act with all diligence both in buying and selling, and forwarding his customer's instructions to the brokers accurately and without variation. When the transaction is completed he must obtain possession of the proper documents of title in a purchase, or of the proceeds in a sale. If the banker negligently fails to secure a purchase or to effect a sale, he will be liable to the customer for any loss that may ensue. So, also, will he be liable for any loss if he varies the instructions which the customer has sent him. The banker makes his profit on these transactions by sharing the standard commission charge with the broker.

Unit trusts

An investor who wishes to spread his risks will often purchase units in a unit trust. A unit trust combines the savings of a large number of investors who subscribe to the initial issue. The managers of the trust then invest the funds in a cross-section of securities. The trust is divided into units, and each investor applies for a certain number of units. The issue is made at an advertised price per unit which includes an initial charge levied by the managers. Thereafter it is still possible to apply for units, with the price of each unit depending upon the progress of the investments included in the portfolio.

Most of the major clearing banks operate a range of unit trusts covering, respectively, capital appreciation, income opportunities, investment in British companies, or a spread of investments in overseas companies. Various unit trusts have been introduced to provide attractive investment benefits for members of professional associations, people under 18 years of age and for shareholders of quoted stocks who wish to exchange them for investment in a unit trust with the minimum of formality and expense.

Units may be realised at any time because the managers undertake to purchase all units offered to them and the price paid depends upon the value of the underlying securities at that time.

Managers of unit trusts derive their profits from three sources:

1 From the initial charge made on newly created units;
2 From an annual service charge which is usually deducted from revenue before distribution of dividends is made to unit holders;
3 From dealing in their own units.

The principal expenses incurred by the managers are in respect of office accommodation, salaries and wages, advertising, and the payment of commissions to banks, solicitors and other agents through whom applications for the purchase of units are submitted.

Investment management by the banks

Some banks offer an investment management service which is especially useful for customers living abroad, or for investors who do not wish to concern themselves personally with investment problems. A customer can choose whether the bank is to make purchases and sales of investments with his consent, or whether such changes are to be made without reference to him. Sometimes, a customer's investments are transferred into the name of the bank's nominee company so that communications from company registrars can be sent to the nominee company which is able to deal on the customer's behalf with such matters as new issues of shares.

Financial counselling

Although all major banks offer advice to individuals concerning their financial affairs, only one bank has, at present, introduced a complete personal financial service. The aim is to help people to organise their financial affairs to the best advantage.

Anyone who feels that his financial affairs are not getting the attention they deserve can benefit from this service, such as middle to senior executives, many of whom are so deeply engaged in company business that they have little or no time left to give full attention to their personal financial affairs.

All important aspects of personal financial arrangements are examined in depth by the bank's own specialist in the relevant fields of finance. These may include investment management, personal taxation, the administration of estates and trusts, wealth tax, property management, unit trusts, equity-linked life assurance, pension arrangements, all kinds of insurance requirements, personal savings, loans and other credit facilities.

This advisory service attracts a 'consultancy' fee, normally in the region of £20 to £25, depending on the complexity of the individual's financial affairs.

Questions

1 What are executor and trustee services?
2 What is a 'credit open' arrangement?
3 Describe the service of 'safe custody' and its legal implications.

9

Banking Operations

Computers and automation

All the clearing banks have been developing substantial computer systems designed to handle accounting – both at branches and at head offices. Although the main objective of all the various systems is the same, methods of approach have differed. For instance, some statements of account produced by computers show no details of entries other than the dates of transactions and the amounts, while others set out each transaction in considerable detail.

The two types of computer operations employed in branch banking are 'on-line' and 'real-time'.

On-line

On-line is a term indicating that a terminal unit in a branch is connected directly to a central computer by a rented Post Office telephone line. Entries are made by each branch and are accumulated in the central computer for subsequent updating of the relative accounts at the end of the day. Customers' balances and details of posted entries can be obtained by the branch direct from the computer.

Real-time

A typical installation in the system is one in which the computer stores data, handles on-line transactions and maintains a central file. Telephone, telegraph and data communications lines are used for remote inquiry and data input. For example, a cashier can 'ask' the file for any kind of stored information on a customer and can enter special instructions into the system depending on the needs of the customer or the bank.

The difference between the real-time and on-line systems is that the former provides continuous up-dating while the latter does not include transactions which have taken place since the last up-dating – usually completed overnight.

The advent of computer systems has removed much routine work from the direct responsibility of branch personnel. This has a number of advantages, such as the clarity and accuracy of statements of account. However, the relationship with customers could become remote, while the computer might be blamed by customers for inefficient service at branches.

The development of sophisticated computer systems and techniques has made possible the provision of a whole new range of customer services. To date, these include:

(*a*) Payroll for customers, e.g. calculating wage and salary schedules for businesses;
(*b*) Reconciliation of paid cheques;
(*c*) Investment portfolio valuation;
(*d*) Credit card system;
(*e*) Accounting and invoicing;
(*f*) The automated clearing system;
(*g*) Share registration;
(*h*) International business.

Computer technology is unlikely to supplant traditional banking skills and automated techniques are no more than a means to an end.

Apart from on-line and real-time processes the following systems are being operated or, at present, are under research.

Integrated file concept

Most large banks are using in their clearing departments automatic sorting machines which read, electronically, sorting code numbers printed on cheques in magnetic ink and conforming to a standard character form. The installation of encoding machines, which enables branches to print in magnetic ink the amount on each cheque, make it possible for any cheque bearing these characters to be sorted and 'posted' entirely within a computerised system.

Voice return, random access, audio response

Updating and making inquiries of computerised account information is an area in banking where communications devices are having their greatest impact. Computer responses which are almost instantaneous with recorded words or visual displays, with associated printers to obtain printout information requested while updating accounts, are other pace-setting trends that banks are seeking from a data communication standpoint.

Thus, this method of presenting information lies in the ability of new computers to speak an answer to a query. A spoken reply can be fed directly into an ordinary telephone line and is, therefore, likely to be extremely useful where branches on a computer system are remote from the computer itself.

Signature verification

This is a system designed to aid in solving the problem of verifying signatures. When verification is requested, the specimen signature is automatically retrieved from a microfilm file, displayed on a monitor and then refiled.

The further developments visualised in the field of communications will call for even more radical changes in banking processes than have so far taken place. In the business of banking, which has always prided itself on the quality of personal service provided, the introduction of mass production techniques to handle many millions of entries a year is inevitable. Far-seeing bankers recognise this and, at the same time, appreciate that the adoption of these techniques should, in fact, free them to give more personal attention to the other aspects of banking which are of more significance from an individual point of view.

Cash dispensers

The idea of installing some kind of mechanical device capable of dispensing cash in response to printed requests was one that intrigued bankers for many years. The basic problems to be solved were concerned with security. For example, instructions to the dispensing machine had to be formulated in such a way as to make fraud or forgery virtually impossible. The answer, eventually, has been to employ specially designed and extremely sophisticated machines which, by incorporating electronic circuits, can accept and 'read' special instruction cards.

Cash dispensers were first introduced in the banks in 1967 and, largely as a result of the decision to close the banks on Saturdays (from July 1969), the installation programme was accelerated.

Most dispensers are built into walls of existing bank offices, although some have been installed in hospitals, in factories and at railway termini. The advantage of this service is that customers who use the dispensers may obtain amounts of cash at any time and on any day of the week.

The 'automatic teller' is a machine linked to a computer, consisting of a small video terminal and a bank of key buttons. The bank customer activates the machine by inserting into a slot a small plastic card and punching a six digit identification code on the keyboard. The terminal then displays a message offering a choice of transactions, e.g. withdrawing or depositing money, transferring funds between current and savings accounts, and account information. The customer punches a key for the function desired; if money is requested the machine checks the account and then passes out notes through a revolving drum. If cash is to be deposited it must be placed into a specially designed envelope and dropped through a slot. All transactions are recorded on a receipt printed and issued on the spot. Hence retail banking revolution has begun, much to the delight of many customers who prefer swift clinical transactions rather than suffering delay at the end of a queue in order to secure personal services.

Electronic funds transfer at point of sale (EFTPOS)

The acceleration of technology is likely to bring the banks much closer to a cashless society, and this is becoming apparent with the introduction of EFTPOS. This system allows, if a person so desires, all purchases or payments for services to take place through a 'personalised' card bearing the bank account and credit information needed to initiate such transactions, and this card would be used mainly in supermarkets and departmental stores. EFTPOS presupposes a very high degree of interconnection between banks and stores.

The operation of EFTPOS is regarded as simple. The customer would hand the personalised card and cheque for the amount of the purchase to the cashier in a store. This would be inserted into a machine connected to a central computer, which would check the balance of the account (to determine if sufficient funds are available), verify the signature, approve the purchase, debit the bank account of the purchaser automatically and credit the account of the vendor. All details would be recorded in the computer and on a computer printout, so that a check could be made if a dispute arose later between the customer and the bank.

It is estimated that a five-year implementation period should bring in about 20% of the larger retailers who have Barclaycard or Access card franchises and they would operate some 20 000 terminals linked into the network, but before any decision to implement can be taken a consensus will have to be reached on accepted terminal types, clearances and settlement methods, legal points, security, timetables, operational costs, tariffs and benefits. Of all the points to be settled, that of security is possibly the most difficult, both from the aspect of card falsification and because the main banks will have to allow for more frequent access to centrally-held accounts than ever before. Thus the security of their accounting systems will be at a greater risk. In Britain there are about six million active credit card users and about 9½ million cheque guarantee cards. Both types may disappear eventually in favour of EFTPOS cards, requiring large and complex control and accounting systems for support.

Equity investment

Many progressive private companies have found that inflation and the incidence of tax have made it increasingly difficult to expand through retained profits, and internally generated funds have been used to finance higher stocks, works-in-progress and debtors. A company in this position may intend to expand through the installation of additional productive capacity, improved processes or greater penetration at home or abroad. It may also have the opportunity of acquiring another business for cash. However, in many cases the capital base of the company will not support the additional external finance that is needed because borrowing lines and other financial facilities are fully employed.

The answer may lie in the provision of share capital by the directors or their friends and the flotation of the company, or (for smaller public companies) a rights issue, but conditions may not always be favourable for the smaller company. As a result, the banks have begun to enter the equity investment market where the purpose is to make equity investment in progressive companies or take up shares in small publicly quoted companies.

The criteria involved in assessing equity finance deals differ considerably from those employed in the provision of normal bank lending, requiring specific negotiations with potential clients to be undertaken generally only by specialists.

The following are the main functions:

(*a*) Subscribing for additional shares to enable a company to expand on a sound financial base;
(*b*) Acquiring existing shares from directors wishing to retire, or from directors or shareholders who have actual, or potential, capital transfer tax or other financial liabilities. The solution of problems of this sort can help to ensure the continuity of a family business;
(*c*) A director may wish to retire and sell his shareholdings;
(*d*) Some family shareholders who have, perhaps, inherited their shares and have little direct interest in the company, may want to switch their investment to a more marketable security.

By raising new money from the banks in this manner companies can solve not only the problem of finding the capital they require, but do so in a way which carries other advantages:

1 Existing borrowing power is not used up: often it is increased because the borrowing base of share capital has been increased.
2 Capital is provided in stable form, not subject to fluctuations in the availability of money or interest rates.
3 The company's creditworthiness is improved in the eyes of its bankers, suppliers and other creditors by the presence of an institutional shareholder.
4 Equally its trading reputation with customers and potential customers is enhanced.

5 Particular ease of access to other bank group services is acquired.
6 Advice is made available on the company's affairs and particularly upon its financial strategies.

The investment is restricted to a minority stake only and control of the company remains with the shareholders. In addition to investing in equity, a bank may support its investment by term loans on normal commercial terms to make up the total finance required.

Specialists and industry advisers

Developments in the industrial environment and certain legislation assisted the banks in pursuing a policy to acquire specialist information and advice. This emerged mainly by the recruitment of specialist advisers, some of them drawn from appointments in industry and not necessarily from the ranks of those in the sphere of banking. The specialisation was not intended to refer to advances in service development or operations, such as insurance, factoring, leasing and so on, but in major sectors of industry, e.g. oil, property, agriculture, shipping, aerospace, electronics, etc.

The demand for finance to exploit North Sea oil exploration accelerated the appointment of specialists by the major banks. Their role has been essentially non-executive, designed to maintain close contact with the oil industry and to respond quickly to enquiries. The non-executive activities were developed with greater emphasis on the international aspects of banking business, while the scope steadily widened to encompass all opportunities relating to energy rather than just oil and gas. This became a logical and desirable extension because, to an increasing extent, the oil companies began to diversify into the energy business as a whole. Ultimately, these specialists have become involved with monitoring the energy field in coal, wind power, wave power, nuclear fusion and nuclear fission.

Another area which drew attention was property. The débâcle that occurred in property in 1973 and 1974 encouraged some banks to recruit property specialists, although many of these came from within their own ranks. Their role involved the evaluation of implication of current and proposed legislation on property, advising on specific lending and other financial transactions, and maintaining contacts within the building and construction industry, including also the leading firms of estate agents, valuers and surveyors. The Community Land Act 1975 and the Development Land Tax proposals which received the Royal Assent in August 1976, further complicated the property scene, reflecting the need for specialist advice.

The demand for advisers and specialists is certain to continue as changes occur in the industrial and commercial environment – the advance of technology, depressions and slumps in particular industries, innovation, new discoveries and sudden growth in specific fields – each marketing a deflection of the rudder and having a variety of implications for the banks, often when competition is at its fiercest. As such, an awareness for information and advice has grown, and with it the need for specialist assistance.

Changes in branch banking

A perennial problem for UK banks has been the costing and control of their branch operations. Although the banks pursue a policy whereby profitability should prevail, there are two aspects which sometimes affect the situation:

1 Provision of a public service; a social responsibility.
2 A change in local demand that has a substantial impact on the operations of a branch.

In some cases branches have been improved and enlarged; in others, they have been down-graded to sub-branches (opened for a few hours each day by members of staff of the nearest main branch) or closed. Following high inflation and a period of recession, the banks began to look more critically at the vast amount of prime site property they controlled which needed to be manned at an ever increasing cost.

There is little doubt that the major banks give a great deal of thought to rationalisation and reduction of branch networks in the light of rapid increases in staff salaries. While rationalisation for strictly economic reasons may be justified depending on external factors, there are increasingly valid reasons for functional rationalisation. Analysing customer requirement and deciding whether to up- or down-grade a branch, or open or close in a community, and when to turn a branch into a corporate business centre is eminently sensible for the purpose of marketing as well as good banking.

As a result of this, some banks have embarked on reorganisation of their networks to establish specific branches designed to assist businessmen and corporate development. Under this scheme, normal branches, i.e. satellite branches, are used for personal accounts only. Other banks have been motivated to make changes of a different nature, aiming to cater for the differing requirements of corporate personal customers by encouraging them to make use of branches designed to meet their individual needs, rather than by trying to provide a universal range of service for every sort of customer at every branch. Thus concentration has been focused on redesigning city centre offices in London and other major cities into larger units, while certain existing central offices have been closed, ultimately offering fewer but larger branches in the city centres. In the suburbs, on the other hand, the approach has been to group branches into 'families' with a full range of services available only at the parent office, where a management team is located.

Other changes in branch banking locations relate to 'on-site' banking. In many cases the customer is unable to get to a bank so the bank has arranged to go to the customer. The simple idea is to set up branches in factories, hospitals, offices, places of further education, military bases, etc. At present, some 800 'on-site' branches have been established by the major clearing banks.

Clearly, the major banks are conducting a number of experiments in the branch banking process. Since banking began small businesses, retailers and professional men have all needed the 'High Street' branch, and a great deal of effort may be required to make them alter their habits. Nevertheless, the method of branch banking operations is undergoing change, which may be accelerated by the techniques applied by modern technology. In time, preference for automatic telling-machines may redefine the needs of customers, and the banks might have to alter their policies accordingly.

Questions

1 Automatic telling machines: what is their likely impact on banks/customers?
2 How are banks able to compete by equity investment?
3 Identify measures which may streamline future development for the branch network system.
4 How will EFTPOS change the nature of retailing and banking?

10

Securities

When a customer has agreed to lodge items of value for a proposed advance, the manager has to consider the following points. Is the security:

(*a*) Of a value easily ascertainable and relatively stable?
(*b*) Readily marketable and realisable?
(*c*) Acceptable as banking security?
(*d*) What it is described to be?
(*e*) Readily available to be transferred to the bank?
(*f*) Adequate cover for the advance?
(*g*) Being charged freely and voluntarily, if it is a third party security?

Security is not taken with the intention of obtaining repayment by its realisation, for no banker wishes to be repaid this way. It is taken in case the normal source of repayment fails, which, unfortunately, it does at times.

A customer should never feel insulted or that his integrity and financial standing are being doubted because of the request for security. Old-established firms in the London discount market and on the London Stock Exchange whose reputations are beyond question regularly deposit first-class securities as cover for advances from their bankers to meet any unforeseen contingencies. Certain things may be of considerable value to the individual, such as jewellery, furs, silver or a car, but these items are not acceptable to a banker as security for an advance, for he has neither the requisite experience nor the facilities for valuing or storing these articles, of which the physical possession may be essential to give him a good title. A banker is interested only in items whose ownership is evidenced by documents of title, and the ownership of which may be transferred by means of these documents.

Security can be either direct or collateral. Direct security is that lodged by a customer to secure his own account, while collateral security is that lodged by a third party to secure the account of another. A complete, and the most satisfactory, title is given by what is known as the full legal title, for the banker taking such a title should be in an unassailable position. The banker has full rights of possession and sale, evidenced by some document of charge, while the customer retains his 'equity of redemption', that is, his right to redeem the property by repaying the advance plus accrued interest, according to the terms of the agreement with the banker. Anything short of a legal title gives an 'equitable title' only.

This is less sound as security for a banker. For example, a mere deposit of documents of title with the banker, with the intent that it shall be security for an advance, will, in most cases, be sufficient to give an equitable title. When, therefore, a customer of undoubted character and adequate means requires an advance for a short period and deposits security as backing, the banker, to save trouble and expense, is happy with an equitable interest in the security. Taking a legal title is a much more expensive business than taking an equitable title, although it could be wiser to take that course of action in the long run.

Rights over security

The banker's right over security may, in law, be:

(*a*) Pledge;
(*b*) Mortgages;
(*c*) Hypothecation;
(*d*) Lien;
(*e*) Guarantee;
(*f*) Indemnity.

Pledge

To pledge or pawn is the most obvious manner in which a right may be obtained over security. An item of value is pledged, or pawned, as security for a debt and is deposited for that specific purpose. When that purpose is fulfilled, i.e. when the debt is repaid, the property is returned to its owner. The essence of a pledge is that while possession passes to the pledgee, the legal ownership remains with the pledger. Negotiable instruments, such as bearer bonds, can be 'pledged' to a banker as security for an advance.

Mortgages

A mortgage differs from a pledge in that legal ownership of the item mortgaged (apart from land which is subject to special conditions of mortgage) is conveyed to secure the debt, to the party granting an advance, subject to it reverting to the mortgagor on repayment of the advance. The advantage to the mortgagor is that physical possession of the items mortgaged may remain with him.

Hypothecation

This is a special kind of mortgage which covers goods or documents of title to goods. It defines how the banker may deal with them on default of repayment of a debt and, generally, confers a power of sale in this event.

Lien

A banker's lien is an implied pledge. It is a general right over documents of title subject to pledge, such as negotiable instruments, passing through his hands ordinarily as a banker, while a debt is owing to him. In other words, the banker has the right to assume that the negotiable instruments passing through his hands are pledged against any money owing to him, unless they are deposited for a special purpose inconsistent with such a right. However, the banker prefers to have the position made quite clear in an agreement in writing. The form used by a bank for this purpose, known as a charge form, often contains a clause giving a specific right of lien and defining its scope.

Guarantee

Perhaps the best-known type of collateral security is a guarantee by which one person makes himself 'collaterally answerable for the debts or defaults of another'.

There must be three parties for a contract of guarantee:

1 The principal creditor;
2 The principal debtor who is primarily liable;
3 The guarantor who is liable if the principal debtor doesn't pay.

A guarantee must be in writing, and it cannot be set aside on the grounds of failure to disclose material facts.

Where a person offers himself as a guarantor, the bank manager does his best to ensure that the potential guarantor fully understands the precise nature of the obligations to be incurred, which is a real financial liability. A guarantee is not something, therefore, that a person should undertake lightly. In spite of the care that is taken to inform them, many guarantors still imagine that they are merely vouching for a customer's integrity or giving him a reference and are genuinely surprised if they are called upon to honour the guarantee by the payment of money. Guarantees are often signed by a number of persons together, in connection with borrowing by clubs, societies, churches, firms and limited companies. Although the same care is needed in explaining their responsibilities, the signatories are usually well aware of what is involved.

Indemnity

Whereas a guarantee is a contract concerning three people, an indemnity consists of only two parties to the contract – the person giving the indemnity being primarily liable. It arises when one person shoulders direct responsibility for the liability of another by saying, for example, 'If you lend £1000 to my brother I will see that you are repaid'.

An indemnity does not require evidence in writing, although a banker will generally ensure that a document of indemnity is signed.

Banks often enter into engagements and indemnities on behalf of customers. These may involve joining with the customers in an indemnity to a company or corporation in respect of documents, such as share certificates, which have been lost and for which issuing companies require a form of indemnity to be signed, both by the shareholder and his banker, before they will issue a duplicate. This is no mere formality because if the original certificates come to light in the future, and two separate holders claim ownership or rights in the same shares, the bank would be liable to reimburse the company for any loss sustained.

Trading customers quite often require indemnities in connection with missing shipping documents. For example, there may be postal or other delays, or the ship carrying the goods may arrive at the port of destination before the documents have reached the consignee. The shipping company will deliver the goods only against an indemnity, signed by both the consignee and his bankers, covering them against any loss. Without this protection, it is possible that the rightful owner might later present the bill of lading to find that the goods have already been delivered.

A further type of indemnity is the bond given by bankers to HM Customs and Excise in respect of dutiable goods imported by their customers into this country, on the understanding that the goods will be re-exported or, failing this, that duty will be paid.

There are many other purposes for which different types of guarantees, bonds and indemnities are given by banks on behalf of their customers. One particularly important example is the guarantee by a bank of the due fulfilment of major contract work for overseas buyers, such as the supply of locomotives or electrical equipment, or the construction of buildings, roads or harbours. Similarly, in the home market, builders and contractors are usually required by local authorities to supply bonds guaranteeing the fulfilment of contracts for the building of houses, schools and other constructional work, in accordance with the terms of their tenders to local authorities. Banks generally do not regard the giving of these due-performance bonds as part of their normal business, usually referring customers to insurance companies and other institutions that handle this type of business. There may be exceptions, of course, and each case is considered on its merits.

Before becoming involved with arrangements of this kind, which are contingent liabilities of a bank on behalf of its customer, the banker will satisfy himself that the customers have the necessary financial resources and the ability and experience to undertake the work successfully.

Life policies

Compared with the guarantee, a life policy, provided that it has an adequate surrender value, is a much more reliable and acceptable banking security.

The advantages are:

1 The surrender value, i.e. the amount which the insurance

company is willing to repay on the premiums paid for the surrender of the policy which may be ascertained. This tends to increase the longer the policy is held. There is, also, the possibility of greatly increased cover in the case of a certain type of policy should the assured party die.
2 Taking a charge over a policy is a comparatively simple matter.
3 Endorsing the security, i.e. making a claim under an assignment, can be made at low cost and with a minimum of formality.

The disadvantages are:

1 A policy of life assurance is a contract of *uberrimae fidei* (of the utmost good faith) and any misrepresentation or withholding of material facts at the time the policy is taken out may, and probably will, affect the validity of the contract.
2 If his customer defaults, there is the possibility that the banker will have to pay the premiums in order to keep the policy alive, and this may well increase the amount of the advance, making it still more difficult for the customer to repay.

When a life policy is offered as security, the bank will read the policy through carefully, bearing in mind the following:

1 What sort of company is it?
   (*a*) Is the policy issued by a well-known and reputable insurance company?
   (*b*) Is the company domiciled in Great Britain? If not, there may be some difficulty in obtaining the policy moneys if, or when, a claim arises.
   (*c*) Is the policy issued by a mutual insurance company? If so, it may not necessarily be a desirable type of security, as the policy holder may also be a member of the company and, as such, incur certain liabilities.
2 What sort of policy is it?
   (*a*) *Whole life:* payable at death.
   (*b*) *Endowment:* payable at a future stated time or at death – whichever is earlier.
   (*c*) *Short-term:* payable only if death occurs within a certain specified time; not a desirable form of banking security.
   (*d*) *Family protection:* designed to protect the widow and her children in the event of the death of the husband.

3 Is it the kind of policy which can be assigned? Certain policies, called industrial policies – premiums on which are usually paid weekly and recorded in a premium book – are issued upon the express condition that they shall not be assigned, mortgaged or sold without the express agreement of the insurance company.
4 Are there onerous or restrictive clauses written into the terms of the policy? These may relate to air travel, kinds of occupation, travel abroad, etc.
5 Whose life is assured and to whom will the policy money be payable? All interested parties must join in an assignment.
6 Are there any trust interests? Where, for example, a policy is taken out by a husband in favour of his named wife, a trust is created in her favour and both must sign the bank's form of charge.

An assignment does not confer upon the assignee (in this case, a bank) any right to sue for the policy until written notice of the date and purpose of the assignment have been given to the insurance company at its principal place of business. The date on which such notice is received relegates the priority of all claims under any assignment. The company must acknowledge receipt of the notice.

Stocks and shares

Traditionally, stocks and shares have been used as cover for bank advances. They have all the advantages required in suitable security, except for the fact that their stability of value may be suspect, especially in times of economic uncertainty. Fluctuations of values for securities which are saleable in the open market, i.e. through stock exchanges, may vary, and price variations from which neither Government stocks nor first-class industrial stocks are immune may be embarrassingly abrupt. Consequently, they involve the banker in constant vigilance, to ensure that the value of the stock remains above, or at least equal to, the amount of the advance.

Stocks and shares offered by customers as security fall into groups as follows.

Stock Exchange securities

These securities embrace stocks and shares of the many companies quoted on the London and other Stock Exchanges. They include ordinary shares, preference shares, debentures and loan stock.

Stocks such as bearer bonds, bearer scrip, share warrants to bearer and debentures to bearer are, perhaps, the ideal security. A mere deposit of these bonds with intent to pledge gives the banker a good title, for this passes by simple delivery.

American-type share warrants

American and Canadian share warrants are usually registered in the name of a stockbroker or bank nominee company, which acts as trustee for the owner. As the broker or nominee company endorses the form of transfer on the back the warrants can be passed from owner to owner via the Stock Exchange merely by delivery. When offered this type of security, the bank has to be satisfied that the warrant is stamped. It is then readily saleable and can be taken as security. However, American and Canadian securities, although treated as 'bearers', do not have all the characteristics of a fully negotiable document, since the holder cannot sue in his own name unless, and until, he has registered the security in his own name.

National Savings Bank issues

These include British Savings Bonds, Premium Savings Bonds and other stocks. Certificates of Government loans purchased through National Savings Stock Register are sometimes offered to the banker as security for small personal advances. For this purpose they have some disadvantages. They cannot be sold on the Stock Exchange and application for repayment must be made through the National Savings Stock Register. In certain cases, they may be subject to a term of notice; the National Savings Bank will not accept notice of any charge; and there is always the possibility that a duplicate certificate or book may be issued to the holder on application.

Thus, it is not possible to take a satisfactory charge over these stocks.

Nevertheless, stocks are, in fact, quite often taken as security, the possible risk being fully understood and accepted by the banker. The customer is asked to sign a memorandum of deposit and to lodge the certificate of stock, and also to sign an undated form of application to sell or repay.

National Savings Certificates

National Savings Certificates are not satisfactory security for a loan for the same reasons as for other National Savings issues. However, they have the merit that they increase slowly but steadily in value during the period they are held as security.

Building society shares and deposits

In view of the special nature of these shares and deposits, they are not strictly desirable as security for an advance. With regard to shares, the bank will require the share certificate or pass book; a covering memorandum of deposit to be signed by the borrower; and a signed but undated notice of withdrawal together with an authority for the payment of the moneys to the bank.

Notice is given to the society at the same time, asking if any prior notices have been registered, whether notice of withdrawal has been lodged by the shareholders and whether the society itself claims any lien or set-off in respect of the holding.

Occasionally, a building society deposit may be taken as security, with the bank insisting on taking a letter of assignment.

Unquoted stocks and shares

Unquoted shares fall into two distinct classes from the standpoint of banking security. These are:

(*a*) Shares of public companies not quoted on any Stock Exchange or the unlisted securities market;
(*b*) Shares of private companies.

Both classes are generally unsuitable as banking security because they are difficult to value with any accuracy and often difficult to realise if the need should arise.

Land

The first practical step when taking land as security is to decide how much it is worth from the standpoint of the bank. The bank manager is not expected to be a professional valuer, but he has to be able to estimate the value of any property within his area with reasonable accuracy. The services of a professional valuer will not normally be required in practice, because the bank is taking the security as a form of insurance in the background, relying primarily upon the borrower to repay the advance from trade or other known sources.

The main points to be considered by the banker are:

(*a*) The valuation of the security;
(*b*) The question of fire insurance in respect of any buildings;
(*c*) The title – examination and report;
(*d*) The mortgage to the bank – legal or equitable?
(*e*) The priority of charges required;
(*f*) Repayment of the advance;
(*g*) Remedies available to the bank as a mortgagee;
(*h*) Is there a second mortgage or a sub-mortgage?
(*i*) Whether or not the land registered, i.e. land recorded by the Land Registry establishing the ownership, or title of the land, in contrast to unregistered land where the title has to be identified from a large bundle of deeds.

As security for a bank advance, land has certain disadvantages.

1 Although unlikely to fluctuate widely in value over a long period, the land may be difficult to value with any degree of accuracy on a short-term basis and realisation may be a protracted and expensive matter if there are no willing buyers in the market.
2 Unless a title to the land is registered, the chain of title may be complicated and defects may be discovered which limit the value of the security.
3 The costs to the borrower are, generally, higher in the case of land than they are with many types of security.
4 The security could well depreciate in value unless it is well maintained. Repairs and decorations are essential over the years and difficulty may arise if the mortgagor neglects the building. There is, additionally, the need for the bank to verify that the property is fully insured against all known risks.
5 There is the danger that some advances granted against property (particularly private houses) may develop into long-term mortgage loans.

Notwithstanding these disadvantages compared with more marketable securities, land in all its forms is acceptable banking security provided there is ample margin in the value and a satisfactory title can be proved and, if necessary, obtained by the bank.

Debentures

Long-term loans made to trading companies against the security of mortgages or debentures represent loan capital, as distinct from share capital. When the security is by way of mortgage the lender has a fixed charge, usually a legal mortgage, over specific assets such as land, buildings and, perhaps, machinery. The debenture is a specialised form of security given by companies, and may be either a fixed or a floating charge, or even a combination of both.

A fixed charge prevents the company disposing of fixed assets or property. A floating charge allows the company to deal freely with its assets on the basis that should certain events take place to affect the safety of the loan or the value of the security given by the debenture, the charge would 'crystallise' and become fixed.

While a fixed charge gives a perfectly satisfactory charge over fixed assets such as land and buildings, a floating charge is of particular value as a security over a company's floating assets; cash, stock, work-in-progress, trade debtors and so on. It would be troublesome and expensive to take a fixed charge over such a variety of changing assets.

Produce

The basic theory of advances against produce is that goods are pledged as security. They are then deposited in a warehouse in the name of the bank, and the customer obtains a loan for an agreed amount. In the majority of cases, when the customer has arranged a sale of the goods or part of the goods, he will need to have possession in order to deliver them to the buyer. The bank will then appoint the customer as its agent to deal with the sale; as such the customer will complete the sale and in due course deliver the proceeds to the bank in order to repay the loan.

Should bankruptcy, a receivership, liquidation or a warrant for execution fall upon the customer while he has possession of the goods as agent for the bank, the bank will be able to claim the goods as being pledged to it. Similarly, if the goods have been sold but not paid for, the bank can claim, as principal, from the person to whom the goods have been sold.

The appointment of the customer as agent of the bank and the instructions to him to account for the proceeds of the sale are made by means of a trust letter: these arrangements are known as trust facilities. However watertight the bank's position may be at law, this protection will be of little comfort if, upon sale, the goods actually yield much less than the amount lent. A close watch must, therefore, be maintained on the market price of the produce or goods concerned, and an adequate margin maintained between buying and selling prices in order to meet possible depreciation in market value. Equally, it is essential to ensure that the goods or produce representing the security are fully insured against all known risks until such time as they are sold.

Statute of Limitations

For debts other than specialty debts, i.e. debts for which documents are prepared under seal, an action must be started before the expiration of six years from the date on which the cause of action occurred.

Adding interest to a dormant loan does not entitle a banker to extend the term if six years have elapsed since the loan or overdraft become repayable.

Where written acknowledgement is made by the debtor, or any repayment has been made by him, the course of action is determined from the date of the last acknowledgement or payment.

If a loan or overdraft is secured by a mortgage or other charge on property, the Limitation Act does not come into effect for twelve years from the date when the right to receive the money occurred. Equally, where a guarantee is signed, the banker's right of action is barred in six years after the date upon which the debt was first recoverable by action, but a guarantee for payment of a mortgage debt secured on land has a limitation of twelve years, both as regards the mortgagor and the guarantor.

The right of 'set-off'

It has already been explained that the banker must cash the cheques of his customer, provided they are in order and funds are available. This can raise difficulties, however, where the customer has several accounts, some in debit and some in credit, because the banker then has to decide the amount of the available balance. The main difficulty, in practice, occurs when a cheque is presented by a third party but, while the credit balance on the account on which it is drawn is sufficient to meet it, the banker has in fact been looking to that credit balance as cover – or 'set-off' – for another account which is overdrawn. In law, the banker may set-off debit amounts against credit amounts of the same customer, despite the fact that they are in different accounts. A right of set-off exists immediately between all accounts, including loans, on death, bankruptcy and liquidation. However, if the customer has one account for his own money and another for trust money, the banker cannot set-off a credit balance on the trust account against a debit balance on the personal account.

Questions

1 What does a banker require in a security when it is offered as collateral?
2 Explain the term 'lien'.
3 Who are the parties to a guarantee?
4 How does a guarantee differ from an indemnity?
5 What are the advantages and disadvantages of a life assurance policy as security?
6 When taking land as security, what points must the banker consider?
7 Explain the right of 'set-off'.

11

International Trading

The expansion of international trade within every sphere of industry has been supported and facilitated by banks, merchant banks and the Export Credits Guarantee Department. As far as the UK is concerned, since April 1980 imports and exports were no longer subject to the requirements of exchange control.

Selling goods abroad is often more complex than selling in the home market. Exported goods are sold to buyers who are likely to be less well known to the seller than are buyers in the seller's own country. In international trading, there is the problem that the legal system, the language and trade customs are all different, and exporting tends to entail a greater risk of non-payment than domestic sales. Additionally, the time taken for goods to pass from seller to buyer is generally longer for exports than for goods sold at home. This poses a problem because buyers prefer not to pay until they have inspected goods, while suppliers want payment on or before shipment.

Exporting also involves payment in a currency foreign either to the buyer or to the seller, or to both, and hence entails exchange risk. Any movements in the relative values of currencies which take place between the date a contract is signed and final payment will mean that the seller obtains less (or more) in terms of his own currency than expected, or that the buyer has to pay more (or less) than planned, and exchange control regulations may exist in both the seller's and the buyer's country.

Dealing with buyers abroad entails a variety of further risks, ranging from that of a delay in foreign currency payments by a foreign buyer to outright default. Shipping documents normally include invoices and marine insurance cover notes, certificates or policies, but it is the bill of lading that is most important; only the holder of this document can normally claim the good from the shipping company. A bill of lading is a receipt, issued on behalf of the shipowner, for goods accepted for shipment, and is an undertaking by the shipowner to deliver the goods to the specified destination in the same condition as they were when he received them. Bills of lading are normally made out in sets of two or three originals, each of which gives the holder title and claim to the goods. Two bills are usually sent to the overseas buyer by alternative routes.

The precautions taken before the bill of lading and other shipping documents are released by the exporter (or his banker) to the buyer (or his banker) vary according to a number of factors depending on the method of payment applied described below.

Methods of payment

1 Advance payment

The greatest security which an exporter can obtain is advance payment of the full contract value – also known as *cash with order*. It requires the buyer to extend credit to the exporter – a practice usually unattractive to the buyer, who has no guarantee that the goods will arrive, or, if they do, that they will be in a satisfactory condition. For this and other reasons, advance payments are rarely used.

2 Open account

This method offers least security to the exporter. The documents of title are sent direct to the buyer, and the latter agrees to pay at a certain time, generally according to the exporter's normal terms of payment as laid down in the conditions of sale. Under this arrangement, an exporter loses control both of the goods being exported and of title to them. A high degree of trust in the importer is required and occurs where a satisfactory relationship has been established between the two parties over several years.

Settlement can be effected as follows.

(*a*) *Cheque.* The buyer could draw a cheque payable at his own domestic bank and dispatch it to the exporter. It may take some weeks for such a cheque to be cleared through the banking system, though it is sometimes possible for the exporter to obtain funds against the cheque by having it negotiated by his own bank.

(*b*) *Banker's draft.* This is a cheque drawn by the buyer's bank, normally on a correspondent bank in the exporter's country. The buyer sends the draft to the exporter, who then obtains payment through his own bank.

(*c*) *Mail transfer* (MT). In this case, the buyer's bank sends instructions by airmail to a correspondent bank, asking it to credit the exporter or his bank with sterling or foreign currency.

(*d*) *Telegraphic transfer* (TT). This is identical to the mail transfer method except that the instructions are conveyed by telex or cable. Transfers can also be made via the SWIFT (Society for World-wide Inter-bank Financial Telecommunications) network.

3 Bills of exchange

A third method of payment for exports is by means of bills of exchange, which provide a very flexible method of settling international trade transactions. They may be at sight or at term/at usance. In the former case, the drawee of the bill (the buyer) has to pay cash on presentation of the bill. With a term/usance bill, a credit period (known as the tenor or usance of the bill) is allowed to the buyer, who signifies agreement to pay in the due date by writing his acceptance across it.

In the simplest case, the bill of exchange is handed to the exporter's bank, which in turn sends it to its importer's country. The latter bank, known as the collecting bank, then obtains payment (if a sight bill) or acceptance (if a usance bill) from the importer. Documents may be released against acceptance or payment according to the exporter's instructions. It is common practice for the collecting bank to retain the bill of exchange once it has been accepted and to present it for payment by the acceptor (drawee/importer) on the due date. Proceeds are then remitted, as with a sight bill, in accordance with the remitting bank's instructions.

The collection of a bill of exchange without documents is known as clean collection. The main difference between clean collection and documentary collection, in which the documents of title are sent together with the bill of exchange to the collecting bank, is that with clean collection the bill can be sent without reference to the original contract. With documentary collection, instructions are given as to the conditions under which the documents may be released to the buyer. The generic term for methods of payment involving such bills is *bills for collection*. A method similar in principle is to omit the bill of exchange and allow release of the documents against payment. This is known as *cash against documents (CAD)*.

From the exporter's point of view, settling an international transaction involving a period of credit by using bills of exchange may have two advantages. First, it may enable him to obtain cash for the goods before payment by the importer, because he may be able to sell the bills for cash at a discount before the overseas buyer has made his payments, and second, he can provide the exporter with a measure of security which is absent when trade is conducted on open account terms.

4 Promissory notes

Another means of payment, a promissory note, is simply a promise to pay. Whereas a bill of exchange is drawn by the exporter on the buyer, a promissory note is written out by the buyer promising to pay the exporter (or bearer) an amount of money at a specified time. It provides a degree of security similar to that afforded by an accepted bill of exchange.

5 Letters of credit

Payment through the medium of a bill of exchange can be made still more secure by the associated use of a letter of credit. This is issued by the buyer's bank at his request in accordance with the payment terms of the underlying contract; it is a guarantee of payment by that bank (although the beneficiary would be well advised to seek the advice of his own bankers on the value of the issuing bank's guarantee, as there may be exchange control problems, political risks or even a question about the credit standing of the issuing bank).

If the credit is made irrevocable, the issuing ban is unable to amend or cancel its terms without the consent of all the parties, including the beneficiary. Further security can be obtained by the exporter if the bank through which the letter of credit is transmitted to him confirms it, making it a *confirmed irrevocable letter of credit*

(CILC): this bank (the advising bank) has added its name to the credit guaranteeing payment. Because payment is thus guaranteed by two banks, this is the safest method of payment. The exporter is responsible for presenting the appropriate documents to the advising bank, thus giving the generic name of *documentary credits* to such instruments. Documentary credits may call for bills of exchange to be either at sight or at term, on the advising bank or the purchaser, or the bank which opened the credit. If it is at sight and is drawn on the advising bank, the exporter receives payment in cash from that bank on production of the relevant documents. If the bill is at term and an *acceptance credit* facility has been arranged under an irrevocable letter of credit, the advising bank accepts it, thus enabling the exporter to sell it for cash at a discount. When the bill matures (usually within 180 days), the holder obtains payment from the advising bank which is then reimbursed via the issuing bank by the overseas buyer.

It is essential that the documents relating to a letter of credit conform in all details to the requirements of the letter of credit; discrepancies in the documents may result in non-payment.

Acceptances

Acceptance credits are widely used by UK companies as a means of financing the production and sale of goods for export. These credits are usually for a specified sum and are available by, say, three months' date or sight drafts by the UK company on the opening bank. The drafts are then accepted by the opening bank and handed to the UK company which discounts them, usually on the London discount market. In this way, the UK company is able to raise finance by making use of the name of the opening bank as acceptor, and can discount the drafts at much 'finer' rates than would be the position if it sought to discount its own unbacked paper.

The system of acceptances works well from the banker's point of view. Very rarely does he have to part with any actual money. The whole transaction is based upon the credit, not the cash, of the banker and for the 'loan' of his reputation the banker charges a commission. In some cases security is deposited as cover, while in others the credits are documentary so that the banker gets the documents of title to the goods as security for the bills. If the customer does not provide for the bills the banker must, nevertheless, pay them, and it is on account of the banker's liability on the one hand and his customer's liability to him on the other hand, that the item appears on both sides of the banker's balance sheet.

Foreign currency advantages

The easiest way for an exporter to avoid exchange risk is to invoice in sterling. Nevertheless, there can be advantages in foreign currency invoicing, particularly if the exporter supplements this by using the forward exchange markets.

1 In some export markets, foreign currency – often the US dollar – is the normal trading currency, and so its use can make exports from the UK more attractive to the buyer.
2 The exporter can quote in the buyer's own currency and relieve the buyer of any exchange risk, thus enhancing the attraction of the export package.
3 When sterling is at a discount on the forward exchange markets, an exporter can sell his expected foreign currency receipts forward for more sterling than he would get at current spot rates. This can enable him to quote a more competitive price in foreign currency or provide him with more profits than would otherwise be the case.
4 Foreign currency receipts from exports can be held for limited periods in special accounts to pay for imports, thereby saving some at least of the commissions payable on foreign exchange transactions and eliminating exchange risk to the extent that income from exports matches payments for imports.

Forward exchange

A UK supplier selling goods abroad may have the option of invoicing in sterling or in a foreign currency. If quoted in sterling, he will know what the sterling receipts will be, leaving the buyer to bear the exchange risk.

On the other hand, if the UK exporter quotes in foreign currency, then he will bear the exchange risk, since he cannot be certain of the amount of sterling he will get for the foreign currency paid over to him in due course. However, it may be possible for the exporter or the buyer, or both, to minimise the exchange risk by using forward foreign exchange markets. This is by means of a forward exchange contract, under which a bank agrees to buy the foreign currency proceeds for sterling at a future date at a rate of exchange specified when the forward contract is made. This rate is known as the forward rate. It is related to the spot rate by a premium (i.e. the forward rate produces less sterling than the spot rate) or a discount (the converse). Thus, by use of the forward market an exporter can assure himself of a fixed amount of sterling at a future time.

The important fact is that the amount is fixed when the forward exchange contract is made. Even when an exporter does not know precisely when he will receive his foreign currency payments, he may still be able to use the forward foreign exchange market by employing an option contract. Under this arrangement, he may deliver currency at any time between two future dates (say, three months apart) at a fixed forward rate of exchange. Alternatively, he may prefer to undertake a forward transaction for a specified future date, this forward exchange contract then being rolled forward (i.e. replaced by a new forward contract) if there is still uncertainty as to when he will receive his currency.

ECGD insurance

Export Credits Guarantee Department (ECGD) is a Government department responsible to the Secretary of State for Trade. It is required to operate an export credit insurance business, and to support British exports. Where *supplier credit* is concerned, ECGD provides insurance to exporters and, if required, guarantees to lending banks that their credit will be repaid. In the case of *buyer credits*, the credit is provided by a loan agreement between the lending bank(s) and the buyer (or other approved borrower), guaranteed by ECGD, with the exporter usually receiving payment of the credit portion from the lending bank according to a payment schedule agreed with the buyer.

Comprehensive short-term credit guarantee

ECGD applies the principle of comprehensive insurance to all goods where the business is of a continuous and repetitive nature. Goods which qualify for short-term credit (up to six months) are generally of this type and the exporter is normally expected to insure all his export business involving credit terms of up to 180 days. However, cover may be agreed for selected markets, provided these comprise a spread of countries acceptable to ECGD and represent a reasonable proportion of the exporter's total overseas business.

The exporter is insured against the risks of loss arising from:

1 Insolvency of the buyer;
2 Failure by the buyer to pay within six months of the due date for goods delivered and accepted;
3 A general moratorium on external debt by the Government of the buyer's country, or by that of a third country through which the payment must be made;
4 Any other action by the Government of a foreign country which prevents performance of the contract;
5 Political events, and economic, legislative or administrative difficulties occurring in other countries, which prevent or delay the transfer of payments;
6 Legal discharge of the debt in the buyer's country but delay in transfer of currency;
7 War, civil war, etc., in other countries preventing performance of the contract;
8 Cancellation or non-renewal of an export licence, or legal restrictions on exports.

Once a credit limit is granted on a buyer, it is normally revolving; as payments are received, the exporter can grant further credit, bringing outstanding debts up to the value of the approved limit.

Medium- and long-term credit

Sales of capital goods and higher value engineering goods often give rise to medium- and long-term supplier credits. For this, two types of ECGD supplier credit insurance are available.

(*a*) *Supplemental extended-terms guarantee* Business of a repetitive kind involving semi-capital goods such as machine tools, commercial vehicles or contractors' plant, where credit terms of between six months and five years are frequently necessary, is covered by ECGD's supplemental extended-terms guarantee. This policy is only available to holders of the basic comprehensive short-term guarantee. Cover is given on a comprehensive basis, the exporter normally offering ECGD all his business on six months' to five years' terms. Each contract is, however, underwritten separately.

(*b*) *The specific guarantee* This is applicable to non-standard, individual contracts for which whole turnover cover is not suited. Cover under the specific guarantee is available either from the date of shipment or from the date of contract, though long manufacturing periods usually make the latter more appropriate.

Buyer credits

A medium- or long-term buyer credit takes the form of an ECGD-guaranteed loan by a bank or syndicate of banks based in the UK, direct to an overseas buyer, or to an overseas borrower acting on the buyer's behalf. The loan normally covers 80% or 85% of the contract price (70% in the case of new ships), the remainder being paid by the buyer to the exporter out of his own resources or from additional borrowing not guaranteed by ECGD – an international convention requires payment of at least 15% by delivery. ECGD's guarantee to the bank is unconditional for 100% of the loan, and covers non-payment, according to the terms of the contract, from the lending institution in the UK, whose loan to the foreign borrower is drawn down accordingly. The borrowing arrangement, however, lies solely between the overseas buyer (or other approved borrower in the buyer's country) and the lending bank. ECGD's guarantee does not relieve exporter, lender or borrower of their commercial responsibilities towards each other.

Individual buyer credits are used for capital goods contracts and overseas projects with a minimum value of £1m, although buyer credits can be used to finance much lower valued exports (£10000 and over) if this is done through a *line of credit* (see below).

A considerable proportion of UK exports of capital goods is financed under ECGD-supported supplier credit arrangements but, for a number of years, the proportion of capital goods contracts financed by means of buyer credits has been growing. The advantage of buyer credits is that they enable exporters to arrange progress payments more easily at intermediate stages of manufacture, provided that these can be negotiated with the buyer. Another benefit is that the exporter is freed from the problems of recourse attendant on supplier credit finance. The buyer credit, however, does have some drawbacks. The principal one is the complicated documentation required, which is more cumbersome than under supplier credit. In addition, customers may resist the use of buyer credit financing. They may prefer to use the traditional supplier credit practice of the industry, or they may object to taking loans direct from foreign banks, perhaps for political reasons.

As well as the supply contract between the UK exporter and the overseas buyer, a buyer credit entails three separate agreements:

1 A financial or loan agreement between the lending bank and the overseas borrower;
2 A guarantee agreement between ECGD and the lending bank;
3 A premium agreement between ECGD and the exporter.

With ECGD's guarantee, such banks are normally prepared to lend to foreign buyers at fixed rates of interest, set in each case by ECGD in accordance with the international consensus on export credit terms.

Lines of credit

ECGD-backed lines of credit take the form of loans by banks in the UK to overseas banks or other institutions, which can be used to finance a number of contracts for capital goods. The finance normally covers 80% or 85% of contract values. As with buyer credits, ECGD's guarantees to the financing banks are unconditional and for 100% of loan values; and credit is made available at preferential fixed interest rates.

With a project line of credit, the loan is tied to UK supplies for a particular overseas project. For example, such a line might be set up to finance the sales of equipment for an oil or natural gas development. In such cases, the borrowers are often governments or government agencies, who determine which contracts may be financed under the line.

In contrast to a project line of credit, a *general-purpose line of credit* can be used by an overseas country to finance a number of different contracts for capital goods and associated services placed with exporters. It includes a time limit for the placing of contracts: in some instances, contracts with values as low as £10 000 may be eligible.

Forfaiting

Forfaiting is an arrangement whereby exporters of capital goods can obtain medium-term finance, usually for periods of between one and seven years. Under this arrangement, the forfaiting bank buys at a discount bills of exchange, promissory notes, or other obligations arising from international trade transactions. Promissory notes are the preferred instruments of payment because it is then possible for the exporter to free himself from all recourse obligations. The purchasing bank (forfaitist) may commit itself to buying promissory notes even before the supply contract is signed. A commitment fee is then payable.

For paper to be eligible for forfaiting it has to carry an internationally-known banking name as guarantor. The guarantor's name is obtained by the buyer, his guarantee being commonly called an *aval*. The bill or promissory note must also be unconditional and not dependent upon the exporter's performance, since the forfaitist has no right of recourse against the exporter.

Bonds and guarantees

In recent years, overseas buyers of capital goods and projects have increasingly demanded that suppliers and contractors provide bonds or guarantees. This is particularly true in the Middle East, where cash or short-term credit contracts are more common than the longer term arrangements demanded elsewhere, so that buyers need an alternative sanction to that of withholding payment.

In the context of export finance, a bond or guarantee is a written instrument issued to an overseas buyer by an acceptable third party (that is, by a surety, normally a bank or insurance company). This instrument guarantees compliance by an exporter or contractor with his obligations, or that the overseas buyer will be indemnified for a stated amount against the failure of the exporter/contractor to fulfil his obligations under the contract. Most bonds are issued by banks and insurance companies. There are three main types of bond or guarantee on export contracts.

1 Tender or bid bond/guarantee

A tender or bid bond/guarantee provides the buyer with an assurance that the party submitted the tender is making a responsible bid.

The bond ensures that, if the contract is awarded to the bidder, the latter will comply with the conditions of the tender and enter into the contract. If he does not, the surety is liable to pay the costs incurred by the buyer in re-awarding the contract, subject to a limit of liability set by the amount of the bond.

2 Performance bond/guarantee

A performance bond/guarantee is a guarantee to the buyer that the exporter will carry out the contract in accordance with its specifications and terms. The liability of the surety is limited to the total amount of the bond, which is generally 10% of the contract price, but can be as low as 5% or as high as 100%.

3 Advance payment or repayment bond/guarantee

Many export contracts contain provisions for advance payments, and in these circumstances the buyer often requires a bond guaranteeing that if the contract is not completed, the surety will make good any loss suffered by the buyer as a result of making the advance payment.

Any of the above bonds may be conditional or unconditional (the latter commonly known as *on demand*). It is normally the buyer and the laws of his country which specify which type of bond has to be supplied by the exporter. In the case of a conditional bond the onus is on the buyer to prove default by the exporter, and payment under a bond is generally limited to the extent of the buyer's actual loss or the amount specified in the bond, whichever is less. On-demand bonds, by contrast, can be called for any reason, at the sole discretion of the buyer, whether or not the exporter has fulfilled his contractual obligations. Moreover, the payment is not limited to the amount of the buyer's loss – if indeed there is a loss at all. Any such on-demand instrument should consequently be regarded by the exporter as a letter of credit (since it has none of the true characteristics of a guarantee within the meaning of UK law). If there is a claim under an on-demand bond, then the surety is bound to meet the call immediately but has recourse against the exporter.

The Euro-currency market

The term Euro-currency is actually a misnomer, because currencies are deposited or lent on a world-wide basis and do not relate specifically to Europe. A Euro-currency is a currency which is available for deposit or loan in a country in which it is not the domestic currency. For example, for banks in the UK, Euro-currency business comprises deposits and lending in currencies other than the pound sterling. This definition embraces all currencies in the Euro-market, but the US dollar is so prominent that the market itself is often referred to as the Euro-dollar market. Development has been so rapid that the Euro-currency market is now the largest international deposit money market in the world, with London the most important centre for its operations (see p. 190).

A considerable expansion of the Euro-dollar market took place in the spring of 1964 when US banks realised that it was possible to escape Regulation Q, which limited the amount of interest that could be paid, by keeping dollar balances with European banks and thus obtain higher rates of interest. The practice spread and a European market developed quickly in dollar balances which became known as Euro-dollars. The banks holding the dollar balances met the ready demand for Euro-dollars by lending them at rates allowed on the deposits, and these were often lower than the borrower would have had to pay for finance in his own country or the USA. The market is essentially a deposit market and the periods of time for the deposits most commonly range from 'call' to six months, although some business is concluded on periods of up to three years or even longer. When a deposit is made it is in a currency, for example US dollars, and when the time for repayment arrives this will be made in the same currency. Exactly the same principle applies to borrowing (or lending) transactions.

Over the past few years, the Euro-currency market has become an established source of providing additional liquidity during strict credit-restriction periods, at the same time providing a means for surplus cash throughout the world to be employed profitably. For British companies, however, there were hurdles to overcome before finalising a transaction of this nature, e.g. Bank of England permission to borrow Euro-currency had to be obtained. However, apart from that the lending bank had to assess the credit risk according to normal banking criteria.

Euro-bonds

When the amount and period for which a borrowing is required is too great and too long for normal Euro-currency operations, a

Euro-bond is often issued. It is arranged in much the same way as a capital loan raising is effected on a stock exchange market in the country of the borrower. Euro-bonds are all bearer securities and issues are usually underwritten by an international syndicate and sold in a number of countries. The tendency with these bond issues has been for them to carry a fixed rate of interest, but some issues have variable rates. Fixed repayment dates soon become unpopular and now most bonds carry some form of conversion rights to enable purchasers to gain access to the equity of the company.

International credit clubs

Some finance houses can arrange finance through associated companies in other countries for imports and exports between their respective countries. Credit can be arranged for all classes of durable goods for periods normally up to two years, but longer in special cases. Credit can also be provided to enable foreign buyers to take stock goods imported from the UK, and to hold them pending their sale.

International credit clubs, which are reciprocal agreements between leading finance houses in Europe, have also been formed to help exporters of substantial items of capital equipment, so that foreign customers can obtain instalment credit finance quickly and cheaply. Similar organisations also offer many ancillary services such as market research and shipping and forwarding advice on all matters relating to export credit.

Banks and international trading

The policy adopted by the clearing banks concerning international finance has not been uniform in the past. Some chose to operate through separate subsidiaries for their overseas business. The alternative was to employ a strategy based upon the development of links with correspondent banks throughout the world. From the late 1950s, however, it became clear (with regard to the latter) that other forms of international representation were required. This was caused by fears about the future role of sterling as a trading currency, the emergence of increasingly large multinational concerns, and the movement towards closer economic and monetary co-operation throughout the world.

In the early 1960s, the first consortium bank was formed, i.e. a number of banks grouping a limited amount of funds for capital development projects in the international field, particularly by geographical area. Expansion of consortia took place in the early 1970s associated especially with the rapid growth of the Euro-dollar and Euro-bond markets, and the advantage over traditional forms of banking at that time was the availability of flexible and imaginative credit packages.

During the 1970s, many joint ventures and agreements were made between both individual and groups of banks and representative offices were opened in financial centres throughout the world. The main attention of the clearing banks, however, was directed towards North America where some degree of penetration has taken place.

As well as providing finance, the clearing banks offer the following international services:

1 Report on the general standing and creditworthiness of overseas buyers and agents;
2 Information on opportunities available to exporters in overseas markets and on political and economic conditions there;
3 Introduction to local branch offices and/or correspondent banks as a means of gaining access to first-hand knowledge of local trading conditions;
4 The supply of travellers' cheques and foreign currencies;
5 Assistance with exchange control problems;
6 Advice on the avoidance of financial loss occasioned through changes in trade and payments regulations;
7 Provision of names of suitable firms of forwarding agents;
8 Establishment and confirmation of documentary letters of credit;
9 Advice on invoicing in foreign currencies, the forward exchange market and financing in foreign currencies.

The clearing banks, their subsidiaries and associates are involved with various forms of international finance and services, including leasing and factoring, and their international departments are able to put importers and exporters in touch with specialists who can provide the types of requirement appropriate to their needs.

Questions

1 By what means is it possible to make payments abroad?
2 What are acceptance credits?
3 Describe the advantages of forward exchange.
4 Outline the value of ECGD.
5 What is the difference between 'supplier credit' and 'buyer credit'?
6 Identify the international services provided by the clearing banks.
7 What is forfaiting?
8 What type of bonds or guarantees are used for export contracts?

12

Saving and Investing

One of the functions of money, as we saw in Chapter 1, is to act as a store of value, that is, it allows people to set aside amounts which can be used at a later date. If these savings were simply put in a box under the bed, they would be of no use to anyone else other than the saver (and at times of inflation even the value of the money he had put aside would fall).

While some people are putting money aside as savings, others need to borrow money to expand their businesses. So it makes sense for those who are saving their money to lend it to those who want to make use of it. In this way, the saver keeps the value of his capital and obtains a rate of interest, while the borrower uses that money to invest in new capital equipment with which to expand his output. Savings can be put to work.

The need for savings 'intermediaries'

There are many problems associated with a saver directly putting his money with someone who is going to use it. First, there is the problem of *risk*. The borrower may not be successful in his enterprise and so may lose both his own money and that which he has borrowed. Second, there is the problem of *liquidity*. A manufacturer will invest his money in capital equipment – buildings, machinery and so on – and in raw materials from which he will make the finished product. So he does not keep all the money he has been lent in cash. But the lender of the money might want it back at any time to meet an unexpected bill, or just because he has decided to spend some of his savings.

Savings institutions or 'intermediaries' as they are sometimes called, help the process of saving and investment by channelling savings to those who need them. By standing between the original savers and borrowers, they help overcome the difficulties which would be experienced by lending and borrowing directly:

1 They collect together the savings of a large number of individuals and lend money to a variety of borrowers. In relation to the total of savings, each individual one is small, and the institutions will make sure that their lending is widely spread, so that they are not dependent upon the success or failure of one person or company. So by pooling their risks, savers are protected from losing their savings.
2 By keeping a proportion of their funds either in cash or in assets which can be quickly turned into cash without loss, the savings institutions can provide the saver with the ability to withdraw his savings, while allowing those to whom they have lent money to continue to have the use of it.

Savings and investment

Who saves and who invests? All the various sections of the economy – the general public, companies and the Government – do both, but generally speaking it is the general public (usually referred to in official statistics as the '*personal sector*') which collectively saves money while companies and the Government use these savings to invest, as is shown in Table 12.1.

Table 12.1 UK Savings and investment (1982)

	Personal sector (£m)	*Government* (£m)*	*Companies (£m)*
Savings	22 438	5 809	20 215
Investment	9 404	12 543	21 566
Net savings (+) or investment (−)	+13 034	− 6 734	− 1 351

* including local authorities and public corporations

Types of saving and saving institution

Deposit saving: banks and building societies

People may want to save for a variety of reasons and for different periods of time and some indication of how the personal sector chooses to save can be obtained from Table 12.2, which shows how much new money savers put into various types of saving in 1982.

Table 12.2 Personal sector savings (1982)

	£m
Deposits with:	
banks	3 809
building societies	10 059
other financial institutions	–
National savings	3 462
Government stocks	546
Other public sector debt	–60
Life assurance and pension funds	13 333
Company securities	–2 092

In the first place, a person will simply want to keep money available so that he can settle his bills as they fall due between one pay-day and the next. He will keep his savings in a bank current account where he can write a cheque on it or draw out cash as required.

If he has some money which he does not need before the next pay-day, but nevertheless does not want to tie up for too long, he may put it on deposit account with a bank, or place it with a building society or savings bank. By doing this, the saver will give up the right to be able to transfer part of his balance by cheque to another person immediately, but in return he obtains a rate of interest and has reasonably quick access to the funds when he needs them.

Long-term savings: The Stock Exchange, unit trusts and investment trusts

Looking further, many people want to save over a much longer period, perhaps to build up savings for when they retire. Here they will be looking not only for a rate of interest, but also some growth in the capital value of their savings as well. A saver here may invest his savings directly in the shares of a number of companies. When he wishes to sell them, he will use the services of a stockbroker to sell his shares on the Stock Exchange.

Unit trusts

One method of investing in company shares but at the same time spreading risk over a wide number of companies is to invest through the medium of unit trusts. An investor buys a number of units, and collective contributions are invested in a range of company shares. A new investor may buy new units at any time, while an existing unit holder may sell his units back to the unit trust management when he wishes. If demand for units is high then more will be issued and the unit trust managers will have more funds to invest. It is called an 'open-ended trust' because the amount of funds available can increase (or fall) at any time. The value of the units is calculated regularly – often daily – and varies according to the value of the shares in which the funds are invested.

Investment trusts

Investment trusts, like unit trusts, enable small investors to spread their risks by pooling their savings. Unlike unit trusts, however, the investment trusts are listed on the Stock Exchange and are traded just like ordinary shares. An investor wanting to get his money back sells his investment trust shares through a stockbroker to another investor. The investment trusts retain the use of their total capital, and they are often called 'closed-end' funds since the amount of money the investment managers have for investment stays the same.

Long-term savings: life assurance and pension schemes

Many more people, however, invest their savings in industry indirectly through other types of savings institution.

Over 14 million people in the UK have at least one life assurance policy and many have more than one. These life assurance policies may be 'whole-life' policies which simply pay out to dependants when the policy-holder dies, or they may be 'endowment' policies which mature on a specified date in the future or on the policy-holder's death. Endowment life assurance is a major form of saving for use after retirement, and is encouraged by granting tax relief to people who take out long-term (i.e. over ten years) life assurance policies. The money paid regularly as premiums is not 'liquid', i.e. it cannot be immediately withdrawn, although in case of need it is usually possible (if not financially sensible) to surrender the policy and get some cash back.

A further and increasingly popular method of saving is through company pension schemes. Employees who join such a scheme may make a contribution from their salaries, which is fully tax allowable, and which goes into a pension fund, administered by a group of trustees. Their employer will also make a contribution to the fund. Indeed many employers will contribute the whole amount and not ask their employees to make any contribution. Nevertheless, these are amounts which are being saved on behalf of those employees who are in pension schemes, and are quite rightly regarded as savings of the personal sector. Over 11 million people are now members of pension schemes, while a further 2¼ million receive pensions from them.

In recent years, pension schemes have expanded very rapidly for two main reasons. First, more employers have made pension schemes available to their employees as part of a policy of improving their conditions of employment; second, and perhaps more important, since contributions are calculated as a percentage of salary, the payments to pension funds have automatically risen in line with salaries. However, for the individual, this is a very illiquid

Table 12.3 Investments by insurance companies and pension funds

(£m – end 1982)

	Pension funds	*Long-term insurance funds*
Short-term assets	2 609	2 588
British Government securities	18 164	22 777
Local authorities	254	768
Company securities*	47 112	32 171
Overseas government securities	432	738
Land and property	12 643	19 705
Other assets	2 337	1 230
	83 551	79 977

* including unit trust units

form of saving because he cannot turn it into cash at times of his own choosing.

Both pension and life assurance funds use the contributions collected to invest in a wide range of financial assets. They will keep some of their funds in a liquid form, either in bank deposits or in very short-term assets, so that they can meet their liabilities when they arise: paying out on maturing policies or making payments to their pensioners. The vast majority of their funds, however, will be invested in Government securities, company shares, property and perhaps a little in works of art.

Some idea of the amounts of funds invested by the pension funds and insurance companies are given in Table 12.3.

In this chapter we have examined, briefly, some of the types of savings institutions which exist to help channel the savings of individuals, made possible by the existence of money, into productive investment. In the following chapters, we shall look more specifically at the working of the banking system in the UK.

Questions

1 How many types of savings intermediaries can you name?
2 What functions do the savings intermediaries perform?
3 What are the differences between the types of financial intermediary?

13

The Commercial Banking Institutions

In this chapter, we shall look at the institutions which make up the banking sector in the UK, describing the different roles they play within the overall framework. Just a few years ago this would have been a much easier task than it is now. Then, each type of institution had a clearly defined function and, for the most part, kept to it. A retail or deposit bank, for example Midland or Barclays, gathered deposits through its widespread branch network and undertook essentially short-term lending by way of overdraft facilities to companies and individuals. A company requiring long-term funds looked not to its deposit bank, but to one of the merchant banks, Barings or Hill Samuel for example. These merchant banks, originally concerned primarily with the financing of overseas trade, had become increasingly active in providing financial advice and long-term funds for companies. The distinction between the type of short-term finance provided by the deposit banks and the medium-term funds made available by the merchant banks, was a clear one in theory, although perhaps blurred occasionally in practice.

Then, too, finance companies provided finance on a hire-purchase basis for personal borrowers. For many years it was considered rather shameful to buy consumer goods on hire-purchase, or indeed any form of credit, and the deposit banks, regarding themselves as institutions of virtue as well as keepers of their customers' deposits, were most reluctant to enter the consumer credit field.

In addition, a number of British-registered banks, whose main business was retail or deposit banking in countries overseas, principally in the British Commonwealth, had offices in London which were used to invest surplus funds gathered overseas in the London money market. A number of foreign banks, mainly from North America, also had offices in London to meet the needs of international trade between Britain and their own countries and to provide services for their own nationals here. Each group of institutions had its own sector of the market, therefore, and left the other areas for institutions specially catering for them. There was little overlap and little competition between the groups of banks.

In recent years, this straightforward picture has changed dramatically. The boundaries, once so clear, have become obscure as the different types of institution have sought to extend their influence into other financial markets previously regarded as the 'territory' of one of the other groups. Competition between groups of institutions has become more severe, and the distinctions have become correspondingly less clear cut.

In describing the structure of the banking system today, it is useful to use as the framework that used by the Bank of England for statistical purposes. In following this method, however, the breaking-down of traditional distinctions between one group and another should constantly be borne in mind.

The deposit banks

The London clearing banks

The London clearing banks are still the main commercial deposit banks in Britain. They are called the 'clearing' banks because they are the members of the Bankers Clearing House, through which the majority of cheques are cleared. They are sometimes still called *joint-stock banks*, but this rather old-fashioned name, used originally to distinguish such banks from *private banks*, and arising from the historical development of banking described in the Introduction, is now rather meaningless, the vast majority of all banking institutions now being joint-stock limited companies. At present, there are six of them, listed below in alphabetical order:

Barclays Bank
Coutts and Co.
Lloyds Bank
Midland Bank

National Westminster Bank
Williams & Glyn's Bank (soon to lose its separate identity and be merged with its parent, the Royal Bank of Scotland)

Until 1969, there were eleven: the so-called 'Big Five', Barclays, Lloyds, Midland, National Provincial and Westminster, and the 'Smaller Six', Coutts, District, Glyn Mills, Martins, National and Williams Deacon's. In the amalgamations which took place from 1968 to 1970, the number was reduced to six (with Coutts maintaining a separate identity despite being a subsidiary of National Westminster). In 1974, the Co-operative Bank and the Central Trustee Savings Bank, the latter acting on behalf of the trustee savings banks as a whole, were offered, and accepted, full membership of the Clearing House although they are not included as clearing banks in the Bank of England's statistical classification. By size of deposits, the clearing banks continue to be dominated by the 'Big Four', Barclays, Lloyds, Midland and National Westminster.

The Scottish clearing banks

The Scottish clearing banks carry out essentially the same functions as their English counterparts and the institutional links between the two are very strong. There are three Scottish clearing banks: Royal Bank of Scotland, Bank of Scotland and Clydesdale Bank. Of these, Clydesdale is a wholly owned subsidiary of Midland, and Barclays has a substantial minority interest in Bank of Scotland. In the reverse direction, the Royal Bank of Scotland's parent company, Royal Bank of Scotland Group, also owns the capital of Williams and Glyn's Bank and is in the process of merging the two operations.

Despite the similarities and close links between the two banking systems, the Scottish banks retain some distinctions, the most tangible of which is the right to issue their own banknotes. For the most part, however, such note issues have to be backed by an equivalent holding of Bank of England notes as reserve.

Northern Ireland banks

Northern Ireland banks now number only two, Northern Bank and Ulster Bank, although the commercial banks based in the Republic also maintain a number of branches in the North. Both the Northern Ireland banks are wholly owned by English banks; Midland took over the Northern Bank in 1965 and merged it with the Belfast Banking Company, which Midland already owned, in 1970. Ulster Bank is owned by National Westminster Bank, having been acquired by the old Westminster Bank in 1917. Both the Northern Ireland banks operate in the Republic of Ireland as well as in Northern Ireland and are subject to control not only by the UK monetary authorities, but by the Republic's authorities as well. Like the Scottish banks, the Northern Ireland banks also have the right of note issue.

Other deposit banks

Other deposit banks are small and relatively unimportant, but for completeness' sake should be mentioned. They include the Isle of Man Bank (owned by the National Westminster Bank), Lewis's Bank (operating mainly in retail department stores and owned by Lloyds Bank) and Yorkshire Bank (owned jointly by National Westminster, Barclays and Lloyds banks). In terms of deposits the three combined are tiny, but their separate identities are maintained for historical, geographical or administrative reasons.

The merchant banks

The term 'merchant bank' is a difficult one to define accurately; it is often loosely applied to any deposit-taking and lending institution which does not fit neatly into any other category of bank. This, however, is far too general. The large and reputable merchant banking companies will normally be members of either the Accepting Houses Committee or the Issuing Houses Association, or both, although restricting the term 'merchant bank' in this way may nevertheless omit some large well-known institutions widely regarded as merchant banks.

Accepting Houses Committee

This consists of 16 members, among whom are some of the most highly regarded banking companies in the City. Any bank of sufficient financial standing can undertake acceptance business, but membership of the Accepting Houses Committee is confined to those institutions a major part of whose business is the 'acceptance' of bills of exchange on behalf of others. Thus, although the clearing banks can and do perform the function of accepting bills of exchange and no one would question their integrity or resources, such business is not their major activity, and thus they are not members of the Accepting Houses Committee. The full list of member companies in alphabetical order is:

Baring Bros
Brown Shipley
Charterhouse, Japhet
Fleming (Robert)
Guinness Mahon
Hambros Bank
Hill Samuel
Kleinwort, Benson
Lazard Bros.
Morgan Grenfell
Rea Brothers
N. M. Rothschild & Sons
Samuel Montagu
J. Henry Schroder Wagg
Singer & Friedlander
S. G. Warburg

Many of today's leading accepting houses have their origins in trading activities. As large and trusted merchants in the rapidly expanding international trade of the nineteenth century, they found that as an additional source of income they could lend their 'good name', at a suitable commission, to the bills of exchange of lesser known traders. As the result of such a well-known merchant 'accepting' the bill of exchange the bill could be discounted (sold) in the market at a 'finer' rate of interest than would have been possible with a lesser known name.

The business of accepting bills of exchange proved so profitable for many of the merchants that their trading activities were run down, and they concentrated on their bill-accepting role. Thus we get the name 'accepting house' and the general title 'merchant bank', a merchant who added a banking business to his trading activities. Their acceptance business assisted the growth of international trade in general in the nineteenth century, helped London to become the major world financial centre, and sterling to be established as the world's major currency.

The Issuing Houses Association

With a general decline in world trade after the First World War, the traditional acceptance business of the merchant banks also declined, and they sought new areas of expansion to compensate for this loss. The accepting houses, as well as a number of other non-clearing banking institutions, began to offer their financial expertise to large industrial companies at home, advising them on the best ways of raising finance, and on mergers, take-overs and capital re-organisations. The merchant banks engaged in this type of activity formed the Issuing Houses Association in 1945, and membership now numbers almost sixty and includes all sixteen members of the Accepting Houses Committee.

Services of the merchant banks today

The merchant banks now provide a number of specialised services for company customers and private individuals. They are perhaps best known for their corporate finance work. The accepting houses, as we have seen, developed the practice of 'accepting' bills of exchange issued by traders and thus by lending their good name to a bill enabled the trader to discount it and obtain short-term finance at cheaper rates than he otherwise could have obtained. Today, to be a member of the Accepting Houses Committee, a substantial amount of the merchant bank's business must continue to be in acceptances.

In addition, the merchant banks themselves will lend money to their company customers on short or medium terms. They will also advise companies on the best methods of raising long-term loans or permanent finance by means of share issues. Merchant banks may also run 'marriage bureaux' matching companies wishing to expand by amalgamation. Because of their involvement with company finance, merchant banks are often engaged in helping companies to win – or to fight against – takeover bids.

The merchant banks also provide fund management services. Individuals or companies can place their funds with a merchant bank to manage on their behalf. Merchant banks will give advice on the best methods of using these funds profitably and may undertake the placing of those funds, buying and selling shares, etc. on their clients' behalf. Many merchant banks run their own unit trusts and also manage pension funds on behalf of their clients.

Some merchant banks are involved on an individual basis in providing specialist services which are not common to all of them. For instance, Samuel Montagu is a major bullion dealer while others specialise in the management of Euro-bond issues, that is issues of long-term loans by international companies denominated in an overseas currency.

The British overseas and Commonwealth banks

In the nineteenth century, when Britain was the main provider of long-term development capital for the rest of the world, and London the major money market, many of the banks operating as deposit banks in countries overseas maintained an office – often the head office – in London. This enabled them to assist the growth of trade between Britain and the countries they served, to raise capital for development of their territories more easily and also to employ surplus short-term funds at a rate of interest in the London money market. Many of these banks operated in the British overseas territories, but others were to be found in the Middle East, the Far East and Latin America, in countries which had no political connections with Britain, but were frequently dependent upon the London capital market for the supply of funds to develop their economies.

Several of the British overseas and Commonwealth banks are subsidiaries of domestic commercial banks. Barclays Bank International, for example, is wholly owned by Barclays Bank and is the international banking arm of the group. Lloyds Bank has a similar relationship with Lloyds Bank International, which was formed in 1971 by a merger of Lloyds Bank Europe and the Bank of London and South America.

The role of the British overseas banks has changed quite sharply in recent years. As the territories in which they act as deposit banks became independent, it was natural that the new political leaders wished to exercise some control over the activities of the banks in their countries. In some instances, the state has taken a controlling interest in the bank and restrictions have been placed on the remittance of funds abroad – which of course includes London.

In response to these changes, the overseas and Commonwealth banks have sought to raise deposits by other means, and they have become extremely active in developing some of the newer money markets in London, such as the Euro-currency, inter-bank and the certificate of deposit markets, which are discussed in Chapter 15. Funds taken in these markets have enabled these banks to continue to expand their business, and develop into more widely based international banks than before.

Foreign banks in London

London has been a leading international financial centre for many years, and a number of banks whose main retail banking business is in a foreign country have decided to open a branch office in London. Some of these foreign banks first opened offices in this country a long time ago. For example, Chase Manhattan Bank, an American bank whose head office is in New York, first opened a London branch in 1887. Another example is Crédit Lyonnais, a leading French bank, whose London office was founded seventeen years earlier in 1870. An even earlier arrival was Algemene Bank Nederland, a leading Dutch bank, which can trace its London representation to 1868. These London branches were established to assist trade between the UK and the country in which the foreign bank principally operated, to give assistance to visiting businessmen from that country when they wished to do business in London, and sometimes to help raise capital on the London capital market for use in developing industry, trade or agriculture in their home country. The presence of these banks in London in the late nineteenth century can be seen as the continuation of an earlier development for what, in essence, were the Lombards' London offices but the London branches of foreign banks?

Until 1950, when fifty-three foreign banks had London offices, they continued to fulfil their original functions, but in the last thirty years the growth in the number and the importance of foreign banks in London has been remarkable, as may be seen from Table 13.1.

The main reason for this rapid growth has been the existence of the Euro-dollar market of which London is the major, although not the only, centre.

Table 13.1 Growth of foreign banks in London

	No. of offices	*Total deposits (£m)*
1960	77	2 877
1965	103	4 955
1970	163	17 904
1979	389+	130 172*
1983	460+	350 000+

Source: *The Banker*, November 1983

+ including those indirectly represented by a consortium bank or a stake in a joint venture.

* total assets

Consortium banks

Since 1964, several so-called consortium banks have been established in London and other financial centres. As the name implies, these banks are organisations which have been established jointly by a number of existing banks, these shareholders usually but not always drawn from a number of different countries.

During the 1960s, large international companies, operating in a number of different countries, became more important in the world economy. The size and complexity of their operations often meant that a domestic bank, however large, could not meet all these companies' financial requirements. The banks' response was to establish consortium banks in order to serve the needs of these companies the better.

In 1982 there were twenty-nine consortium banks in London, and through them, around seventy other overseas banks are indirectly represented in London. Among the consortium banks are UBAF, owned 50% by UBIC Nederland and 25% each by Midland Bank and Libyan Arab Foreign Bank; Euro-Latin American Bank, in which Barclays International has a holding, along with twenty-one other European and Latin American Banks; Libra Bank, which has National Westminster as a shareholder; Scandinavian Bank, whose shareholders are drawn from Denmark, Sweden, Norway and Iceland; and Japan International Bank, all of whose shareholders are Japanese banks.

Lending, mainly of a medium-term nature, is carried out by these banks. Apart from the funds subscribed by the original shareholders, they also take funds from depositors on the sterling and currency 'wholesale' markets. The funds for lending come partly from the deposits of the consortium banks themselves, partly from the resources of the shareholder banks, and sometimes from the non-shareholder banks who are willing to participate in a particular loan.

The borrowers are normally large companies, who may wish to borrow in any one of a number of currencies. The major reason for the establishment of so many consortium banks in London has been the fact that the Euro-currency market has been centred there, although some consortium banks have their headquarters in Paris, Brussels and other financial centres.

Other banks in London

In addition to the different types of bank described above, a number of other banks exist in London which do not fit neatly into any other category. These banks include the English offices of Scottish and Irish banks, the National Girobank and some merchant banks which are not members of the Accepting Houses Committee.

Savings banks

The savings banks have their origins in the nineteenth century, when they were established to encourage thrift or savings among the poorer section of the population. Two separate types of savings bank are still in existence, the National Savings Bank (NSB) and the Trustee Savings Banks (TSB) although the TSB organisation is currently developing along the lines which will transform it into a commercial rather than a purely savings bank.

The National Savings Bank

The National Savings Bank (which used to be called the Post Office Savings Bank) was established in 1861. It accepts savings deposits from the public through post offices throughout the country, and permits withdrawals of up to £50 on demand at any post office.

Accounts with the National Savings Bank are of two types. Balances in the *ordinary account* attract a relatively low interest rate, but the first £70 of annual interest is free of income tax. The minimum initial deposit is £1 and the maximum permitted balance £10 000. The *investment account*, first introduced in 1966, pays a higher, market rate of interest, but a depositor must give one month's notice of withdrawal from an investment account. In the investment account, the minimum balance is £1 and the maximum (which may be held in addition to funds in an ordinary account) is £200 000.

The National Savings Bank holds over £1800m on deposit in its ordinary accounts and around £4000m in investment accounts. The bank undertakes no lending to customers. The National Savings Bank is a part of the National Savings Movement, and all the funds of the bank are passed on to a body called the National Debt Commissioners which invests them in government securities. Thus the National Savings Bank acts as a borrowing agent for the Government, taking money on deposit from the general public and lending it to the Government of the day. The latter, in return, guarantees both repayment of the capital and the payment of interest to the account-holders.

Other services offered include regular standing order payments, the easy purchase of national savings and other government securities and the direct receipt from employers of amounts of savings from the pay of employees at the latter's request.

Trustee Savings Banks

The Trustee Savings Banks (TSB) were established even before the National Savings Bank. The first legislation governing their activities dates from 1817. Essentially the Trustee Savings Banks were organised on a local basis and administered by a board of voluntary trustees, while their day-to-day running was in the hands of a general manager, a permanent paid official and his staff.

For many years, the TSBs were run along traditional lines, providing a savings service for small depositors and no more. The situation began to change in 1964 when current account cheque facilities were offered for the first time and a Unit Trust scheme was set up in 1968. These services supplemented the basic savings accounts facilities which had been the banks' traditional business.

The Trustee Savings Banks' role is now becoming much more wide-ranging and they are developing a fully fledged banking service, including lending facilities which were previously unavailable. All this springs from the report of a Government committee – the Page Committee – which provided a blueprint for the changing role of the Trustee Savings Banks in 1973. The banks were reorganised into 18 regional banks and began to prepare for their changed role. The Central Trustee Savings Bank (CTSB) was set up in 1973 to act as banker to the separate Trustee Savings Banks and to be the clearing agent for those which then offered a cheque service; in 1974 it became a member of the Bankers' Clearing House.

Because of their changing role, the Trustee Savings Banks are becoming increasingly similar to commercial banks. They now provide a range of services which includes savings and cheque accounts, direct debits and standing orders, a cheque card and a credit card service, Unit Trust investment, personal loans and travellers' cheques. In line with the banks' new status, depositors no longer enjoy the tax privileges on their savings accounts which are enjoyed by savers with the National Savings Bank, while the banks themselves no longer have to invest their funds through the National Savings Commissioners.

The National Girobank

The National Giro was established in 1968 and renamed the National Girobank in 1978. It was originally set up to modernise the money transmission services provided by the Post Office, which until then had been largely dependent on the postal order and the money order systems. The Giro was an attempt to provide a simple, cheap and efficient money transfer service for the large section of the general public which did not have a bank account.

Originally, the National Giro only accepted deposits and provided its account-holders with a means of settling their bills between one another by a transfer of funds from one account to another. It did not generally make loans available to its customers. The scope of the National Giro was widened when the Post Office (Banking Services) Act was passed in 1976, allowing Giro to provide banking services without the restrictions imposed earlier. Services now provided by the National Girobank include, in addition to money transfer, standing orders, personal loans, cheque cards, deposit accounts, budget accounts, bridging loans and travel facilities. Small overdraft facilities are also available to cheque card holders, providing that the borrowing is repaid when the next salary cheque is credited. Providing that an account is kept in credit there are no charges for using the payment facilities, but on overdrawn accounts a charge is made for each debit item.

National Girobank at present has approximately 700 000 customers, of which about 30 000 are corporate or business accounts. For the personal customer it has the advantage over the clearing banks of operating through over 22 000 Post Office outlets, while for the company users, especially retail stores and the nationalised industries, it offers a major service in collecting takings and crediting them to central Giro accounts one day later.

In 1978, National Girobank was added to the list of banks maintained by the Bank of England for monetary control purposes and it now has to maintain the various ratios applicable to a commercial bank. In 1979, the National Girobank became a member of the London Clearing House system.

Questions

1 Give a brief account of the types of bank existing in the UK at the present time.
2 Outline the principal functions of an accepting house.
3 Why were consortium banks established in London in the 1960s?
4 What is the National Girobank and what service does it offer?
5 Why have so many overseas banks opened London offices in recent years?
6 In what ways do savings banks differ from commercial banks?

14

The Banks' Balance Sheets

Table 14.1 gives a summary of the combined figures for the London clearing banks at the end of December 1982, which is taken from the combined balance sheets of the banks at that date or at the nearest

Table 14.1 The Banks' Balance Sheets

Liabilities	*(£m)*	*Assets*	*(£m)*
Shareholders funds:		Cash	1 485
share capital	990	Cheques in course	2 252
reserves	5 774	of collection	
Loan capital	1 210	Money at call and	8 568
Current, deposit	87 858	short notice	
and other accounts		Treasury bills	185
Other liabilities	475	Other bills	1 100
		Certificates of	672
		deposit held	
		Special deposits	—
		Investments	2 444
		Advances	73 047
		Fixed assets:	
		investments in	3 637
		subsidiaries and	
		associates	
		Premises and	2 854
		equipment	
		Other assets	63
	96 307		96 307

balance sheet date available. It gives only a broad indication of the order of magnitude of one figure in relation to others, and as the amounts of the short-term assets and liabilities are constantly changing, opportunity has been taken in the text to give later figures where possible.

The liabilities of the banks

Share capital

On the liabilities side, a notable feature is the relatively small amounts of paid-up share capital and reserve funds as compared with the total of current, deposit and other accounts.

From time to time it has been suggested that the amount of share capital of the banks should be increased in view of the very considerable rise in the total of deposits, due both to inflation and to the rapid increase in the number of bank accounts. It is relevant to point out that the capital and reserves still exceed the fixed asset items of bank premises and shares in subsidiary and associated companies, which are the 'fixed assets' of a bank, and in any case the public has shown complete confidence in the financial stability of the banks and their ability to meet all demands made on them for repayment. This confidence is justified by the 'liquid' nature of such a large proportion of the items in the assets side of the balance sheet.

Nevertheless, the extremely sharp increase in total deposits which has occurred in recent years caused the ratio of capital and reserves to total deposits to fall below a level which the banks found acceptable. They have, therefore, at appropriate times raised new share capital, mainly by way of 'rights' issues to existing shareholders.

Reserves and profits disclosure

Unlike most companies, banks were for many years permitted to have 'hidden', as well as published, reserves. Although, in the ordinary way, hidden reserves were not considered to be in the best interest of the shareholders because the true trading results and financial strength of a company might be obscured, the knowledge that the banks had accumulated these unspecified reserves was thought to have resulted in increased public confidence in British banks. It was a recognition of this that banks and certain other types of company were permitted by the Companies Act 1948 to continue the practice of having secret or unpublished reserves.

During the 1960s, criticism of this privilege became more and more frequent, and there were many observers who felt that it was only a matter of time before the law was changed to bring the banks into line with other companies. It seems that the banks themselves recognised this and took the initiative by announcing, towards the end of 1969, that they would, in future, voluntarily follow a policy of full disclosure of profits and reserves. As a result, the so-called 'hidden reserves' were removed from 'current, deposit and other accounts' and included in the figure of reserves. This disclosure took place on 20 February 1970 when for the first time the clearing banks declared their true profit figures for the previous year. The public and investment advisers were then able to compare with some accuracy the performance of one bank with another.

Loan capital

In recent years, some of the clearing banks have issued small amounts of loan capital. Some of this loan capital has been issued to shareholders of other financial companies which have been taken over by the clearing banks, and some consists of bond issues made on overseas capital markets. The loan stocks range in maturity up to 20 years. Apart from the overseas bond issues, the loan stocks are usually of the subordinated unsecured type, which is rarely found in the balance sheets of companies other than banks. In the event of a winding-up of the bank, the claims of the holders of these stocks are subordinated to those of the depositors.

Deposits

The great bulk of the banks' liabilities consists of the deposits of their customers. The different types of deposit which a modern bank takes are outlined in Chapter 2. During the past few years, the total amount of the deposits held by the banks has increased very rapidly, and total deposits of the clearing banks now amount to almost £90 000m, of which more than £23 000m consists of deposits taken in foreign currencies; an increasing proportion of deposits is taken on the so-called 'wholesale' markets in large amounts at competitive rates of interest.

One of the most considerable banking developments of the 1970s was the extremely rapid increase in the level of deposits following the introduction of Competition and Credit Control in 1971. In the eleven years from October 1971 when the new measures were introduced, total clearing bank deposits rose from £11 500m to almost £90 000m. Although some of this growth occurred in the increase in ordinary current and deposit accounts, the banks took an increasing amount of deposits by other methods. Deposits from other UK banks, taken on the inter-bank market (see Chapter 15) rose from £260m, which were in effect simply small working balances, to well over £7500m. Sterling certificates of deposit issued by the clearing banks rose from nothing in September 1971 to over £2000m in 1973, and now stand at over £3000m. A further notable feature has been the rise in the amounts of foreign currency deposits held by the clearing banks, which, rising from less than £300m in 1971, totalled over £23 000m by the end of 1982.

Other liabilities

The figure of *other liabilities* is fairly substantial in total, but of little relevance from a banking point of view. They consist mainly of items of an accounting nature, such as provisions for taxation, miscellaneous creditors and dividend provisions.

The assets of the banks

On the other side of the balance sheet, the assets are listed in descending order of liquidity, or the ease with which they can be turned into cash without capital loss. Before the arrangements for controlling the banking system came into force in 1971, various parts of the banks' balance sheets were important from the point of view of monetary control by the Authorities. This was because the old methods of control – the cash ratio and the liquidity ratio – were originally conventions developed by the banks themselves as prudent ratios which they needed to keep in order to run their businesses soundly and maintain public confidence. These ratios were easily seen in their balance sheets. When the new methods were introduced, and then changed again in 1981, these ratios were not readily obtainable from the balance sheet figures. It remains useful, however, to know the items which appear in the balance sheets of the banks and their relationship to each other.

Cash

Under present arrangements, no specified margin of cash need be held (except that ½% of the clearing banks' eligible liabilities must be held in their accounts at the Bank of England). The banks thus hold what they believe to be necessary – around 1¾% of deposits to meet:

(*a*) Day-to-day withdrawals by customers;
(*b*) Settlements with other banks as a result of daily cheque clearing.

Cheques in course of collection

The figure for cheques in course of collection is about 2½% of the total of deposits. As it is not possible for all cheques to be cleared on the same day as they are paid in over bank counters, some time-lag is inevitable, and the figures for cheques in course of collection reflect this.

Money at call and short notice

This represents about 10% of total deposits. This is money lent mainly to various discount houses, at rates of interest which fluctuate daily according to demand and supply. When money is in short supply, market rates will be higher, and vice versa. These loans are very liquid indeed; they are lent either overnight only, or can be called in at very short notice, and are secured by Treasury bills, commercial bills of exchange accepted by banks, or short-dated British Government gilt-edged bonds – i.e. those with less than five years to maturity – held by the discount houses.

Treasury bills

The Treasury bill is, in effect, a promissory note, i.e. a promise to pay, issued by the Treasury and payable in 91 days' time. It is one of the main methods of short-term government finance through what is known as the *floating debt*, as opposed to the long-term *funded debt*, which comprises British Government longer dated securities such as 10% Treasury stock, 1992, 12% Exchequer stock, 1998, etc.

The need for this short-term finance arises through the Government's periodic payments of dividends on and the redemption of its securities, and the regular payments made all through the year by various Government Departments such as those of Health and Social Security, Education and Science, etc., for such things as National Insurance benefits, schools, etc. As taxation, the main source of revenue, does not always match these payments, in that it is received at less frequent intervals, and mainly in the final part of the financial year from January to March, the Treasury bill is the main method by which the gap is bridged. The role of the Treasury bill, its method of issue and its importance to the London discount market, are more fully discussed in Chapter 15.

From the late 1930s until 1971, the clearing banks, by agreement, did not bid on their own behalf for Treasury bills at the tender each week. Although this agreement was abandoned in 1971, the banks still do not in fact tender for Treasury bills at the time of issue, but buy them from the discount market some time after they have been issued. Once a bank has bought a Treasury bill from the market it usually holds it until maturity.

Other bills

This item consists of commercial bills, promissory notes and other negotiable paper held as assets by the banks. It includes UK bank bills, that is bills which have been accepted by a recognised bank operating in the UK. Within the category of bank bills are some which are eligible for rediscount at the Bank of England, i.e. the latter would be prepared to buy them from the commercial banks should the need arise. Only those bills which bear the names of two reputable and long-established banks, one of which must be the 'acceptor' of the bill, will be available for rediscount at the Bank of England. These bills therefore command the finest rate of interest, and other bills, even if they are accepted by the London branch of a highly reputable overseas bank, will qualify only as an ordinary bank bill, the interest rate on which will be slightly higher.

Other types of bill which might be held include 'trade bills'. These are commercial bills which bear the name of a first-class company, and on which risk of default is small, but which do not bear the name of a bank. These will bear a rate of interest higher than that on a UK bank bill.

Finally, the local authority bills eligible for rediscount at the Bank of England are also included under 'other bills'. All such bills can be included as eligible reserve assets of the banks.

Certificates of deposit held

The origins of certificates of deposit, and an outline of their importance, are discussed in Chapter 15. In addition to issuing 'CDs', as they are called, the banks also hold them as assets, and such holdings can be deducted from total deposits in calculating eligible liabilities for the purposes of credit control (see Chapter 18).

Special deposits

Special deposits are amounts which the banks are called upon to place in special accounts at the Bank of England. They are called by the Bank, with the agreement and probably at the instigation of the Treasury, at times when credit is to be restricted. Money placed with the Bank of England in special deposits cannot be used by the banks which have had to place it, nor can it count as part of the liquid assets which the banks must maintain. Again, the use of special deposits in controlling the banking system is discussed in Chapter 18.

Investments

Investments are mainly securities of, or guaranteed by, the Government, all of them having a fixed redemption date. They are often referred to as 'gilt-edged' securities, because the Government is not likely to default on its debts, and thus the security is regarded as first class. In practice, the banks like to hold stocks with less than five years to run to maturity, although a few stocks in excess of this might sometimes be held. The banks hold government stocks as an asset to give themselves a better rate of interest than they can obtain on their more liquid assets, at the same time involving less risk than advances to customers. Thus, a combination of a good rate of return and minimum risk determines the banks' holdings of gilt-edged investments. Such investments account for around 3% of total deposits, a great reduction on their importance twenty-five years ago when they accounted for 38% of deposits and were the largest single asset in the banks' balance sheets.

Changes in interest rates, high rates of inflation and periodic balance of payments crises in recent years have caused wide fluctuations in market values of British Government securities. These values have sometimes been well below the prices actually paid by the banks, and the prospect therefore has to be faced of considerable losses if the banks find it necessary to realise some of their investments. This has helped to determine the banks' preference for short-dated stocks. The prospect of capital loss has become a much more serious problem for the banks since the introduction of Competition and Credit Control in 1971, as part of which the Bank of England no longer stood ready automatically to support prices in the gilt-edged market. This withdrawal by the Bank of England meant that if the banks wished to sell a large volume of gilt-edged securities on the stock market, the prices which those securities would fetch might be sharply reduced.

Advances to customers

By far the largest item on the banks' balance sheets at the present time is advances to customers, which at the end of December 1982 stood at £73 047m, or over 80% of deposits. The amount of advances in the banks' balance sheets tends to vary inversely with the amount of gilt-edged investments held: as advances – both in total and as a proportion of deposits – increase, the figure for investments tends to fall, and vice versa.

The reason for this is simple. A primary function of a bank is to lend money to its customers, and generally it will seek to do this to the best of its ability. The banks recognise, however, that advances to customers are their most risky assets, because they involve a greater possibility of loss than any of the others. In addition, although in theory most of the banks' lending is repayable on demand, in practice this is not always possible. Advances are therefore the least liquid of the banks' assets as well. To compensate for the lack of liquidity and greater degree of risk, the interest rate earned on advances is higher than that available on other assets, and hence advances are also the banks' most profitable assets, even allowing for some bad debts. We shall discuss in Chapter 18 the importance of bank lending in the economy, and the ways in which the authorities seek to control it. It is sufficient for the moment to note that there are times when bank lending is restricted by the authorities, and when such restrictions are in force, the banks are unable to lend as much to customers as they would like. They will therefore seek to put surplus funds into the next most profitable assets, which are gilt-edged securities. Being less liquid than short-term assets, the yield is usually higher, but they are less risky than advances. The yield to the bank therefore tends to be somewhere between that on short-term assets, and that on advances. When credit is easy, the banks will be increasing lending to customers, and probably selling gilt-edged stocks to finance the greater volume of advances, but when credit is restricted the opposite will occur; advances will be held constant or fall, investments will increase.

An analysis of London clearing bank advances by the category of the borrower shows roughly the breakdown given in Table 14.2. The proportions do vary from time to time, but this analysis gives some idea of the relative importance of the various categories of borrower.

Fixed investments

The two items in this category are self-explanatory. They consist of the banks' premises and equipment, such as the computers in which they have invested heavily in recent years. Investment in subsidiary and associated companies has also been tending to rise as the banks have sought to diversify by buying into other organisations in order to provide a wider range of financial services to their customers.

Other banking institutions

The discussion above has concerned only the balance sheets of the clearing banks, but the liabilities and assets of the other banking institutions are similar to those of the clearers, although the pro-

Table 14.2 Analysis of Bank Lending

	%
Manufacturing	19
Other production	10
Property	4
Other financial institutions	15
Transport and communications	4
Public utilities and Government	1
Local government	2
Distribution	10
Personal lending (including house purchase 10%)	22
Professional, scientific and miscellaneous	13

portions are often different. It should be remembered that although the clearing banks remain the single most important group of banks in the UK banking structure, their overwhelming position has been, and continues to be, eroded by the growing importance of the other banking institutions discussed in Chapter 13.

The relative importance of the clearing banks in sterling business can be seen from Table 14.3 which shows the proportion of total sterling deposits accounted for by the different groups of banks in January 1983.

Table 14.3 Distribution of Sterling Deposits

	% of total sterling deposits
London clearing banks	45
Scottish banks	5
Northern Ireland banks	1
Accepting houses	5
Overseas banks:	
American	6
Japanese	2
other	10
Other UK banks	24
Consortium banks	1

The practice of banks in London accepting deposits and making loans in foreign currencies is discussed in the section on the Eurodollar market in Chapter 15. So important indeed has this business become that, surprising as it may seem, the amount of foreign currencies on deposit with the various groups of British banks, both clearing banks and others, is now more than twice the size of the total amount of sterling funds held.

It may also be seen from Table 14.4 that the American and other overseas banks are the principal takers of foreign currency deposits. Of the British banks, the category 'Other UK banks', which includes many of the 'wholesale' deposit-taking institutions, is the most important group, while the clearing banks and accepting houses play only minor parts.

Table 14.4 Distribution of Currency Deposits

	% of total currency deposits
London clearing banks	6
Scottish banks	1
Northern Ireland banks	–
Accepting houses	3
Overseas banks:	
American	22
Japanese	26
other	27
Other UK banks	11
Consortium banks	4

– = less than 0·5%

Questions

1 Outline the main assets on the balance sheet of a commercial bank.
2 What is meant by the 'liquidity' of an asset? What assets do banks regard as liquid?
3 Why do banks lend money to discount houses, and on what terms?
4 What are the liabilities of a commercial bank? Describe the principal characteristics of each type of liability.

15

London's Money Markets

Within the boundaries of the City of London are many different financial markets. Some of these are housed in a particular building, and can be seen as physical entities: into this category fall, for example, the Stock Exchange and the great insurance market, Lloyd's of London. But there are many other markets which do not possess a single place of residence. Among these are the foreign exchange market, the capital market and the various money markets of London. These markets consist of dealings done by telephone or personal contact, and by the getting together of dealers and of brokers to transact business in the financial 'commodities' in which they specialise. Although no one can enter a 'visitors' gallery' to see the discount market at work, it is nevertheless just as real and active as the Stock Exchange, which welcomes over 200 000 visitors a year to its imposing building in Throgmorton Street.

This chapter is concerned with the short-term money markets which exist in London. Until the mid-1950s it would have been accurate to refer to the short-term 'money market' in London in the singular. By that would have been understood the discount market, the traditional market for short-term funds in the City, whose dealers still add a touch of old-fashioned dignity to the area around the Bank of England and Lombard Street by wearing their traditional top hat, on their 'rounds' of the banks. Although a good deal of their business is now conducted by telephone, they still pay regular morning visits in person to the banks with which they deal. The City would be a less colourful place were these visits by the members of the discount houses discontinued. Today, however, it is no longer accurate to talk of a singular money market in London for a number of other short-term money markets have grown up side by side with the traditional discount market. These more recent markets are collectively known by a variety of names, the 'new' markets, the 'parallel' markets and the 'complementary' markets, for instance; these markets include both those which deal in sterling and those which deal in other currencies. They include the *interbank market*, the *local authority deposit market*, the *instalment finance company market*, the *Euro-currency market* and the sterling and dollar *certificate of deposit markets*. One feature characterises all the short-term money markets, whether traditional or more recent, whether dealing in sterling or in other currencies: these markets are dealing in the *lending* and *borrowing* of money, not in the buying and selling of it, in contrast to the Stock Exchange and the foreign exchange market where the dealings are buying and selling transactions.

The discount market

The discount market has its origins among the bill brokers of the early nineteenth century. These firms dealt in inland bills of exchange, which were the most important means of settling accounts between traders at that time. A merchant supplying goods to a buyer would draw a bill of exchange on the buyer in a manner described in Chapter 5. If the supplier did not wish to wait until the bill fell due for payment, in perhaps three months' time, he could raise cash immediately by selling it, less a discount, probably through his own local bank, to a bill-broker in London. The bill-brokers, as the word 'broker' implies, acted mainly as intermediaries, selling, or to use a more technical word, 'rediscounting' the bills with those banks with spare funds to invest, which then held them to maturity.

Two developments of the nineteenth century changed the role of the discount houses significantly. One was the trend towards the amalgamation of the small unit banks described in the Introduction, and the second was the growing popularity of the cheque as a means of settling debts between traders within the UK. The amalgamation movement enabled the branch banks which were emerging to channel funds directly from the branches which had a surplus of deposits to those which needed them for lending purposes. The intermediary role of the bill-brokers was no longer necessary. The growing importance of the cheque, an instrument of payment which did not involve the element of credit which the old bill of exchange had done, removed from the bill-brokers the very instrument on which their business had been built.

The discount houses proved adaptable, and instead of acting as intermediaries in the discounting of inland bills of exchange, they began to buy and sell them on their own account. With the decline of the inland bill of exchange, the houses were fortunate that the international bill rapidly took its place. The growth of world trade, and particularly British trade, in the nineteenth century was rapid, and London was without question the major financial market providing both short-term funds to make the trade possible, and also the long-term capital to assist the development of other countries of the world. The discount market helped to provide the funds, and the Bill on London became a principal method of financing international trade.

The funds the houses used came partly from their own capital and reserves, but mainly from the banks who were seeking a profitable outlet for short-term funds. It was unprofitable for the banks to keep too many of their resources in cash, which was expensive to store and yielded no interest. They found that the discount houses were willing to borrow funds from them, either on an overnight basis or at very short periods of notice, paying a rate of interest on the funds borrowed. The arrangement suited both parties; the banks earned interest on funds which could be turned back into cash very quickly, and this enabled them to keep a smaller amount of cash than would otherwise have been necessary. The funds enabled the discount houses to expand their business, using the funds to invest in assets which earned them a profit. The assets also formed the security which the banks took for the funds lent to the houses.

A further important feature of the discount market emerged during the nineteenth century. The Bank of England began to act as lender of last resort to the banking system through the medium of the discount houses, as described in Chapter 16.

The discount market today

The London discount market today consists principally of 11 discount houses,* which are all members of the London Discount Market Association. In addition, a number of other companies – known as running brokers – carry on a similar type of business and several banks operate money-trading departments.

The market continues to act as an intermediary between those banks which have cash in excess of their immediate needs, and those which are short. The market takes money 'at call' from the former, while the latter call back from the market funds which had previously been placed with it.

The largest of the discount houses is Union Discount, which is also one of the oldest of the present companies, having been founded in 1885. One of the smallest of the houses – Seccombe, Marshall and Campion – has a particular status in the market in that it is the 'special buyer'. The 'special buyer' is the Bank of England's agent in the market; if the Bank wishes to relieve a temporary shortage of cash in the market, but does not wish to force the market to borrow from the Bank at penal rates, it can instruct the special buyer to buy Treasury bills from the other houses, supplying the necessary funds itself. These transactions can thus take place at market rates, rather than at the penal rate.

Assets of the discount market

The discount houses now invest in a wide range of assets; some of these are assets of the public sector, and some are those of the private sector. The amounts shown in Table 15.1, and the percentage of each in relation to the totals are constantly changing, and the changes can sometimes be quite rapid. The discount houses have survived by adapting themselves to changing circumstances, and as one asset becomes less freely available, or less profitable to hold, then switches are quickly made. Equally, if a suitable new instrument is developed and houses can make a profit by dealing in it, they are likely to enter the market wholeheartedly.

* Alexanders Discount; Cater, Allen; Clive Discount; Gerald Quin, Cope; Gerrard & National; Jessel, Toynbee & Gillett; King & Shaxson; Page & Gwyther; Seccombe, Marshall & Campion; Smith, St Aubyn; and Union Discount.

Table 15.1 Assets of the discount market (November 1983)

	£m	*% of total assets*
British Government stocks	514	8
British Government Treasury bills	118	2
Other public sector bills	122	2
Other bills	2 892	46
Local authority securities	134	2
Certificates of deposit:		
sterling	1 788	28
US dollars	154	2
Other assets	638	10
	6 360	100

British Government stocks

In the 1930s, the discount houses began to deal in Government stocks with a short period (of less than five years) to maturity. The houses could earn a better rate of return on this type of investment than on the other securities which were available, principally Treasury bills. By the mid-1950s, short-dated Government stocks had risen in importance to become the major assets of the discount houses. Although Government stocks can be the most profitable of a discount house's assets, because they are of a longer term nature than their other assets, they also involve the greatest risk of capital loss if they have to be sold before they mature. This risk is the greater when interest rates are fluctuating sharply, which has been the case in this country during the past twenty years, and especially since 1971.

When interest rates rise very rapidly the houses may suffer large capital losses on their Government stocks, and so they will reduce their holdings of Government stocks when prices are expected to fall and add to them when they foresee a rise in prices.

British Government Treasury bills

Treasury bills are instruments by which the British Government raises short-term finance to cover its spending, while awaiting the receipt of its income from taxation. They are of two types: 'tap' and 'tender'. 'Tap' bills are issued to Government Departments, which have surplus funds to invest, and to overseas central banks who wish to hold them.

The other type of Treasury bill, that issued each week through the tender – hence the name – is, however, very important both from the point of view of Government finance and of the discount market, which occupies a special place in the method of issue.

Treasury bills are issued by tender for a period of 91 days. The bills are available in denominations of £5000, £10 000, £25 000, £50 000, £100 000 and £250 000, but the minimum tender is for £50 000, so that the market in them is effectively confined to large financial institutions. Each week the Bank of England announces how many bills will be available, and the tender takes place each Friday. Hopeful bidders must submit a tender for a given nominal amount of bills. Since the bills themselves do not carry a rate of interest, the bidder, in order to earn a rate of return, will tender for the bills at a discount, at say, £98 for £100 nominal value. The tenders when submitted to the Bank of England will be ranked in descending order, beginning with the highest tender. The bidder at the highest price will usually receive the full amount bid for and the Bank of England will work down the list of bids until it runs out of bills which are on offer. The discount houses, by agreement with the Bank of England, bid for the full amount of bills on offer each week, so that the Bank is never left with unissued bills on its hands nor the Government short of funds. The banks do not themselves usually bid for Treasury bills, although they may put in bids on behalf of customers.

The Treasury bill was first introduced in 1877, as a method of raising short-term finance using an instrument similar to that with which the discount market was familiar, the bill of exchange. Until the outbreak of the First World War, it was only a small part of the discount market's portfolio of assets, but gained a much greater place from the 1920s onwards. So much so that after the end of the Second World War, as the Government relied heavily on Treasury bills as a means of raising temporary finance, Treasury bills became the single most important asset of the market. During the 1960s, however, the importance of the Treasury bill declined as the

Government sought to finance its borrowing requirement by the issue of longer-term Government stock.

Today, the Treasury bill accounts for between 3% and 20% of the assets of the market. The amount of bills on offer each week may fluctuate quite substantially, depending upon the time of year. The reason for this is that the Government needs to spend money regularly throughout the year, but the majority of revenue from taxation flows into the Exchequer in the final quarter of the financial year, that is between January and March. In the early part of the financial year, when expenditure exceeds revenue week by week, the Government finances the additional expenditure by raising money from the market on Treasury bills; as the tax revenue begins to exceed expenditure from January onwards, some of it is used to pay off maturing Treasury bills which are not being replaced.

Other public sector bills

These mainly consist of bills issued by local authorities. Like Treasury bills they are short-term instruments designed to finance expenditure pending the receipt of revenue from other sources, in this instance principally the local rates.

Other bills

Bills listed as *other bills* among the assets of the discount market, consist mainly of the traditional assets of the houses, namely commercial bills. We have already described the early history of the commercial bill in the discount market, and it is of interest to note that commercial bills have recently re-established their pre-eminent place in the market's assets after a long period of decline. Because of the reduction in world trade during the 1930s and, after the Second World War, the declining importance of sterling as a world currency, as well as other methods of transferring funds internationally, the commercial bill lost so much ground that, in 1959, the Radcliffe Committee was able to speak of 'the irreversible shrinkage in the relative supply of commercial bills'.

However, the commercial bill has revived in importance, partly as a method of overcoming restrictions on the growth of bank lending, partly as a method of export finance, and finally because since 1981 the Bank of England has relieved shortages of funds in the money market by buying bills from the banks.

Local authority securities

These securities consist principally of stocks and bonds which the various local authorities in the UK have issued to help them finance their expenditure. Many of these bonds are negotiable instruments, which means that they can be transferred by delivery. The discount houses provide a 'secondary' market in these bonds, buying them from and selling them to other investors. The houses also hold a substantial amount of these bonds as part of their own assets. As with securities issued by the central Government, the market usually holds local authority stocks of up to five years to maturity.

Negotiable certificates of deposit (CD)

These are the newest types of asset held by the market, and within five years of their first being introduced in London became the most important asset held. This position, however, was not maintained as the commercial bill's popularity revived. A negotiable certificate of deposit (CD) is a receipt issued by a bank, acknowledging that a certain sum of money has been deposited for a fixed period. Being negotiable, title to the certificate can pass by delivery; they are thus very easy to transfer from one holder to another. CDs were first introduced into London by an American bank in 1966. The instrument had been known in the USA for some years, and the first issues in London were denominated in US dollars. At the time, some doubt existed about the legality of issuing such certificates denominated in sterling, but legislation was passed which made such an issue possible, and the first sterling CD issue was made in October 1968.

Sterling CDs are issued by banks in London in multiples of £10 000 with a minimum of £50 000 and a maximum of £500 000. They are issued for a minimum period of three months and a maximum of five years. Each certificate, when issued, shows the date of maturity and the rate of interest payable on it. On certificates which are issued for less than a year, interest is paid along with the capital sum when the certificate matures. For those certificates issued for longer than a year, interest is payable annually. Dollar CDs are similar to those denominated in sterling, except that the minimum is \$10 000 for medium-term certificates, and \$25 000 for short-term ones.

The negotiable CD is a flexible instrument, and gives advantages both to the depositor and to the borrower. A depositor may have available for example a sum of £50 000 on which he is seeking a good rate of interest with maximum security. He calculates that he will not need the money for a year, and so he puts it on deposit with a bank for that period. If he were simply to put it on deposit for repayment after one year without taking a CD he would not be able to get his money back, should he find that he needs it, in the meantime. The bank would quite rightly claim that the money had been placed with them for one year and it had paid a better rate of interest on those funds than they would otherwise have done on that understanding.

But suppose that in return for his deposit of £50 000 the depositor obtains a negotiable CD. The bank has use of the money, as before, for a full year, but the depositor, should he find that he needs his money before the year is over, can take his certificate to a trader in the secondary market – that is, the market for existing certificates – who will buy the certificate from him at a price which reflects the going rate of interest for certificates of that maturity. Thus the CD gives the original issuing bank the funds for the period for which the certificate is issued, but gives the depositor the ability to get his money back before maturity by selling the certificate in the secondary market.

The discount houses form a major part of the secondary market in CDs, both buying them from existing holders who wish to sell, and selling them to new holders who may wish to buy a certificate in the secondary market. Some of the buyers in the market are the banks themselves, who as noted in Chapter 14, not only raise deposits by issuing CDs but also hold CDs issued by other banks as a part of their assets. Between 1971 and 1973, the volume of sterling CDs issued increased very rapidly from around £2000m to over £6000m, and the discount market, participating fully in the development of the secondary market in them, increased its holdings of them. Despite a lull in their growth after 1973, the volume of sterling CDs is now increasing again, and stands at over £9000m. The discount market's holdings of them has shown a similar pattern.

Sources of borrowed funds

Having seen the types of asset in which the market invests its resources, let us now turn our attention to the sources from which it obtains its funds. Very little of the market's resources comes from its own capital and reserves, the major part consisting of short-term borrowing from the banks and other sources.

Table 15.2 The Discount Market

Sources of borrowed funds (November 1983)*

	£m	*% of total*
Bank of England	–	–
UK monetary sector	5 168	87
Other UK sources	771	13
Overseas	21	–

* including the sterling equivalent of funds borrowed in other currencies
– = less than 0.5%

A notable feature of the transactions involving the discount houses is that all lending by the banking and other institutions is secured on the houses' assets. However short the borrowing period, security is taken. This is in contrast to some of the newer short-term money markets, where transactions are usually made on an unsecured basis.

The main supplier of funds to the market is the UK banking system. Prior to the introduction of Competition and Credit Control (see Chapter 18), the market had become heavily dependent on the clearing banks, which usually provided well over 60% of the market's funds, and sometimes as much as 75% to 80%. The 1971 measures, which made money at call with the discount market an eligible reserve asset, caused the other banks, which had tended to use the inter-bank market as a means of transferring cash balances between themselves, to divert funds to the discount market as a means of maintaining the reserve asset ratios which they had to observe from 1971 onwards.

The discount market and monetary control

The special position long enjoyed by the discount market in the British banking system has been confirmed by the various monetary changes introduced during the 1970s and early 1980s. First, competition and credit control in 1971 counted all money placed with the discount houses as an eligible reserve asset without limit for the banks. The discount houses thus became the most important depositary of short-term liquid funds for the banking sector. In return, the discount houses agreed with the monetary authorities that they themselves would restrict the ways in which they used these borrowed funds.

At first they had to keep 50% of their assets in specified public sector assets, such as Treasury bills and short-dated government stocks. This requirement proved too restrictive in practice and it was replaced by one which stipulated that the total of 'non-specified' assets (mainly private sector assets) should not exceed twenty times a house's capital and reserves.

In 1981, the set of measures which made up Competition and Credit Control was largely replaced by a new system of monetary control, as explained in Chapter 18. Within this new system of control the discount houses still retain a special place. The old concept of eligible reserve assets has been abandoned but all members of the 'monetary sector' (a rather wider grouping than the old 'banking sector') agreed to keep an average of 6% of their eligible liabilities with members of the London Discount Market Association on a secured basis, and further agreed that on no day will the level fall below 4%. In mid-1983 these agreed figures were reduced to 5% on average, with a minimum figure of 2½%.

Changes were also made in 1971 in the arrangements for the Treasury bill tender. Previously, the market had tendered as a 'syndicate' for the weekly supply of Treasury bills, a practice which dated back to the 1930s. This practice meant not only that the houses bid for the whole of the Treasury bill issue, but also that they bid at a common 'syndicate' price, which had been agreed beforehand. As from September 1971 the syndicate bid was discontinued. The houses continued to cover the whole of the tender each week, but not at an agreed price. This arrangement was unaffected by the changes in 1981.

Under the revised monetary control arrangements which came into effect in 1981, the Bank of England continues, where necessary, to give lender of last resort facilities to the discount houses. In practice, however, it seldom uses such facilities now, preferring to keep control over the supply of credit in the system by dealing with the discount houses, buying and selling various assets, to create, or alleviate, a shortage of funds. The monetary authorities seek in this way to keep short-term interest rates within a narrow, but unpublished, band.

The revised arrangements, like all their predecessors, continue to give the discount houses a central role in the monetary system of the UK, a situation which is unique in the world's banking systems.

The sterling inter-bank market

During the past twenty-five years several new markets in short-term money have grown up in London alongside the traditional discount market. One of these is the sterling inter-bank market. As the name implies, only banking institutions participate in this market, in which banks lend sterling cash balances to, and borrow them from, other banks.

We saw above that the discount market acts as an intermediary in transferring the surplus cash balances of one bank to another which is short of cash. The interbank market performs the same function, but does so directly, a bank with surplus cash lending directly to another which is short, although in practice the deals are usually arranged through brokers.

There are now over 400 banking institutions in London which deal in the inter-bank market. The sums involved are large with a minimum transaction being for perhaps £250 000, and individual deals of £10m or even higher are made. Figures are difficult to obtain, but a typical deal will probably be around £500 000. Interbank transactions may take place for a period of maturity ranging from overnight up to five years, but the market is essentially a short-term one with the great majority of deals being done for less than one year. All transactions are done on an unsecured basis, unlike those in the discount market, so that every lender is relying on the good name and trustworthiness of the borrower, and not on the security of any underlying asset.

The sterling inter-bank market has its origins in the early 1960s when a number of non-clearing banks began to deal directly between themselves, thus bypassing the traditional discount market. The clearing banks did not participate directly in the market, maintaining the traditional practice of working through the discount houses, but the clearing banks established 'money market' subsidiaries, which dealt in the market, and so the clearing banks were indirectly involved. The main reason for the clearing banks dealing only indirectly in the inter-bank market was that, under the banking controls then in operation, any funds which the parent banks took were subject to ratio controls, i.e. 8% of the funds had to be kept in cash, and a further 20% in liquid assets. On the other hand, the same funds raised through a non-clearing subsidiary were not subject to these controls, and so the subsidiary could on-lend a greater proportion of them.

The Competition and Credit Control measures of 1971, by putting all banking institutions on a more equal basis and making them all subject to ratio controls, made it less advantageous for funds to be taken indirectly in the manner described. Several of the clearing banks therefore began to deal in the market directly.

The size of the inter-bank market increased rapidly in the early 1970s. In 1971, approximately £2000m was outstanding but this figure increased rapidly and by the beginning of 1974 it had reached over £8000m. Today, now that the Bank of England has included many more institutions in the 'monetary sector', the intra-sector sterling balances are over £30 000m.

Closely linked to the sterling inter-bank market is the market in negotiable *sterling certificates of deposit*. These instruments were described above as part of the assets of the discount houses, which provide the secondary market in which CDs are traded, and thus the CD has been the instrument by which the traditional market and the newer markets have drawn closer together.

The Euro-currency market

Undoubtedly the most important of the new money markets in London has been the Euro-currency market. So important has the lending and borrowing of Euro-currencies become that, as noted in Chapter 14, the value of deposits held in foreign currencies by banks in the UK, particularly in London, exceeds the total amount of sterling deposits held by banks throughout the country. The existence of this market has also attracted a large number of overseas banks to London, and by September 1982 the total number of such banks represented in London was almost 450. Another surprising statistic is that there are more US banks with offices in London than there are in New York.

The major part of the Euro-currency market consists of Euro-dollars. These are simply US dollar balances, which, instead of being held directly in a bank in New York, Chicago or Los Angeles, are held as dollar deposits in a bank outside the USA. The advantage to the depositor is that he receives a higher rate of interest on his deposit than he could obtain in New York, because US regulations used to set a maximum limit to the amount of interest which could be paid on bank deposits held in the USA. Furthermore, since many of the holders of dollars are non-American, it is more convenient to hold these balances through a bank outside the USA. Borrowers may take dollar loans in the market, sometimes transferring them into another currency for ultimate use. Many UK companies have borrowed funds on the Euro-currency market, and so too have a number of local authorities and nationalised industries, with the British Government's approval. During 1974, the Government itself, through the clearing banks, arranged a Euro-currency loan of $2500m.

A considerable amount of inter-bank dealing takes place in the Euro-currency market, just as it does in the sterling markets, and the amount of foreign currency deposits held by UK-based banks with each other is over £85 000m. Furthermore, the existence of the Euro-currency market has led to the development of the negotiable dollar CD, the forerunner of its sterling counterpart. The equivalent of some £8000m of dollar CDs are on issue in the London market.

By size, the sterling inter-bank market and the Euro-currency market are the most important of the newer markets to have developed in London alongside the traditional discount market. Other deposit-taking institutions have, however, developed active markets for funds. British local authorities, requiring finance for local projects, bid for large deposits on the local authority deposit market. Deals are usually arranged through brokers and can range from overnight maturity up to one year. Although individual circumstances may make exceptions to the rule, the minimum deposit taken is usually of £50 000 and deals may range up to £1m or even beyond.

Instalment finance company market

A further deposit-taking market is that of the instalment finance companies. This market works in a similar way to the local authority deposit market, but deals are usually arranged for either three or six months. Funds are mainly attracted from financial institutions and other large companies with spare funds. Because the funds are lent on an unsecured basis, the rates paid vary with the individual finance house, those with close connections with a clearing bank being able to attract funds at lower rates than smaller and less well-connected institutions.

Questions

1 Describe briefly the assets of the discount houses.
2 What is a Treasury bill? How do the discount houses assist in the issue of tender Treasury bills?
3 What is a negotiable certificate of deposit?
4 How have the discount houses helped the development of negotiable certificates of deposit in London?
5 From what sources do the discount houses borrow money, and on what terms?
6 Describe the work of the inter-bank market.
7 What is a Euro-dollar? Who borrows them and why?

16

The Bank of England

The Bank of England is now the central bank of the UK, but although the Bank since its foundation has always occupied a leading position in the British financial system, the term 'central bank' only came into use in the second half of the nineteenth century, and the Bank of England acquired the role of a central bank gradually over many years.

Objectives of economic policy

The primary duty of a modern central bank is to assist the Government of the day in carrying out that Government's monetary policy, which itself is used, along with fiscal policy and direct controls, to help achieve various economic policy objectives which a Government sets itself. These objectives are: full employment; a stable level of internal prices; a steady improvement in the standard of living; and balance of payments equilibrium.

Full employment

Strictly speaking, full employment means that there is a job for everyone who wants one, and that no one is therefore involuntarily unemployed. In practice, the regular figures of unemployment record a percentage unemployed, which in the UK has usually varied in recent years between 6% and 12% of the working population.

A stable level of internal prices

In any economy, because of changes in taste and in demand for individual items, and because of the effects of technological change on the supply of individual goods, some goods will tend to be rising in price while others are falling. The objective of maintaining a stable level of internal prices relates to the overall, or general, price level. The best known price index is the *index of retail prices* which records, each month, the average level of prices in the shops. This index has shown a general tendency to rise since the end of the Second World War, and in recent years has risen even more sharply. Thus, so far as the UK – and indeed many other countries – is concerned, the objective of stable internal prices has proved an elusive one.

A steady improvement in the standard of living

By this we mean a steady rise in the volume of goods and services available per head of population year by year. This objective is also sometimes referred to as *economic growth*. In the UK, we have not had a rapid rise in economic growth, and hence our standard of living over the past thirty years compared, say, with West Germany and Japan has not been as great. For the most part, however, some economic growth has been achieved year by year since the Second World War, and represents a long period of steady if slow growth, which this country failed to achieve earlier in the century.

Balance of payments equilibrium

No country can, over a long period, import more in goods and services than it exports. In some years, more may be imported than is exported, and a deficit will be incurred on the balance of payments, but over the longer term surpluses should be earned to replenish the reserves.

On a fixed exchange rate system, one of the objectives of economic policy was that of a stable rate of exchange between sterling and other currencies. In 1972, the British Government decided to 'float' sterling, and instead of supporting the rate of exchange by buying sterling on the foreign exchange market, the Authorities simply allowed the rate to find its own level according to the interplay of supply and demand.

Although it is not possible to achieve all of these objectives at the same time, they are the ideals which all Governments attempt to achieve; at times, however, one might have to be given priority over the others.

Monetary policy and other controls

The Government seeks to achieve its economic objectives by three groups of policies:

1 Monetary policies;
2 Fiscal policies;
3 Direct controls.

Monetary policy consists of actions which work through the banking and financial systems, affecting the supply of funds, the price (the interest rate) at which they are supplied or a combination of both.

Fiscal policy consists of changes in the level of Government spending, on defence, roads, hospitals, schools and so on, and changes in the level of Government revenue, principally in taxation. Fiscal policy is usually implemented by the Government in its annual Budget, although it is becoming more common for fiscal policy to be amended during the year in 'mini-Budgets'.

Direct controls Sometimes a Government may find it necessary to take direct action in order to achieve a given objective. At times of crisis, such as wartime and immediately afterwards when goods are in short supply, rationing schemes may be introduced in order to allocate scarce commodities in a reasonably fair way among consumers. At other times, Governments have felt it necessary, in order to control the rate of inflation, to introduce legal controls on both price and wage increases. Such measures cannot be classified as either fiscal or monetary weapons, but they are controls which are used in pursuit of a particular economic objective which a Government is seeking to attain.

The Bank of England and monetary policy

In this chapter we are concerned with the work of the Bank of England in implementing monetary policy, and the means the Bank has at its disposal in order to play an effective part. We saw above that monetary policy is concerned with the banking system in order to achieve its ends. The Bank of England stands in a particularly central position so far as monetary policy is concerned. The Bank has its roots very firmly in the banking community of the City of London as we have already seen in our brief history of banking in the Introduction. However, as we also noted there, the Bank of England was nationalised in 1946, when the Treasury bought the capital of the Bank from its former private stockholders, and is now a public corporation whose capital is owned by the Treasury. The Bank is therefore a part of the Government sector of the economy, just as are the coal and steel industries, gas and electricity supply, and the Post Office. The Bank of England may be seen both as a part of the Government sector and as a part of the banking community. It is the financial arm of the Government, and works very closely with the Treasury in implementing the monetary policy of the Government in power. So closely in fact does the Bank work with the Treasury that the two are often referred to collectively as 'the Authorities'. Ultimately, because the Treasury owns the Bank of England, and its political chief is the Chancellor of the Exchequer, the Treasury would have the final word if any substantial disagreement arose between the two on a matter of policy.

Functions of the Bank of England

At the beginning of this chapter, we said that the major function of a modern central bank is to assist the Government in carrying out its monetary policy. To help it carry out this major task, the Bank of England performs a number of further functions, many of which are common to central banks throughout the world, although there are differences of detail in the way some of these functions are carried out.

Banker to the Government

From its foundation in 1694, the Bank of England has been the Government's bank. The very reason for its formation was to provide a loan of £1 200 000 to the Government to allow the war against France to be waged, and in return for this loan the merchants of the City of London who subscribed the money were allowed to form themselves into a company under the title of 'The Governor and Company of the Bank of England'.

Thus the Government and the Bank of England were always closely linked. The Government held its accounts at the Bank, and the Bank provided the Government with funds to wage its war. Today, the Government's main accounts are all held at the Bank of England, although the clearing banks throughout the country do hold a number of subsidiary accounts for Government departments. The work of the Bank of England as banker to the Government is sometimes likened to that of a commercial banker providing banking services for his ordinary customers. In some respects this is true, but the comparison should not be carried too far. For example, it is not normal for a bank to be owned by its major customer! Nor is it usual for that customer to have the legal power to issue directives to the Bank if he so wishes. On the other hand, the Bank of England does not now as a general rule perform one of the services which a customer of a commercial bank probably finds the most essential at times; it does not lend money to its customer, the Government, except on a small scale and then only overnight, i.e. for repayment the following day. This may seem surprising, but the Government is such a large borrower in the course of its day-to-day business that it uses the short-term money markets and the long-term capital markets for raising the funds it needs. The methods and instruments it uses are discussed later.

Agent of the Government

The Bank also acts as agent for the Government in a number of ways. First, it acts as registrar of the National Debt. This role was acquired by the Bank at an early stage, for we noted in the Introduction that the Bank was performing this task as early as 1715. The Bank continues to act as registrar of Government stocks as well as those of nationalised industries, some local authorities, public boards and Commonwealth Governments.

Activities of more recent origin are administering the exchange control regulations imposed under the Exchange Control Act 1947 while it was still in force, and managing the Exchange Equalisation Account, established in 1932. The Exchange Control Act was designed to protect the country's reserves of gold and foreign exchange by imposing restrictions on the transfer of funds to countries outside a defined area. At first it applied only to transfers outside the sterling area, which included Australia, India, New

Zealand and many other former Commonwealth countries. It was redefined on a much narrower basis following the floating of sterling in 1972, but late in 1979 all restrictions under the Exchange Control Act were lifted, although the Act itself has not been formally repealed.

The Bank also acts as the agent of the Treasury in dealings for the Exchange Equalisation Account. The Account, which is a department of the Treasury, holds the UK's reserves of gold and foreign currencies. When the UK was on a fixed rate of exchange, and was under an international obligation to keep the rate of exchange within narrow specified limits, the Exchange Equalisation Account was the means by which this obligation was honoured. When sterling was weak on the foreign exchange market, this was caused by a surplus supply of sterling on the market relative to the demand. By the elementary economic law of supply and demand the price would fall. To prevent it falling below the floor price agreed, the Bank of England, acting as agent for the Treasury, would buy sterling on the market, thereby creating a demand for it and steadying the price. To pay for the sterling thus acquired, the Bank had to use some of the gold and foreign exchange reserves held by the Exchange Equalisation Account. Thus support for sterling meant that our gold and foreign exchange reserves would be depleted. Since June 1972, the UK has not been under an obligation to support the sterling exchange rate in this way, although the Bank does occasionally intervene in the foreign exchange market to prevent too sharp a movement in the sterling rate against other currencies.

Banker to the commercial banks

In addition to acting as banker for and agent of the Government, the Bank of England also acts as the banker to the commercial banks, the discount houses, overseas central banks and international bodies such as the International Monetary Fund, the International Bank for Reconstruction and Development (the World Bank) and the Bank for International Settlements.

The main commercial banks all keep accounts at the Bank of England and these perform a useful function in enabling settlements to be made between one bank and another arising from settlements of the clearing of cheques between them. The banks also use their balances to pay for notes drawn from the Bank of England to meet the demands of their customers for cash. Again the role of the Bank of England as the bankers' bank is one of long standing. From the early days of its history, although it was only one bank among many entitled to issue its own banknotes, it was, as has already been noted, the only joint-stock bank to do so. Although the privileges enjoyed by the Bank of England were resented by the private bankers, they found it convenient to keep accounts with it. Thus, the Bank of England became, from the eighteenth century onwards, the banker to the London private bankers as well as conducting accounts for its private customers.

Today the Bank has very few private accounts. Members of staff are provided with banking facilities, and private accounts of long standing are still kept. Occasionally, a new business account may be opened for a special reason. This 'small but active private business has the merit,' it is claimed, 'of giving the Bank first hand experience of some of the practical aspects of day to day commercial banking'.* But otherwise, the Bank acts exclusively as a central rather than a commercial bank.

Monopoly of the note issue

The Bank of England now has a complete monopoly of the note issue in England and Wales. Although the Scottish and Northern Ireland banks still retain the right to issue their own banknotes their issues are small and for the most part are fully backed by the Bank of England notes.

The monopoly position of the Bank came about as a result of early nineteenth-century banking legislation. Although the Bank lost its powerful place as a commercial deposit bank, its position as a note-issuing bank was being strengthened. This process led to the introduction of the Bank Charter Act 1844, a piece of legislation which laid the groundwork for the Bank of England acquiring the sole right of note issue later on.

The basic framework laid down by the Act was noted in the Introduction. One of the details of the Act was that it divided the Bank of England into two parts for statistical purposes, the Issue Department and the Banking Department. The former was devoted

* *The Functions and Organisation of the Bank of England* (2nd edition, 1970).

exclusively to the note issue, and the Bank had to issue a weekly statement of account of both these Departments. This statement, known as the 'Weekly Return', is still published, and in form it has changed little since 1844.

The object of this section of the Act was to make sure that the note issue of the country did not become excessive, and in ruling that a weekly statement be made by the Bank, the Act ensured that the Bank's note issue could be quickly and regularly supervised.

The Bank of England was empowered to issue notes up to the value of the gold held in its vaults. This ensured that all the Bank of England's notes were fully convertible into gold; in other words, that anyone with a Bank of England note could exchange it for the equivalent amount of gold at all times. The Bank of England could therefore only issue more banknotes if it succeeded in attracting a

Table 16.1 Bank of England Weekly Return

Issue Department

	£m		£m
Notes issued:		Government Debt	11·0
In circulation	11428·6	Other Government securities	5318·9
In Banking Department	11·4	Other securities	6110·1
	11440·0		11440·0

Banking Department

	£m		£m
Capital	14·6	Government securities	394·1
Public deposits: including Exchequer, National Loans Fund, National Debt Commissioners and dividend accounts	40·8	Advances and other accounts	1240·7
		Premises, equipment and other securities	1020·8
		Notes	11·4
		Coin	0·2
Bankers deposits	559·4		
Reserves and other accounts	2052·4		
	2667·2		2667·2

larger amount of gold. It was realised that such a provision might prove too restrictive to the development of industry and trade, and so a clause was inserted in the Act allowing an additional amount of £14m of notes to be issued over and above the value of gold held. This additional amount was called the *fiduciary issue*, a term coming from the Latin '*fides*' meaning '*trust*'. This extra £14m based on trust did, however, have to be backed by Government securities.

The Bank Charter Act was designed to control the growth of the money supply, and it was based on the view that banknotes were the primary source of money in the country, but during the second half of the nineteenth century the cheque drawn on a commercial bank became an accepted means of payment. We saw in Chapter 1 how anything which is acceptable as money *is* money, and so bank deposits transferred by means of the cheque became regarded as money. As a result, the Bank Charter Act, with its restrictions on the supply of banknotes, became less effective as a means of controlling the total money supply. Recognising this, the Bank of England allowed the fiduciary issue to increase if necessary. The Bank of England finally became the only bank issuing notes in 1921, but control of the banknote issue was no longer considered to be of great importance in the economy, as bank deposits were by then the major element of the money supply.

When gold coin ceased to circulate in 1914 it became less important for the Bank to maintain gold supplies to meet the needs of the note issue. Nevertheless, for some time the Bank of England continued to hold gold in its Issue Department as backing for the note issue, and this was again of some importance between 1925 and 1931 when partial convertibility of notes into gold bullion was allowed. Between those two dates, anyone could buy a gold bar of 400 ounces from the Bank of England. At the price of gold even in those days, such a bar would have cost nearly £1700.

In 1931, the Bank of England suspended the sale of gold, and this situation continues still and is unlikely to be changed. As a result of this action, the Bank of England had no need to keep gold to meet the demands for repayment by holders of its notes, and in 1939 most of the gold held in the Bank of England's Issue Department was transferred to the gold and foreign exchange reserves (although physically remaining in the Bank of England's vaults). For 'window-dressing' purposes, some gold to the value of about £400 000 continued to appear among the assets of the Issue Department in the Weekly Return until 1970. At that time it was decided that such a figure no longer had any importance and it was taken out.

From that time onwards it has been true to say that the entire note issue of the Bank of England has been a fiduciary one, backed not by gold but only by Government securities.

Although the control of the note issue is not now regarded as being of any great economic significance, it is still nominally controlled by law. The Currency and Bank Notes Act 1954 supposedly limits the maximum amount of the note issue to £1575m, but it also provides that it may stand in excess of this figure with the approval of Parliament. This is readily given and the note issue is now permanently in excess of the stated limit. This is permitted because it is realised that control of the *total* money supply, including bank deposits, is the important thing, and the Authorities allow the general public to decide what proportion of the total they wish to hold in cash and what in the form of bank deposits. The element of cash in the total money supply tends to be high at certain times of the year, for example just before Christmas when people draw cash to finance their Christmas shopping and again in the summer at the height of holiday spending; notes in circulation tend to increase, only to be reduced again as payments flow back into the banks.

Lender of last resort

It is a prime duty of a central bank to support the banking system under its control. If the commercial banking system is short of funds it has the right to expect assistance from the central bank, and *in the last resort* a commercial banking system will always be able to borrow from the central bank. Although the central bank must make the funds available, it will do so at a rate of its own choosing and against specified securities; that rate charged will probably be an expensive or penal rate, and the securities those on which there is no possibility of loss. It should not be thought that 'lender of last resort' assistance is provided only when a banking system is in trouble. Although help certainly will be provided in those circumstances, a central bank will constantly be in action, ironing out shortages of cash in the system, or perhaps trying to manipulate the level of interest rates.

The Bank of England acts as lender of last resort to the British banking system, although it does so in an indirect way through the London discount houses. These discount houses are the modern-day equivalents of the bill-brokers of the early nineteenth century (see the Introduction). At that time, the bill-brokers took funds from banks with surplus cash, and lent it on to those who were in need of funds to assist their customers. The most reputable of these bill-brokers, like the banks themselves, held accounts at the Bank of England, and the Bank began to take on its role as lender of last resort during this period. It did so in the main by purchasing acceptable bills from the bill-brokers in exchange for cash, if the banks which had previously lent money to the brokers on a short-term basis were calling it back. Thus cash was immediately available to tide over any shortage, and, assuming that a temporary crisis was averted, the bills on maturity would be paid, and the Bank would recoup its assistance. Such an arrangement suited the banks, because they could argue that it was not they who were borrowing from another bank but the bill-brokers. One bank borrowing from another – even from the Bank of England – in the early part of the nineteenth century would have been considered a sign of weakness, and could well have provoked a run on that bank.

Thus began the practice of lending to the bill-brokers rather than directly to the banks themselves, and this practice still exists today. In other countries of the world, the central bank gives lender of last resort assistance directly to the banks themselves. The fact that in the UK the assistance is given indirectly through the discount market should not obscure the fact that the Bank of England is providing lender of last resort facilities to the banking system.

The work of the Bank of England as a central bank, its functions and how it acquired them, have now been described. The methods which the Bank uses in carrying out its major task of controlling the financial system are the subject of the next two chapters.

Questions

1 Describe the objectives of economic policy.
2 What functions does the Bank of England perform?
3 Explain the circumstances in which the Bank of England might (*a*) buy and (*b*) sell sterling on the foreign exchange market.
4 What is a 'fiduciary issue' of banknotes?

To what extent is or was the Bank of England note issue fiduciary:
(*a*) in 1844?
(*b*) today?

5 Trace the steps by which gold lost its role in English currency.
6 What is meant by lender of last resort? How does the Bank of England fulfil this role?

17

Supervising the Banking System

In the last chapter we examined the role of the Bank of England in general terms. In the next two chapters we shall look at the way in which it carries out its duties in more detail.

There are two areas in which the Bank of England has a major role to play: the first, supervising the safety of the banking system, is the subject of this chapter; while the second, the implementation of the Government's monetary policy, is dealt with in Chapter 18. Although it is useful for the purposes of explanation to separate the two in this way there may be areas in which they overlap.

A banking system must maintain the confidence of those who use it: if depositors lose confidence in a bank they will rush to draw out their deposits and the bank will have to close its doors. In today's complex banking system such a situation would be highly dangerous, not only to the bank concerned, but also to the other banks in the country, while, because of the international nature of banking, a major failure of a bank in one country could cause serious problems on a world-wide basis.

Every central bank must, therefore, try to ensure the safety of the banks within its own country, and the Bank of England is no exception.

In recent years, the method of supervising the British banking system to make sure that confidence is maintained has become more formal than it used to be. In 1979, the Banking Act was passed which gave the Bank of England much greater legal control over the system than it had needed previously, but the Banking Act itself was the final touch to a much more formal system which had been developing over the preceding 10 years.

Previously the system of supervision in the UK had been an informal one. Banking was dominated by the large clearing banks which could be relied upon to maintain adequate cash to pay out to their depositors on demand, absorb any debts which occurred, etc. The banks produced balance sheets once a month, but the main interest in these was the level of deposits and lending and how they were changing rather than checking that the banks were 'safe'.

The banks had developed certain ratios in the course of time which they kept in order to make sure they could repay their depositors. These ratios were set by the banks themselves as a matter of prudence and, by convention, 10% of deposits was held in cash, while 30% (including the 10% cash) was held in 'liquid' assets which could easily and quickly be turned into cash without loss. It was only after the Second World War that these 'prudential' ratios were adopted by the authorities as a means of monetary control. The development of these controls is the subject of the next chapter, but it is mentioned here to indicate how 'prudential' and monetary controls can overlap.

The background to the Banking Act 1979

Since the end of the Second World War, a wide range of banking institutions has grown up offering banking services. Some of these new institutions, notably the overseas banks in London, were described in Chapter 13; alongside them were British registered organisations other than the major clearing banks, which offered some banking services. Some of these were known as secondary banks to differentiate them from the major banking institutions – the primary banks – although a few did have close links with the major banks themselves. In addition, there was a group of banks known as 'tertiary' banks. The methods of controlling these groups of banks were haphazard. Some of the larger secondary banks received requests from the Bank of England in a credit squeeze asking them to restrict lending, and usually they complied with them, but they did not prepare monthly statistical information as did the clearing banks. The only checks on their safety were the standing of the major banks with which they were associated, if any, and their annual and interim reports. Even less controlled were the tertiary banks, whose activities were controlled by the Department of Trade under the provisions of the Companies Acts. They were controlled in their competition for deposits by restrictions on how they could advertise their services, but otherwise were controlled no more closely than any other company. They were certainly outside any regular monitoring of their affairs by the Bank of England, but, by the very nature of their business, mainly in personal lending and property development built on a very short-term deposit base, they were perhaps the most in need of close surveillance.

A first step towards greater control of the secondary banking system was taken by the Bank of England in 1971, under the provisions of Competition and Credit Control. Under these regulations, as we shall see in the next chapter, many more banks had to give statistical returns to the Bank of England on a monthly basis, and the Bank was thus able to monitor more closely the growth of the activities of those organisations. Nevertheless, the tertiary banks remained outside this control.

The problem came to a head in late 1973. London and County Securities, a bank heavily involved in property lending, failed when the property market, which had been booming in the early 1970s, suddenly crashed, leaving London and County Securities unable to repay its depositors on demand. The essential element of a banking system, namely that of confidence, had been lost and a number of other secondary and tertiary banks suffered a run on their deposits, and a number of these collapsed too; even some widely known secondary banking institutions suffered a sharp withdrawal of deposits.

In order to ward off a major collapse, the Bank of England established, with the major clearing banks, a 'lifeboat' scheme designed to help these smaller banks over their liquidity difficulties to prevent the collapse having a 'domino effect' on other parts of the system. The major banks agreed to provide up to £1200m to the institutions in difficulties. The object of the 'lifeboat' scheme was to steady depositors' nerves and allow the companies a chance to sort out their affairs without the threat of a further run on their deposits.

Some of them had been heavily involved in the property market boom and in its subsequent collapse found that the value of the properties was well below what they had lent; as a result some of the banks themselves were eventually wound up. Others, who were simply suffering from liquidity difficulties, remained in the 'lifeboat', receiving help from the clearing banks until such time as it was possible to realise the values of the property they had financed and they were in a position to stand on their own feet again.

The events of 1973–4 had demonstrated that the British banking system was not immune from the possibility of collapse, and while a major financial problem had been averted by the 'lifeboat', the crisis demonstrated to the Authorities quite clearly the need for greater control of the secondary and tertiary banking system than had been exercised previously.

Faced with this situation, the Authorities began to look at methods of controlling the entire system more effectively.

There was a further consideration. In 1973, the UK had joined the European Economic Community (EEC) whose Commission was attempting to co-ordinate legislation relating to banking law and control. The countries of continental Europe had long had a more legalistic approach to the control of their banks, so it was almost inevitable that any European-wide framework of control would contain legal backing; a policy which the British financial system had not previously felt necessary.

The Bank of England issued a White Paper in 1976, 'The Licensing and Supervision of Deposit-Taking Institutions', and this was followed by a draft Bill. The object of the White Paper was to set out the Bank's thoughts on the way in which banks and other deposit-taking institutions should be supervised and to stimulate constructive discussion. The major banks were unhappy about the establishment of a deposit protection fund, to which they would have to contribute the largest share, but which would basically be for the protection of depositors in rival and less well-managed institutions. Despite their objections, the Bank stuck to its original proposals and, as noted below, a deposit protection scheme has been introduced.

The Banking Act 1979

The Banking Act 1979, which came into force on 1 October 1979, is a milestone in British banking history comparable to the Bank Charter Act 1844. Without doubt it is the most important piece of banking legislation this century (including the nationalisation of the Bank of England in 1946) and the conduct of banking in the UK will never be quite the same again.

The Act is divided into four parts. The first deals with the control of deposit-taking by institutions; the second sets up a deposit protection scheme to safeguard depositors who hold deposits in any bank which fails; the third deals with the question of advertising for deposits and the use of the name 'bank' or 'banking' in the title; while the fourth part deals with various miscellaneous items, such as penalties for infringements, etc.

1 The control of deposit-taking

In the past it has been possible for a company to set itself up and invite the public to place deposits with it quite easily. It had to comply with certain laws, notably the Protection of Depositors Act 1963, but no prior permission was necessary. The Banking Act changes that situation fundamentally. In future, no one may seek deposits from the public without first obtaining a licence to do so from the Bank of England. The Banking Act prohibits anyone other than a company specified in the Act from seeking deposits from the public. Furthermore, it divides those companies which are permitted to seek deposits into two categories: those which are classified as 'banks', and secondly, 'licensed deposit takers' (LDTs).

Banks As we noted at the beginning of this book, there is no satisfactory definition of a bank in UK legislation. Even the 1979 Banking Act goes only part of the way towards a full definition. How an institution qualifies as a 'bank' is defined in the Act in Schedule II, which outlines certain services an organisation must provide if it wishes to be recognised as a bank. The following services are listed:

(*a*) Current or deposit account facilities in sterling or foreign currency for members of the public or for bodies corporate or the acceptance of funds in sterling or foreign currency in the wholesale money markets;

(*b*) Finance in the form of overdraft or loan facilities in sterling or foreign currency for members of the public or for bodies corporate or the lending of funds in sterling or foreign currency in the wholesale money markets;

(*c*) Foreign exchange services for domestic and foreign customers;

(*d*) Finance through the medium of bills of exchange and promissory notes, together with finance for foreign trade documentation in connection with foreign trade;

(*e*) Financial advice for members of the public and for bodies corporate or investment management services and facilities for arranging the purchase and sale of securities in sterling or foreign currency.

This list describes the sort of services which the Bank of England will expect an institution to provide if it wishes to be recognised as a bank. But the Bank of England still has discretion in deciding whether a company can qualify for the title of Bank and be allowed to use that status in its literature when competing for deposits. The Act also says that the institution must enjoy a high reputation in the financial community. So recognition as a bank is not automatic, even though it may provide the full range of services which the Act outlines.

Licensed deposit-taking institutions An organisation not qualifying as a bank may in future only seek deposits from the general public if the Bank of England recognises it as a licensed deposit-taking institution.

The Bank now issues a full list of those institutions to which it has granted recognition in either category. The Bank also has the power to withdraw recognition if it decides an institution fails to comply with the provisions of the Act or no longer, in the Bank's view, justifies the status of a bank or licensed deposit-taking institution.

Exemptions Because certain bodies which take deposits from the public have their own special legislation they were exempted from the provisions of the Banking Act 1979. These include the National Savings Bank, other central banking institutions, the Post Office, the Trustee Savings Banks, the building societies, stockbrokers and stockjobbers, friendly societies, insurance companies, Credit Unions and local authorities.

2 The deposit protection scheme

We saw earlier that the fringe banking crisis of 1973 had left depositors in a position where they might well lose the value of their deposits. In the event the 'lifeboat' arrangement saved most, if not all of them, from any loss, but the experience did cause the Authorities to look at a form of deposit protection for the general public, so that they would automatically be protected in the event of a similar occurrence in the future, rather than being dependent on a group of organisations voluntarily rallying round to protect them.

The idea of a deposit protection scheme is not a new one. In the early 1930s, a large number of banks failed in the USA. The response there was the establishment in 1933 of an organisation called the Federal Deposit Insurance Corporation (FDIC), to which all American banks were obliged to belong, and which gives a degree of protection to depositors in the event of a bank failure. The system in the USA has been extremely successful and despite the unit banking system which exists there (a large number of individual banks and very few branches), there have been very few failures since the establishment of the FDIC. Each bank in the system contributes a proportion of its deposits to the FDIC which now gives protection of up to \$100 000 for each depositor in the event of failure.

The deposit protection scheme established in the UK under the Banking Act 1979 gives any depositor with a balance of up to £10 000 in a recognised bank or deposit-taking institution protection against loss up to 75% of the value of the deposit. In practice, the scheme is not as beneficial as that in the USA, where deposits of up to \$100 000 are covered to a full 100%.

Protection will be given by the establishment of a fund of between £5m and £6m contributed by the recognised banks and licensed deposit takers at a rate of up to 0·3% of their sterling deposit base, subject to a minimum contribution of £2500 and a maximum contribution of £300 000 for each institution.

The deposit base of the bank is defined as sterling deposits, other than deposits which are secured on assets, money which was originally deposited for a period in excess of five years, and any deposit against which a certificate of deposit has been issued.

In addition to the initial contribution which the bank will levy in order to build up the fund to its level of £5–£6m, the contributing institutions may also be called upon to make further contributions if at the end of any financial year the amount in the fund is less than

£3m and also make special contributions if at any time it appears likely that the resources of the fund may be exhausted.

A deposit protection board has been set up to manage the fund and to levy contributions to it to maintain its value and the protection for depositors. The board consists of the Governor, the Deputy Governor and the Chief Cashier of the Bank of England, while the Governor appoints to the board three people who are directors or managers of institutions which are members of the scheme and a number of people who are officers or employees of the Bank of England. Thus the deposit protection board will be heavily dominated by the Bank of England.

The funds collected by the board will be invested in Treasury bills while the board has the power to borrow up to a further £1m in order to carry out its activities, should this be necessary.

It is too early to say how the scheme will work in practice, but it is hoped that by having the scheme in place, together with the close supervision of the banking and deposit-taking institutions which the Bank of England has now set up, any recurrence of the 1973 secondary banking crisis will be prevented. The object is to tackle the problem at source. If, however, in any particular instance the supervisory system fails to prevent the failure of an institution, then the deposit protection fund will be available as a last resort.

3 Advertisements and banking names

This third section of the Act gives the Treasury the authority to regulate the issue, form and content of advertisements seeking deposits from the general public. In future, no institution will be able to advertise for deposits unless it is recognised by the Bank of England, and, unless it is granted recognition as a bank, will not be able to use the name 'Bank' or 'Banking' in its title or in the description of its activities. In future, only the Bank of England itself, the central bank of any EEC country, a bank recognised under the Banking Act, a Trustee Savings Bank or the Post Office in carrying out its banking services may use the word 'Bank' in its title.

The section in the Act dealing with banking names and descriptions was felt to be necessary because of the rather loose legislation previously in existence which enabled companies to give the impression that they were of a certain standing, either by the use of the word 'Bank' in their titles or, more frequently, by suggesting they offered banking services in the body of the text. This was felt to be misleading, and hence the need for more effective control contained in the Banking Act.

This chapter has given a description of how the control of and supervision of the banking system in this country moved from a state of persuasion to one in which the law has been found to be necessary. It is a significant milestone in British banking history and has fundamentally altered the methods of supervising the banking system in the UK.

Questions

1 Why was the Banking Act 1979 thought necessary?
2 Distinguish between banks and licensed deposit-taking institutions.
3 What were the major changes introduced by the Banking Act 1979?

18

Control of the Banking System

In Chapter 16 we saw that it is the function of a modern central bank to assist the Government in carrying out the monetary part of its overall economic policy. We saw, too, that the Authorities place particular emphasis on controlling the growth of bank deposits in trying to restrict the growth of the money supply. We now turn our attention to the methods which the Authorities use in the UK to exercise this control over the banking system.

Unlike the situation in the USA and several countries of western Europe, the banking system in the UK is not subject to a set of legal restrictions governing the ratios which the banks must keep. No law exists stating how much capital and reserves must be kept for a given level of deposits, nor is there a *legal* requirement that a bank must keep a given amount of deposits in specified assets. This remains true even after the passing of the Banking Act 1979 which does not lay down any legal constraints on ratios, etc. Although the Bank of England does possess the legal right, under the Bank of England Act 1946, to give directives to the banks, this power is expressed in very general terms, and, in practice, the legal power to issue directives has never been used. Instead, the Bank of England relies on an informal approach. The Bank's wishes in the matter of credit control are nonetheless effective.

The need for control

In discussing the workings of a banking system one fact should be constantly remembered, and that is that a banking system can create its own deposits. A banker may protest that this is not so and that he can lend to his customers in the form of advances only a proportion of what he has received from other customers on deposit. Contradictory though these two statements might at first appear, they are both true.

The paradox is explained in that a banker does not need to keep all the deposits he receives from his customers in the form of cash in his vaults. The seventeenth-century goldsmiths discovered this, as have bankers both before and since. Only a fraction needs to be kept in cash in order to repay depositors on demand. So long as the banker keeps enough to do this, confidence will be maintained. Experience teaches him what proportion he must keep in order to fulfill his commitments to repay on demand. This principle, that of keeping only a fraction of total deposits in the form of cash, is what gives a banking system the ability to create its own deposits.

To explain more fully how this comes about, let us take the example of a commercial banking system receiving an extra £1000 of deposits, and keeping a reserve of 10% in the form of cash.

The initial impact is:

1	Deposits	+1000	Cash	+1000

But only 10% of the extra deposits needs to be kept in cash; the remainder can be lent to customers by way of advances. At the second stage, the addition to the balance sheet will read:

2	Deposits	+1000	Cash	+ 100
			Advances	+ 900
		+1000		+1000

Bearing in mind that these balance sheet figures represent the situation of the commercial banking system as a whole, we should ask ourselves the question 'What will happen now?' Customers of the bank obtaining the advances will use those funds to buy goods and services from suppliers, paying for them by cheque. The suppliers, on receiving the cheques, will pay them into their own bank accounts. The receiving banks will credit the cheques to the customers' accounts and they will be honoured by the paying banker. The receiving banker does not know whether the funds have come from the drawing down of credit balances or as a result of the granting of an overdraft. At this next stage, the whole of the £900 granted as overdrafts earlier will come back into the banking system as further deposits. Again on the assumption that only 10% has to be kept in cash, the additional £900 will be used thus:

3	Deposits	+900	Cash	+ 90
			Advances	+810
		+900		+900

Working on the same principle as before, the £810 will come back into the system in the form of deposits:

4	Deposits	+810	Cash	+ 81
			Advances	+729
		+810		+810

and so on.

From the initial increase of £1000 the banking system has created further deposits as we have seen: £900 at the second stage, £810 at the third, etc. To the individual banker, however, he is simply lending out 90% of extra deposits he has received and his balance sheet will always show an excess of deposits over advances.

The final total for a given initial increase, when the full effects have worked through the system, depends upon the amount which has to be kept in the form of cash. The formula is:

$$\text{Final amount} = \frac{1}{\text{percentage retained in cash}} \times \begin{array}{l}\text{Initial}\\\text{increase}\\\text{in deposits}\end{array}$$

In the above example therefore:

$$\text{Final amount} = \frac{1}{10\%} \times £1000$$
$$= £10\ 000$$

The final balance sheet, after the full effects have worked themselves through, will be:

Deposits	+10 000	Cash	+ 1 000
		Advances	+ 9 000
	+10 000		+10 000

The multiple creation of deposits, assuming a retention of 10% in cash reserve, is therefore 10 times the original amount deposited. If the amount which had to be retained were 50%, the multiple creation would be only twice the original amount. At the two extremes, if no reserve at all had to be kept, the multiple creation of deposits would be equal to infinity, and if the amount which had to be retained in reserve were the full amount, the multiple creation would be nil.

In practice, the multiple creation of bank deposits cannot be so precisely calculated. We assumed in the above example that there were no 'leakages' from the system. By that we mean that we assumed that all money which went out in the form of additional lending came back into the system in the form of increased bank deposits. In the real world, leakages do in fact occur. Sums of money may be paid to foreign suppliers, thus causing a leakage from the domestic banking system. Again, advances may be used to pay a sum of money to the Government, for example to settle an outstanding tax liability. Because the central bank is not a part of the commercial bank network, such a payment to the Government would take funds out of the private financial sector and into the public sector, thus causing a leakage from the commercial bank network. Despite the difficulties of calculating a precise increase in total bank deposits arising from a given initial increase, multiple creation of bank deposits can certainly be brought about through the operation of the banking system, and the monetary authorities therefore seek to set limits to it in order to control the money supply.

Methods of controlling the banks' creation of money

Because of the power of the banks to create extra deposits in the way described, the monetary authorities will try to control the growth by a variety of techniques. For ease of explanation, the techniques are described below in simplified and theoretical terms. We then go on to describe some of the techniques which the British Authorities have used during the 1970s as Governments have placed greater emphasis on control of the money supply to achieve their economic objectives.

1 Open market operations

Open market operations are a means of controlling the ability of the banking system to lend money. Quite simply, open market operations are the buying and selling of Government securities on the Stock Exchange by the Authorities themselves, designed to expand or restrict bank credit by causing changes in the structure of the banks' balance sheets. Open market *sales* of stock by the Authorities are designed to *reduce* the ability of the banks to grant advances; open market *purchases* of stock *increase* the banks' lending power. The technique of open market operations has been used for many years in the UK and other countries which have a developed market in Government stocks. In Britain, official transactions in Government stocks are carried out by the Government Broker, who is a member of the Stock Exchange. He receives instructions from the Bank of England, acting on behalf of the Government (just as an ordinary stockbroker receives instructions from his own clients) and goes into the market either as a buyer or a seller.

To illustrate the workings of open market operations through the banking system, let us trace the effects of open market sales of stock on the balance sheets of the commercial banking system. (As with the previous illustration, we shall assume that a 10% cash ratio has to be maintained. It is stressed that this is used simply for illustration of the principle and is not the situation as it exists in the UK.)

At the outset, the banks' balance sheet looks like this:

Liabilities		*Assets*	
	£m		£m
Deposits	10 000	Cash	1 200
		Investments (Government stocks)	1 000
		Advances	7 800
	10 000		10 000

The cash ratio is 12%, 2% above the minimum needed.

The Authorities wish to restrict the ability of the banks to lend money to their customers by way of advances. Through the Government Broker, they sell £300m of Government stock on the market. These stocks are purchased by savings institutions such as pension funds and insurance companies and by private individuals, all of whom pay for them by drawing cheques on their bank accounts. When these cheques are presented, they will be paid by the commercial banks out of their deposits at the central bank. Customers' deposits at the commercial banks and the commercial banks' own balances at the central bank will both be reduced by £300m. The position will now be:

Liabilities		*Assets*	
	£m		£m
Deposits	9 700	Cash	900
		Investments	1 000
		Advances	7 800
	9 700		9 700

The effect of this action has been to reduce the cash ratio from 12% to a little over 9¼% and the minimum of 10% must be restored. Since the Authorities are themselves sellers of stock on the market, the banks may feel it would be unwise to try to sell any of their own investments as such action might depress the prices of Government stocks. Instead, let us assume that the banks choose to reduce customers' advances and transfer the funds into cash. We further assume that this has no effect on the level of deposits.

Liabilities		*Assets*	
	£m		£m
Deposits	9 700	Cash	970
		Investments	1 000
		Advances	7 730
	9 700		9 700

Advances have been reduced by £70m, the amount which it was necessary to turn into cash to make up the required 10%.

On the other hand, should the Authorities wish to allow the banks to expand their advances, they would instruct the Government Broker to buy Government stock on the market. This stock would be purchased from investors, who would be paid by cheques drawn on the central bank. On presentation, the proceeds would be paid into the investors' bank accounts and would swell both the commercial banks' deposits and the banks' cash balances at the central bank. This would have the effect of raising the cash ratio and allow the commercial banks more freedom to expand lending and hence deposits.

2 Interest rate control

An interest rate is the price of money in a lending and borrowing transaction. If *A* lends £100 to *B* for one year at an interest rate of 10%, *B* will have to pay back £110 to *A* at the end of that year. *A* is willing to do without the goods which that £100 would have been able to buy, but requires some benefit – in the form of the rate of interest – in exchange. *B*, on the other hand, wishes to purchase goods and services now, rather than waiting a year, and for that privilege is willing to pay the rate of interest demanded.

If the rate of interest (the price of money) rises, it is reasonable to expect that more people will be willing to refrain from consumption in order to obtain the interest; savings are therefore likely to increase. But as the interest rate rises, those who wish to borrow money to buy goods now are likely to be fewer in number, because the cost to them of immediate enjoyment of the goods is higher. In very simple terms, therefore, the interest rate can be seen as the price which equates the demand for money (spending or investment) with the supply of money (from savings).

Given that, monetary authorities will try to push interest rates up and so restrict the *demand* for credit when they want to restrict credit and the money supply. Conversely, the Authorities will allow interest rates to fall when they wish to see credit expanded. The methods the British Authorities have used during the 1970s are discussed on pages 222–33.

3 Varying the cash base

A further way of restricting the banks' ability to lend money is to vary the requirement for holding cash or other liquid assets. We saw above that the higher the amount which has to be retained in cash, the smaller will be the multiple credit creation. Monetary authorities therefore, in seeking to influence the level of credit granted by the banks can vary the level of cash which has to be held by the banks or they may demand that the banks place some of their cash or reserve assets in special accounts which do not count as part of the cash base. In the USA variable cash ratios are used; in the UK the latter technique is used by means of calls for special deposits.

4 Direct requests for restraint

When other techniques fail, the Authorities resort to direct 'requests' to the banks to conform to official policies. Such requests may be of the 'quantitative' type, under which the banks are asked to restrict the total of their lending to a specific figure, or 'qualitative', where categories of borrower – such as exporters, farmers, etc. – are given priority in lending, while others (e.g. property development and personal lending) are restricted.

The British Authorities have used all these techniques and more in running their monetary policies. Let us look now in some detail at the British monetary techniques of the 1970s, the way in which they were operated and the new developments which are now taking place.

Control of bank deposits in the UK

In Chapter 1, we saw that bank deposits have become the major form of money in this country (and indeed in every other developed economy). In recent years, Governments in the UK have relied increasingly on monetary measures – as opposed to fiscal policy, incomes policy or other direct control – to try to influence the level of demand in the economy, the rate of price increases and so on. As a result, control of bank deposits has become a crucial issue of economic policy.

The reliance to such a large extent on control of the money supply has been called *monetarism*, and the policy is by no means without its critics. Underlying monetarism is the self-evident principle that if the supply of money rises faster than the supply of goods and services, then prices will rise, and the greater the gap, the faster will be the rise in prices. In other words, the greater will be the rate of inflation.

So the basic principle of monetarism is to allow the money supply to rise in line with the growth of output which an economy can sustain. In that way, so the argument goes, a country can achieve its maximum rate of economic growth without excess money supply causing inflation.

The argument is a simple one, perhaps too simple for today's complex economic world, but whatever the rights or wrongs, British Governments have placed great reliance on it, which has meant that they have had to try to control the level and growth of bank deposits, the major element of the money supply.

Monetary policy in the 1970s and 1980s

Because of the great emphasis placed on monetary policy during the past decade, the methods by which bank deposits are controlled have become the subject of a great deal of close study, and not a little controversy.

From 1971 the banking system was controlled by methods collectively called Competition and Credit Control. The methods were introduced by the Bank of England with, as the name implies, a two-fold objective. In the first place they sought to stimulate competition on a fair and equitable basis among the various banking institutions and secondly they sought to provide a better framework than had previously existed within which the Authorities could regulate the overall amount of credit granted by the banking system.

The major elements of the system were as follows:

(*a*) There was a *reserve asset base* which had to be maintained by the banking institutions.
(*b*) *Special deposits* could be called from the banks by the Bank of England, which had the effect of removing liquidity from the banking system.
(*c*) *Open market operations* (the buying and selling of Government securities by the Bank of England on the 'open market' of the Stock Exchange) were used to expand or restrict the supply of deposits with the commercial banks.
(*d*) *Interest rates* were used to try to restrict the demand for advances from the banks' customers.
(*e*) *Selective guidance* was given on the direction of lending; e.g. lending for property development was officially frowned on after 1972.

Competition and Credit Control, as it related to the balance sheets of the banks, introduced two new features, namely *eligible liabilities* and *eligible reserve assets*.

Eligible liabilities

These were basically bank deposits, from which long-term deposits (i.e. those over two years) were removed, and an allowance made for *items in transit* (those cheques deposited with the collecting bank and credited to customers' accounts, but not yet debited to the payers' accounts). The importance of the eligible liabilities figure was that it was the basis on which various other ratios were worked out.

Eligible reserve assets

The most important of the figures which was based on the total eligible liabilities was the *eligible reserve assets ratio*. Eligible reserve assets consisted of the following:

(*a*) Balances with the Bank of England* (other than special deposits);
(*b*) British and Northern Ireland Government Treasury bills;
(*c*) Money at call with the London money market;
(*d*) British Government stocks and nationalised industries' stocks guaranteed by HM Government with one year or less to final redemption;
(*e*) Local authority bills eligible for rediscount at the Bank of England;
(*f*) Commercial bills eligible for rediscount at the Bank of England up to a maximum of 2% of eligible liabilities.

1 Open market operations

For much of the 1970s, successive Governments spent more each year than they received in taxation. So money was flowing out of the Exchequer and into the banking system. Throughout this period, the Authorities sought to syphon off such excessive spending by persuading investors to buy Government stock. This stock the Authorities were prepared to supply in almost limitless quantities when investors were prepared to buy, which meant that higher and higher interest rates have had to be offered to sell the stock.

Thus the Authorities pursued open-market sales of Government stock throughout the 1970s, mainly to diminish the effects on bank deposits of their own overspending, rather than to contain bank advances.

Prior to 1971, the Authorities pursued a policy of interest-rate stability (so far as this was possible). In practice, they did not try to oppose a tendency for interest rates to fall or, more frequently, to rise; but they did try to smooth out sharp fluctuations in the rate of interest.

So when rates of interest were rising (i.e. prices of Government stock were falling as investors sold) the Bank of England would tend to buy the stock close to, but a little below, the existing price. Such a

* Cash in the banks' own tills was not an eligible reserve asset, and the London clearing banks (but not others) agreed to keep 1½% of eligible liabilities in balances at the Bank of England to ensure that there were sufficient funds to meet the day-to-day demands of the clearing system and to ensure the smooth working of the Bank of England's operations in the money market.

policy, which was designed to maintain confidence and so help long-term sales of Government stock, meant that the Authorities were often buying stock and adding to bank deposits when they really wanted to pursue a tight money policy. So in 1971 this system was ended.

2 Interest rates

Prior to 1971, Bank rate was an important factor in determining the rate of interest of the clearing banks. Officially, Bank rate was the rate at which the Bank of England would rediscount first class bills for the discount houses when called upon to act as lender of last resort, and was fixed each Thursday by the Bank of England. But Bank rate had a much more important part to play in the financial markets because clearing banks had a number of agreements among themselves which fixed the level of interest rates. The principal ones were:

(*a*) No interest was paid on a current account.
(*b*) The rate of interest on seven-day deposit accounts was fixed at an agreed percentage below Bank rate (this figure had normally been 2% below Bank rate).
(*c*) The minimum rate of interest charged on overdrafts was 1% above Bank rate.

It is clear that because of these agreements, movements in Bank rate had an important and immediate effect throughout the entire clearing bank system. Whenever the Bank of England announced a change in Bank rate, all those borrowers from the clearing banks, whose borrowing rates were linked to Bank rate, found that the rate which they were paying had changed immediately and automatically. Equally, those who held deposit accounts with one of the clearing banks found that the rate of interest earned was also changed as a result of the alteration in Bank rate. The Bank of England, therefore, before 1971 had a direct control over a wide range of interest rates because of the link between Bank rate and the clearing banks' own rates.

The Government, however, decided that these interest rate agreements were hindering competition among the banks, and so as part of Competition and Credit Control arrangements the clearing banks agreed to abandon them. Instead of linking their own deposit and lending rates to Bank rate, each clearing bank fixed its own deposit rate, and a base rate to which its lending rates were linked. Changes were made from time to time in accordance with changes in market conditions.

Bank rate temporarily lost its central place in the monetary system in 1971 and in October 1972 it was replaced by minimum lending rate (MLR). For six years, MLR was calculated according to a formula based on the discount rate at the regular Treasury bill tender, but in 1978 the formula was abandoned, and although the name minimum lending rate remained, it was, after 1978, fixed by the Authorities and changes were usually announced on a Thursday. The banks' base rates, while not strictly fixed to MLR, followed it very closely.

During the late 1970s, interest rates became a central policy weapon, with the Government trying to bring about a substantial reduction in the money supply, and hence in inflation, by allowing interest rates, led by MLR, to rise to extremely high levels. For instance, in 1979–80 MLR stood at 17% for almost a year. Under the influence of Competition and Credit Control, interest rates were designed to play a much more important role in the regulation of credit than they had done before. The experience of the 1970s suggests, however, that interest rates did not necessarily allocate credit in the most desirable manner, and that they might have to rise to extremely high levels before they reduced borrowers' demands. Nevertheless, the British monetary Authorities still place great emphasis on interest rates in the conduct of their monetary policy.

3 Special deposits

We noted in Chapter 14 the presence of special deposits in the banks' balance sheets. Special deposits were devised originally in 1958 and first brought into operation in 1960. They were thus a part of the old arrangements for controlling the banking system, and were retained in 1971 in a slightly modified form. Whereas, prior to Competition and Credit Control, special deposits had been called only from the London and Scottish clearing banks, in 1971 the scope was widened, and they are now called from the whole banking system. A further change at that time was that they were then called as a percentage of eligible liabilities and not as a percentage of total deposits.

Special deposits remained in operation throughout the period of Competition and Credit Control from 1971 onwards. They were, however, used very flexibly by the Authorities in order to take liquidity from the clearing banks.

The Authorities sought to push the banks down towards their reserve asset base of 12½% and thus force them to restrict advances. In practice, however, the reserve asset control was never very effective and special deposits in practice became used simply as a means of indicating general tightness of credit in the banking system, rather than forcing the banks to any specific curtailment of advances.

4 Supplementary special deposits

The introduction of Competition and Credit Control was followed by sharp increases in the level of bank deposits and advances. The clearing banks began to bid for large deposits on the so-called wholesale markets, such as the inter-bank market, and to offer certificates of deposit as a means of attracting new funds. The ease with which the banks were able to increase their resources in this way gave the Authorities cause for serious concern, and in December 1973 they introduced a scheme variously called 'supplementary special deposits', 'IBELs control' or, more picturesquely, the Bank of England's 'corset' (particularly appropriate, perhaps, as the Bank is often called 'The Old Lady of Threadneedle Street').

The scheme, which operated from 1973 to 1975 and again from 1978, allowed the banks to increase their interest-bearing eligible liabilities only by a specified percentage. If they exceeded the permitted growth, they had to place some of the excess, interest-free, at the Bank of England. However, the supplementary special deposits scheme led to all manner of distortions as the banks arranged their balance sheets so as not to have to bid for IBELs in the market and so incur the Bank's very severe penalties under the scheme. So the Authorities finally abandoned the scheme in the summer of 1980 as a prelude to a wide-ranging reform of monetary control.

5 Selective guidance

When ceiling controls on advances were abandoned in 1971, the Authorities retained the right to provide the banks with guidance as to which categories of borrower were to be given priority and which categories should be deprived of bank funds. Although such guidance was outside the spirit of Competition and Credit Control, the Authorities wished to preserve this power in case of need. It was, in fact, found necessary to resort to this guidance as early as August 1972, less than one year after the introduction of the new system, when the banks were asked to restrict lending for property development and stock exchange transactions. Such guidance, strengthened and changed from time to time, continued to be a part of the Authorities' control.

The fall of Competition and Credit Control

There were a number of reasons why Competition and Credit Control, introduced in 1971 as a milestone in British monetary history, had by 1981 all but disappeared. First, the system was designed to put all banks on a fair and equal footing in terms of competing with one another. Yet it succeeded only in creating new barriers between those banks which were controlled and those which were not. The so-called fringe banks referred to in Chapter 17, were still outside the Bank of England's control, and so were able to compete with less restrictions than those which had to keep to the Bank's reserve assets and other requirements. The major banks' base rates, free from their link with Bank rate, still moved very closely in line with one another. This, however, is not particularly surprising as the major banks operate in such a similar environment that in practice one could not effectively stay out of line with the others for very long.

Secondly, on the question of credit control, the system clearly failed. However, in defence of the architects of Competition and Credit Control it should be pointed out first that virtually no system of monetary control could have coped with the massive increases in money put into the system by the large Government Budget deficits of the 1970s, and secondly, Britain was far from being the only country in the world to suffer banking and financial difficulties in the 1970s. So all the blame cannot be laid at the door of Competition and Credit Control.

The Authorities themselves began to lose confidence in the system to control the growth of bank lending and the money supply.

Qualitative control – the power of the Authorities to give directives to the banks regarding the direction of their lending – was retained in 1971, although the Authorities clearly hoped it would only be used as a back-stop in an emergency. Yet it was back in force as early as mid-1972. Quantitative control, nominally completely abandoned in 1971, was back in the guise of IBELs control by 1973.

In addition, the reserve asset ratio was never effective in forcing the banks to cut down on their lending, in the way theoretically described earlier in this chapter. Such an adjustment of the assets side of the balance sheet is called simply *asset management.* What the banks did, however, was to indulge in *liability management.* That is to say, they allowed the assets on their balance sheets – particularly advances, etc. – to rise to meet the level of demand for them and then 'buy-in' the deposits in the inter-bank and other wholesale money markets to finance them and to make up reserve assets. Thus the fulcrum did not work, the Bank of England had to resort to penalising the banks through supplementary special deposits. Whereupon the banks responded by finding ways of lending money – by means of leasing or bill finance – which avoided bidding for IBELs in the market and hence paying the interest-rate penalty. The supplementary special deposits scheme merely succeeded in distorting the figures while failing to control the effective amount of credit in the system. Finally, the abolition of exchange control, enabling individuals to hold foreign currency accounts abroad, and the banks to channel lending through overseas subsidiaries to UK borrowers, rendered the control of the money supply through the Competition and Credit Control system impossible.

New methods of control

In the previous chapter, we saw that the Bank of England has sometimes in the past adopted, for monetary control purposes, ratios which the banks themselves worked to as a matter of banking prudence. The liquidity and cash ratios were both in this category. Competition and Credit Control introduced new ratios for the purposes of credit control, but took relatively little notice of the degree of risk associated with particular types of liability. We have seen how the problems of the 1970s eventually produced the Banking Act 1979.

Alongside the legislative moves to improve the stability of the banks and other financial institutions, was the increasing disillusion with the monetary controls. Prudential and monetary controls however, were now being seen as quite separate issues, and we now look at some of the suggestions for improving monetary control.

Monetary base control

Early in 1980, the Bank of England issued a discussion paper on possible new methods of controlling the banks' ability to create additional deposits. Among suggestions which were discussed was the adoption of *monetary base control*.

Monetary base control is a simple concept. Each bank has to keep a known proportion of its liabilities (deposits) in the form of *base money*, which includes deposits held with the central bank and may include cash held by the banks and the general public. Taking this proportion, which might be fixed by banking prudence or by the Authorities, the latter then

1 Control the amount of such base money available to the banks, and hence the total money supply, since the banks' balance sheets cannot exceed a specified multiple of the base; or
2 Use divergences of the growth of this monetary base from its desired trend to trigger changes in interest rates intended to correct this divergence.

In the first case, banks would compete for a limited supply of base money by bidding up the interest rates in the market and using interest rate movements to bring the money supply back to the desired rate of growth. In the latter case, interest rate changes would be automatically triggered but the control of the rates would be determined, not by the market forces, but by the monetary Authorities.

The Bank of England, in discussing these methods, was rather sceptical about their effectiveness, and to date no scheme for monetary base control has been introduced.

However, towards the end of 1980, the Bank did produce a series of proposals which were introduced in August 1981 and which substantially affect the methods by which the banks' balance sheets are controlled.

The changes in monetary control in 1981

To all intents and purposes, the ground rules laid down in Competition and Credit Control were all but swept away. The new methods of control made quite fundamental changes.

In broad outline, MLR was put into abeyance, so that an official Bank of England lending rate no longer exists. At the same time, the reserve assets ratio, first introduced in 1971, was also discontinued, while the Bank of England changed its methods of operating in the gilt-edged market. Now let us look at the details.

1 Interest rates

Perhaps the most important change was the ending of MLR and the new methods of interest rate control. The avowed object of discontinuing MLR was to allow market forces a greater say in the determination of interest rates. The Bank of England now seeks to keep short-term interest rates within an unpublished band through its bill dealings with the discount houses (see Chapter 15). The Bank of England may change its views on the range of interest rates from time to time (as it did in September 1981 when it engineered a rise) when it will seek to implement its wishes through its activities in the market. MLR, however, has only been 'put on ice', it has not been abandoned. The authorities can re-activate it, should they so wish.

2 Acceptable bills

The rules regarding what the Bank of England would recognise as an 'acceptable name' on a bill of exchange were also changed in August 1981. Gone is the requirement that an acceptable bank name has to be British. The list now includes many overseas banks in London, and the extension has given the Bank a wider range of bills which it may use in its money market operations.

3 Cash ratio

The reserve assets ratio was abandoned in August 1981, as was the requirement that the clearing banks alone had to keep 1½% of their eligible liabilities in cash at the Bank of England.

The Bank of England now requires members of the 'monetary sector' whose eligible liabilities exceed £10m to keep ½% of their deposits at the Bank of England. The 'monetary sector' includes:

(*a*) All recognised banks and licensed deposit takers (LDTs);
(*b*) National Girobank;
(*c*) Those banks in the Channel Islands and the Isle of Man which opt to join the cash ratio scheme;
(*d*) The Trustee Savings Banks (TSBs);
(*e*) The Banking Department of the Bank.

Some redefinition of eligible liabilities has been necessary under the new arrangements. The following can be offset against a bank's liabilities in arriving at its eligible liabilities figure:

(*a*) Funds (other than cash ratio deposits or special deposits placed with the Bank) lent by one institution in the newly defined monetary sector to any other;
(*b*) Money at call placed with money brokers and gilt-edged jobbers in the Stock Exchange, and secured on gilt-edged stocks, Treasury bills, local authority bills and eligible bank bills.

4 Undertaking by 'eligible banks'

As noted in Chapter 15, each bank whose bills are recognised as 'eligible' under (*b*) above has undertaken that:

(*a*) It will maintain 5% of its eligible liabilities on a secured basis, with members of the London Discount Market Association (LDMA) and/or with money brokers and gilt-edged jobbers.
(*b*) The proportion held with the LDMA will not fall below 2½% of eligible liabilities on any day.

Each bank aims to meet the daily average over either a six- or twelve-month period (the choice of period being notified to the Bank of England), with the ratio on any particular day in the month related to the banks' eligible liabilities on the last-but-one make-up day. Thus the relevant eligible liabilities each day of the 'banking month' of March (i.e. the four- or five-week period to the third Wednesday in March) will be the eligible figure at the January make-up day. In addition, it must not go below the average figure on a daily basis, except in exceptional circumstances, which it must justify to the Bank of England.

5 Liquidity

Although the reserve asset ratio no longer applies, the banks have agreed to discuss in advance with the Bank of England any change they may be contemplating in their liquidity management and the composition of their liquid assets. In addition, prudential guidelines on liquidity and capital adequacy have been established following the Banking Act 1979.

6 Bank of England operations in the gilt market

The Bank of England now confines its automatic purchases of gilt-edged stock in the market to a maximum of three months to maturity, rather than the previous one-year rule.

These, then, are the methods by which the Authorities will seek to control the lending policies of the banking system in the 1980s. They are far more complex than the arrangements of earlier days, but then the whole system has become more diverse. As the structure changes, so methods of control themselves will have to adapt.

We hope that in this area, as in all the other areas of banking which we have covered in this book, readers will have found some enlightenment and a context into which they can put the ever-changing developments in the banking world.

Questions

1 'A bank can create its own deposits.' Trace briefly the steps by which this occurs.
2 How do special deposits assist the control of the British banking system?
3 How do open market operations affect a bank's balance sheet?
4 How does the Bank of England seek to influence the level of interest rates?
5 Why did 'Competition and Credit Control' fail?
6 Outline the methods by which the UK monetary authorities are seeking to control the banks in the 1980s.

Glossary of Banking Terms

Acceptance credits Used mainly by companies as a means of financing the production and sale of goods for export, credits are usually arranged for a specified sum and period and then discounted to enable the company to secure a large proportion of the finance required.

Assets Everything owned by a business, e.g. current assets (cash, short-term deposits, debtors, stocks), fixed assets (buildings, machinery) and intangible assets (patents, good will).

Automatic tellers Machines linked to a computer – often built into the wall outside branch banks – which provide cash and other services at all hours.

BACS Bankers Automated Clearing Services. This processes, on behalf of the English and Scottish banks, magnetic tape information of customers' bankers orders, Bank Giro credits and direct debits.

Balance sheet A statement showing the nature and amount of a company's assets, liabilities and capital on a given date. A consolidated balance sheet shows the financial condition of a holding or parent company and its subsidiaries.

Bankers' draft A draft drawn on the bank itself which may be regarded as cash by the person receiving it. (Drafts are used generally in the purchase of a property; the deeds will not be passed to the purchaser's solicitor in exchange for an ordinary cheque for there is no guarantee it will be paid on presentation.)

Banker's lien An implied pledge over documents of title subject to the pledge, such as negotiable instruments, while the debt is still owed.

Bank Giro A means of transferring funds to the bank account of a customer of any bank in the UK as an alternative to paying by cheque.

Base rates The floating rate upon which interest rates on bank loans are based.

Bridge-over loans Temporary finance where an assurance is given that fresh capital is to be introduced shortly to repay the advance, e.g. on the sale of a property.

Cash flow The net income of a company, plus non-cash charges such as depreciation and charges to reserves.

Central Bank The official Government-owned bank; in the UK, the Bank of England.

Certificates of deposit (CD) A certificate of deposit is a receipt issued by a bank, acknowledging that a certain sum of money has been deposited for a fixed period.

Collateral Securities or other property pledged by a borrower to secure repayment of a loan.

Competition and Credit Control The method of controlling bank deposits used in the UK from 1971 to 1981.

Credit scoring A method of assessing loan applications by a pre-arranged point system of scoring for various categories, e.g. house ownership, business capacity, age, etc.

Direct debiting Payments of fixed amounts on regular recurring dates, similar to a standing order but direct debits are originated by the third party requiring payment and sent to the customer's bank.

Discount market A market which acts as an intermediary between banks which have cash in excess of immediate needs and those which are short. The twelve members purchase and sell bills, Treasury bills, and other (usually short-dated) securities.

ECGD Export Credits Guarantee Department: a Government Department, which operates an export credit insurance business to promote British exports.

Electronic funds transfer point of sale (EFTPOS) A system being tested which will allow customers to purchase goods in retail outlets and pay by a special card bearing the bank account and credit information needed to initiate such transactions.

Eligible liabilities Bank deposits from which long-term deposits (those over two years) are removed and an allowance made for items in transit (cheques in the course of payment not yet debited to payers' accounts).

Eligible reserve assets Specified assets under Competition and Credit Control (q.v.), now no longer in operation.

Endorsement The signature by a holder of a cheque (usually on the back) or his authorised agent, whereby it is negotiated to another person who takes it as a new holder.

Equity investment Investment by a bank in a company by way of taking part of the equity for funds provided. In many cases, the return on investment accrues on flotation of the company.

Euro-dollars A deposit in dollars held outside the USA.

Factoring A type of finance under which the borrower sells his trade debts to a factoring company, which takes over the customer's sales ledger and becomes responsible for the collection of debts.

Forward exchange A contract for the purchase or sale of currency proceeds at a future date at a rate of exchange specified when the contract is made.

Guarantee Collateral security whereby one person makes himself collaterally answerable for the debts or defaults of another.

IBELs Interest-Bearing Eligible Liabilities.

Inter-bank market A market operated by banks to adjust surpluses and shortages of cash flows.

Lender of the last resort The Bank of England is the lender of the last resort to the discount houses. Any discount house, which at the end of a day requires to borrow to balance its books, may approach the Bank for this facility; although the latter will assist at a rate of its own choice.

LIBOR The London Inter-Bank Offered Rate of interest.

Long-term loan A loan arranged for a period of between ten and twenty years.

Medium-term loan A loan arranged for a period of between two and ten years.

Minimum Lending Rate (MLR) An interest rate quoted by the Bank of England for its short-term lending operations with the discount houses; put into abeyance in 1981.

Money at call Funds deposited on agreement that they will be returned immediately, i.e. at call. This applies frequently to money lent by a bank to a discount house.

Mortgage A pledge or assignment of security of particular property for payment of debt.

Near-money/quasi-money Assets which perform some of the functions of money but which either cannot be transferred immediately into money or lack transferability, e.g. building society accounts, share certificates, bills of exchange, etc.

Note issue The amount of notes in circulation. Currently the responsibility of the Bank of England, but some Scottish and Irish banks issue their own banknotes.

Not Negotiable crossing Writing the words 'Not Negotiable' between two lines across the face of a cheque is a means of safeguard when issuing the cheque.

Open market operations The buying and selling of Government securities by the Bank of England to expand or restrict the supply of deposits with the banks.

Revolving loans Loans repayable by regular repayments. The borrower need not take up the full amount of the loan at the outset. Further, the loan can be 'topped up' by borrowing more, provided that the total debt outstanding does not exceed the agreed credit limit.

Set-off The right of a bank to apply the credit balance of a customer's account against an overdrawn account of the same customer.

Sovereign risk The political risk that an overseas Government may default on its debts.

Special deposits Calls for deposits on the banks by the Bank of England which have the effect of removing liquidity from the banking system.

Standing orders Payments of fixed amounts on regular recurring dates made on a customer's instructions which are credited to a third party and debited against the account of its customer.

Treasury bills Promissory notes issued by the Bank of England to provide short-term finance for Government Departments.

Working capital The difference between current assets and current liabilities.

Index

BUSINESS STUDIES

PETER FEARNS

A modern, integrated approach to business studies which examines organisational activity in the economic, social, political and legal environment. The emphasis throughout is on people as both producers and consumers of goods and services.

This introductory text shows how the separate disciplines of economics, administration, marketing, accounting and law are all interrelated in the real world of business decision-making. Peter Fearns looks at the nature of markets, the formation of organisations, and the acquisition and management of resources, and then examines the concept of efficiency within organisations. Further chapters deal with central and local government, and the impact of technological change. Examples of the main types of financial records and analytical techniques are also included.

TEACH YOURSELF BOOKS

ECONOMICS

Edited by DAVID BURNINGHAM

A lucid introduction to the economics of contemporary society and a comprehensive analysis of the key issues behind the media headlines.

This sound introductory text explains complex ideas simply and clearly, and emphasises the links between economics and politics. Part One focuses on the economics of the market place and the first principles of supply, demand and price. Part Two then examines economic activity at a national and international level, exploring the impact of corporate power, government and overseas influences on output, employment and prices. A wide range of examination questions, a detailed plan for further study and a comprehensive index are special features of the book.

This established text will appeal to the general reader as well as to students preparing for 'A' level, first year university and professional examinations.

TEACH YOURSELF BOOKS